Legalines

Editorial Advisors:
Gloria A. Aluise
Attorney at Law
David H. Barber
Attorney at Law
Robert A. Wyler
Attorney at Law

Authors:
Gloria A. Aluise
Attorney at Law
David H. Barber
Attorney at Law
Daniel O. Bernstine
Attorney at Law
D. Steven Brewster
C.P.A.
Roy L. Brooks
Professor of Law
Frank L. Bruno
Attorney at Law
Scott M. Burbank
C.P.A.
Jonathan C. Carlson
Professor of Law
Charles N. Carnes
Professor of Law
Paul S. Dempsey
Professor of Law
Jerome A. Hoffman
Professor of Law
Mark R. Lee
Professor of Law
Jonathan Neville
Attorney at Law
Laurence C. Nolan
Professor of Law
Arpiar Saunders
Attorney at Law
Robert A. Wyler
Attorney at Law

FEDERAL COURTS

Adaptable to Tenth Edition of Wright Casebook

By President Daniel O. Bernstine
Portland State University

THE
barbri®
GROUP

Harcourt
Professional Education Group, Inc.

EDITORIAL OFFICES: 111 W. Jackson Blvd., 7th Floor, Chicago, IL 60604

Legalines

REGIONAL OFFICES: Chicago, Dallas, Los Angeles, New York, Washington, D.C.
Distributed by: **Harcourt, Inc.,** 6277 Sea Harbor Drive, Orlando, FL 32887 (800)787-8717

SERIES EDITOR
Angel M. Murphy, J.D.
Attorney at Law

FIRST PRINTING—2000

SHORT SUMMARY OF CONTENTS

TABLE OF CONTENTS AND REVIEW OUTLINE

I. "JUDICIAL POWER" OVER "CASES AND CONTROVERSIES"

A. FEDERAL COURTS ARE COURTS OF LIMITED JURISDICTION

1. **Federal Court Subject Matter Jurisdiction Must Be Expressly Granted.**

   a. **Source of jurisdiction—Constitution and Congress.** Article III, Section 1 of the United States Constitution states that there shall be one Supreme Court and such other inferior courts as Congress may from time to time establish. Thus, federal courts are courts of limited subject matter jurisdiction because these courts derive their adjudicatory authority solely from the Constitution, which describes the classes of cases that Congress may then give federal courts jurisdiction to hear.

   b. **Narrowly construed.** The courts have generally interpreted the constitutional jurisdiction limitations narrowly.

2. **The Plaintiff Must Plead the Existence of Federal Subject Matter Jurisdiction.** The plaintiff, as the party seeking to invoke the jurisdiction of the federal court, must plead and, if necessary, prove the existence of federal subject matter jurisdiction. *See* Form 2, Federal Rules of Civil Procedure for examples of jurisdictional statements.

   a. **Alien plaintiff vs. persons of unstated citizenship--Hodgson v. Bowerbank,** 9 U.S. (5 Cranch) 303 (1809). Hodgson v. Bowerbank

   1) **Facts.** Bowerbank and others (Ps), all aliens and subjects of the United Kingdom, sued Hodgson and others (Ds) in federal court. Ds were identified as "late of the district of Maryland, merchants," but they were not stated to be citizens of the state of Maryland. On appeal to the Supreme Court, Ds argued that this omission deprived the federal courts of jurisdiction. Ps contended that the Judiciary Act gave the circuit courts jurisdiction over all cases in which an alien was a party.

   2) **Issue.** May the federal courts entertain suits by foreigners in which the defendants are not specifically identified as being citizens of any state?

   3) **Held.** No.

      a) The federal courts have no jurisdiction over a suit by a foreigner if the action does not clearly state that the defendants are citizens of some state. The Constitution specifically permits the federal courts to take cognizance of actions between a foreigner and a citizen of one of the states, and so it is essential that the parties be specifically described. Therefore, the failure to identify Ds as citizens of the state of Maryland constitutes a fatal defect in the complaint.

3. **Congress May Limit Federal Court Subject Matter Jurisdiction Beyond What Is Otherwise Required by Article III.**

a. **Introduction.** Congress has not given to the federal courts all of the jurisdiction described in Article III, Section 2. For example, Congress has established a jurisdictional dollar amount requirement for suits based on diversity of citizenship under 28 U.S.C. section 1332 even though no monetary limitations exist in Article III.

b. **Limitations on suits involving individuals--Sheldon v. Sill,** 49 U.S. (8 How.) 441 (1850).

   1) **Facts.** Sheldon (D), a Michigan citizen, executed a bond and mortgage obligating him to the Bank of Michigan. Hastings, president of the bank, assigned the obligations to Sill (P), a resident of New York, who sued D in federal court to recover on the bond and mortgage. By way of defense, D cited a provision of the federal Judiciary Act that denied federal courts jurisdiction to consider suits by assignees of choses in action unless the assignor could also have sued in federal court. P argued that Article III of the Constitution vests the federal courts with jurisdiction to decide "controversies between citizens of different states," and that the provision of the Judiciary Act cited by D was invalid. The trial court rendered judgment in favor of P, and D appeals.

   2) **Issue.** May a federal statute enacted by Congress limit the jurisdiction conferred on the federal courts by Article III of the Constitution?

   3) **Held.** Yes.

      a) Congress has the power to remove a case or a controversy from the jurisdiction of the federal courts. The lower federal courts were created by Congress, not by the Constitution. Since Congress established these courts, it has the power to determine the scope of their jurisdiction. It has long been recognized that Congress has the right to do so by restricting the authority conferred by Article III of the Constitution, which may be construed as applying only to the Supreme Court anyway, since the Constitution set up no system of subordinate federal courts. Therefore, the cited provision of the Judiciary Act requires reversal of the judgment in favor of P since he satisfies the Act's definition of an assignee of a chose of action.

   4) **Comment.** Some of the earliest constitutional scholars argued that Article III required Congress to vest the inferior federal courts with jurisdiction to resolve all suits enumerated in the article. This view, however, never achieved preeminence. Today, the authority of Congress to enact laws circumscribing the jurisdiction of the federal courts is seldom questioned. Congress has frequently acted to deprive the federal courts of jurisdiction over suits that they would otherwise have had the authority to decide. One way that Congress accomplishes this objective is to confer upon the Supreme Court original jurisdiction to resolve certain cases.

c. **Limitations on suits involving corporations--Knee v. Chemical Leaman Tank Lines, Inc.,** 293 F. Supp. 1094 (E.D. Pa. 1968).

   1) **Facts.** Knee (P), a Pennsylvania citizen, sued Chemical Leaman Tank Lines, Inc. (D) in federal district court, alleging that she had sustained injuries as a result of the negligence of D. As a basis for federal jurisdiction,

P alleged diversity of citizenship, citing the fact that D was a Delaware corporation. D filed an answer in which it admitted the allegation that it was a Delaware corporation. Later D served interrogatories. After the statute of limitations had run, D for the first time raised the contention that its principal office was in Pennsylvania and that diversity jurisdiction was therefore lacking.

2) **Issue.** Will federal subject matter jurisdiction attach if the plaintiff is a citizen of the state in which the defendant corporation maintains its principal place of business?

3) **Held.** No. D's motion to dismiss is granted.

    a) For purposes of federal diversity jurisdiction, a corporation is deemed a citizen of any state in which it is incorporated and of the state in which it maintains its principal place of business. This is the rule that derives from 28 U.S.C. section 1332(c). Since D maintains its principal place of business in Pennsylvania, it is a citizen of that state. There is, therefore, no diversity of citizenship in this case. Although it is unfortunate that D's tardy assertion of the jurisdictional defect has disadvantaged P, objections to jurisdiction may be interposed at any time and federal jurisdiction cannot be conferred by waiver, estoppel, or consent. It follows that the motion to dismiss for lack of jurisdiction must be granted.

4) **Comment.** Diversity of citizenship has never been a favored basis for establishing federal jurisdiction. 28 U.S.C. section 1332(c), the basis for the *Knee* decision, was enacted for the purpose of contracting the scope of diversity jurisdiction in cases in which a corporation is a party. One purpose of federal diversity jurisdiction is to protect litigants against the local bias that theoretically pervades the state court system. But a corporation is unlikely to suffer significant prejudice in the courts of a state in which it maintains its principal place of business. Thus, 28 U.S.C. section 1332(c) does not seem to undermine seriously the objective of diversity jurisdiction.

B. "CASES" AND "CONTROVERSIES"

1. **Introduction.** Among the nine grants of jurisdiction given, Article III states that the federal judicial power shall extend to "cases" and to "controversies." While the parameters of the case or controversy limitation are far from clear, the concept reflects a concern that there are certain categories of cases where the federal courts should exercise judicial restraint as well as certain requirements that must be satisfied before a court is competent to hear a suit. The concept manifests itself in a number of limitations on the federal judicial power, which are discussed in the paragraphs that follow.

2. **Political Questions.** The political question doctrine is based on the relationship among the three coordinate branches of government—Congress, the Executive branch, and the Judicial branch. This doctrine does not involve

the federal courts' relationship to the states. When a federal court invokes the doctrine and refuses to extend federal jurisdiction to a case, the court is, in essence, characterizing an issue as one that the Constitution has committed to the discretion of one of the other coordinate branches of the federal government. In practice, the political question doctrine affords the courts a considerable measure of discretion, since countless cases that are controversial or otherwise unappealing may be dismissed on the ground that they are of a political nature. An activist court, needless to say, is less likely to invoke the political question doctrine than is a tribunal that conceives of itself as a passive and reluctant decisionmaker.

Baker v. Carr

a. Malapportionment of representation in the state legislature is a justiciable issue--Baker v. Carr, 369 U.S. 186 (1962).

1) **Facts.** Baker and other residents of five Tennessee counties (Ps) filed suit in federal district court against Carr and other state officials (Ds). The suit, commenced on behalf of voters in the five counties and all other similarly situated voters in Tennessee, alleged that the state's apportionment statute (assigning voters to various voting districts for the purpose of electing members of Congress) so inaccurately reflected actual population statistics that it violated the Equal Protection Clause of the Fourteenth Amendment. The district court dismissed the suit, holding that the federal court lacked jurisdiction over the subject matter and that Ps had failed to state a claim upon which relief could be granted. Upon review of the case, the Supreme Court was confronted with the argument that the case involved a political question, and thus was nonjusticiable.

2) **Issue.** Should an attack on a state apportionment statute be dismissed on the ground that it involves a political question?

3) **Held.** No. Judgment reversed.

a) A political question exists when a case involves a matter that has been constitutionally committed to some political department coequal with the judiciary or when the courts have no discoverable standard for resolving the case.

b) Political questions may also be involved when determination of a case would require a preliminary policy formulation by another branch of government or would entail possible disrespect for a political decision already made by another department.

c) The present case involves none of these situations and thus does not present a political question.

d) Ds argue that the case raises a political question because it is, in essence, an assault upon the Guaranty Clause of the Constitution. It is true that Article IV, Section 4 of the Constitution guarantees that every state shall have the right to maintain a republican form of government and that attempts to interfere with that provision have been deemed to present nonjusticiable political questions. But there is nothing inherent in the Guaranty Clause itself that compels the conclusion that cases involving it necessarily present political questions. As it happens, the Guaranty Clause cases all incidentally involved political questions, but every case relating to the clause need not involve such questions. Although the present case would be thought to involve the Guaranty Clause, it does not present a political question. The action is based on the Fourteenth Amendment and the claims relating to that provision are distinct and involve no political question.

e) Ps have standing to bring this suit, the district court has jurisdiction over the subject matter, and no political question is involved. It follows that the district court should not have dismissed the suit.

4) **Dissent** (Frankfurter, Harlan, JJ.). This case involves the Guaranty Clause and thus, according to a long line of authorities, presents a political question that this Court should not resolve. If the Court embroils itself in political disputes, it will invade the province of other branches of government and will run the risk of losing the public respect and confidence upon which its effectiveness depends. The fact that Ps' claim is cast in terms of the Fourteenth Amendment does not disguise the fact that the case involves the Guaranty Clause and thus presents a nonjusticiable political question.

3. **Standing.** The concept of standing to sue in federal court is premised on the proposition that a plaintiff cannot raise an issue unless that plaintiff has some interest and stake in the litigation.

a. **Basis of the doctrine.** The doctrine is based on both Article III limitations as well as on prudential or policy considerations. Unlike the Article III limitations, the prudential rules may be disregarded by the federal courts if deemed appropriate; in addition, the courts cannot create prudential barriers to standing if Congress grants statutory standing consistent with Article III.

b. **Purpose of the requirement.** The standing requirement guarantees that issues will not be presented and precedents will not be established by individuals who are not serious about the prosecution of their cases.

1) In recent years the courts have been willing to open their doors to parties who can show a legitimate interest in the outcome of an action, be it economic, aesthetic, or otherwise.

2) There is a problem of determining when standing exists because the courts have established several different tests for determining standing, and the test to be applied may vary according to the type of plaintiff involved and the claim asserted. In addition, the courts, in some cases, appear to examine the merits of the claim raised as part of the inquiry into whether a party has a sufficient stake in the outcome of the litigation.

c. **A plaintiff who in fact has suffered economic injury by a statute has standing to raise constitutional claims of third parties also injured by the statute--Craig v. Boren,** 429 U.S. 190 (1976).

Craig v. Boren

1) **Facts.** Craig, a male between 18 and 21 years of age, and Whitener (P), a licensed vendor of 3.2% beer, sought declaratory and injunctive relief against enforcement of two sections of an Oklahoma statute that

prohibit the sale of nonintoxicating 3.2% beer to males under the age of 21 and females under the age of 18. Craig and P claimed that the age differential between males and females constituted invidious discrimination against males 18 to 20 years of age. A three-judge district court found for Oklahoma (D), sustaining the constitutionality of the gender-based differential. After the Supreme Court noted probable jurisdiction, Craig reached the age of 21 and the controversy was rendered moot as to him. The Supreme Court then considered whether P, the vendor, had standing.

2) **Issue.** Can a licensed vendor of 3.2% beer rely on the equal protection objections of males 18 to 20 years of age to establish her claim of unconstitutionality of the gender-based differential?

3) **Held.** Yes.

a) Despite having had the opportunity, D never raised any objection to P's reliance on the claimed unequal treatment to 18- to 20-year-old males as the premise of her own challenge to the state law.

b) Any limitations on a litigant's assertion of jus tertii are not mandated by the Constitution but rather involve prudential concerns to minimize unwarranted intervention into controversies where the applicable constitutional questions are ill-defined and speculative. These prudential objectives, however, are not relevant when the lower court has already entertained the constitutional questions without objections by the parties. Also, when the constitutional questions have been cogently and vigorously presented, it serves no purpose to deny jus tertii standing.

c) In any event, P has independently established her claim to assert jus tertii. The statutes have inflicted sufficient "injury in fact" on P to satisfy the constitutional standing requirements of Article III. P is obligated either to obey the statute and incur direct economic loss, or to disobey the statute and suffer sanctions, including the possibility of loss of license.

4) **Dissent.** (Burger, C.J.). There is no danger of interminable dilution to P's rights if she is not permitted to litigate them here because there are no barriers to other 18- to 20-year-old males asserting any constitutional rights they may claim to purchase 3.2% beer.

Village of Arlington Heights v. Metropolitan Housing Development Corp.

d. **Plaintiff may have standing to challenge a zoning ordinance without a showing of economic injury--Village of Arlington Heights v. Metropolitan Housing Development Corp.,** 429 U.S. 252 (1977).

1) **Facts.** In 1971, Metropolitan Housing Development Corporation (P) applied to the Village of Arlington Heights (D) for the rezoning of a 15-acre parcel from single-family to multiple-family classification. Using federal financial assistance, P planned to build 190 clustered townhouse units for low- and moderate-income tenants. D is a Chicago suburb in which most of the land is zoned for detached single-family homes. According to the 1970 census, only 27 of D's 64,000 residents were black. P is a nonprofit developer organized to build housing in the Chicago area for persons of low and moderate incomes, using federal subsidies available for this purpose. P

contracted to buy a tract of land in the village known as Lincoln Green, but the arrangement was contingent on getting zoning changes and federal subsidies. After D denied the rezoning request, P and others brought suit, alleging that the denial was racially discriminatory and that it violated the Fourteenth Amendment and the Fair Housing Act of 1968.

2) **Issue.** Is economic injury the only kind of injury that can support a plaintiff's standing?

3) **Held.** No. Remanded for further consideration of statutory claims.

    a) D contends that P lacks standing because P has suffered no economic injury, in that its contract of purchase is contingent upon securing rezoning.

    b) However, P is a nonprofit corporation, and its interest in building the townhomes stems not from a desire for economic gain, but rather from an interest in making suitable low-cost housing available in areas where such housing is scarce.

    c) The specific project that P intends to build, whether or not it will generate profits, provides that essential dimension of specificity that informs judicial decisionmaking.

    d) Further, at least one of the individual plaintiffs here will suffer some injury if the project is not built. The injury which this individual asserts is that his quest for housing nearer his employment has been thwarted by official action that is racially discriminatory. If a court grants the relief he seeks, there is at least a substantial probability that the project will materialize, affording this plaintiff the housing opportunity he desires in the village.

4) **Comment.** In a brief excerpt in the casebook, the Court's decision on the merits is summarized. In its discussion of the case on its merits, the Court held that while D's decision had a heavier impact on racial minorities, P had failed to prove that D had acted with the necessary discriminatory intent that is required to state a claim under the Fourteenth Amendment.

e. **Mere claim that plaintiff has suffered injury to personal constitutional rights inadequate for standing without showing of causal connection with constitutional error--Valley Forge Christian College v. Americans United for Separation of Church and State, Inc.,** 454 U.S. 464 (1982).

1) **Facts.** Property belonging to the United States that has outlived its usefulness may be declared surplus and may be transferred to private or other public entities. The price to be paid may be discounted in whole or part on the basis of the benefits to the United States from the use to which the property will be put by its new owner. The Department of the Army had operated Valley Forge General Hospital for many years, but in 1973, it decided to close the hospital and declare it surplus. In August 1976, a part of the property was transferred to Valley Forge Christian College (D). Although the appraised value of the property was $577,500, D was given a 100% public benefit allowance, which allowed it to acquire the property without making any financial payment for it. D is a nonprofit educational

institution operating under the supervision of a religious order known as the Assemblies of God. When suit was brought challenging the conveyance on the basis that it violated the Establishment Clause of the First Amendment, the district court held that Americans United for Separation of Church and State, Inc. (P) lacked standing and dismissed the complaint. The court of appeals reversed, and D appeals.

2) **Issue.** Is the disposal of public property in an allegedly unconstitutional manner an injury sufficient to confer standing on a plaintiff taxpayer?

3) **Held.** No.

   a) The property transfer about which P complains was not an exercise of authority conferred by the Taxing and Spending Clause of Article I, Section 8.

   b) The Article III requirements of standing are not satisfied by the abstract injury in nonobservance of the Constitution asserted by citizens.

   c) This Court repeatedly has rejected claims of standing predicated on the right, possessed by every citizen, to require that the government be administered in accordance with the law.

   d) P has failed to identify any personal injury suffered by its members as a consequence of the alleged constitutional error, other than the psychological consequences presumably produced by observation of conduct with which one disagrees. That is not an injury sufficient to confer standing under Article III, even though the disagreement is phrased in constitutional terms.

4) **Dissent** (Brennan, Marshall, Blackmun, JJ.). The case and controversy limitation of Article III overrides no other provision of the Constitution. One of the primary purposes of the Establishment Clause was to prevent the use of tax monies for religious purposes. The taxpayer was the direct and intended beneficiary of the prohibition on financial aid to religion. Each and every federal taxpayer suffers precisely the injury that the Establishment Clause guards against when the federal government directs that funds be taken from the pocketbooks of the citizenry and placed into the coffers of the ministry.

5) **Dissent** (Stevens, J.). For the Court to hold that P's standing depends on whether the government's transfer was an exercise of its power to spend money, on the one hand, or its power to dispose of tangible property, on the other, is to trivialize the standing doctrine.

Department of Commerce v. United States House of Representatives; Clinton v. Gavin

f. **Individuals affected by voter redistricting satisfy the injury-in-fact requirement for Article III standing--Department of Commerce v. United States House of Representatives** (No. 98-404); **Clinton v. Gavin,** 119 S. Ct. 765 (1999).

1) **Facts.** The Census Bureau announced a plan to use two forms of statistical sampling in the 2000 Decennial Census to address undercounting of certain identifiable groups of individuals. In one case, various counties and individual residents of states that would lose a representative to Congress under the

plan (Ps) brought suit claiming the plan was unconstitutional and requesting an injunction barring the use of statistical sampling. In a second similar case, the House of Representatives also brought suit. Convened as three-judge courts, each of the two suits held that the plan violated the Census Act. It was determined in each case that the plaintiffs satisfied the requirements of Article III standing.

2) **Issue.** Do Ps have standing to challenge the statistical sampling plan under the Census Act?

3) **Held.** Yes. Judgment affirmed.

    a) The expected loss of a representative to the United States Congress undoubtedly satisfies the injury-in-fact requirement of Article III standing.

    b) There is undoubtedly a traceable connection between the use of sampling and the expected loss of a representative and there is a substantial likelihood that the requested relief, a permanent injunction, will address the alleged injury.

4. **Ripeness.** The concept of ripeness is closely related to the concept of standing.

    a. **Rationale.** The requirement that the federal courts exercise jurisdiction only over cases and controversies is designed to insure that those courts will not have to render hypothetical decisions relating to disputes that do not actually exist. Thus, a major purpose of the requirement is to excuse courts from any obligation to render "advisory opinions." The requirement also prevents the courts from exercising jurisdiction over moot cases, *i.e.*, those in which developments subsequent to the filing of the lawsuit have made it unnecessary or impossible to grant relief, and cases that are not ripe for resolution because objectionable conduct has not yet occurred or an alleged cause of action has not yet accrued.

    b. **Declaratory judgments.** In 1934, Congress passed the Declaratory Judgment Act to create actions even though a plaintiff has suffered no actual damages, but there is nevertheless a necessity to adjudicate the rights and obligations of the parties. A declaratory judgment is proper if the controversy is definite and concrete and touches the legal relations of parties with adverse legal interests.

        1) **Status of insurance policy--Aetna Life Insurance Co. v. Haworth,** 300 U.S. 227 (1937).

            a) **Facts.** Edwin Haworth (D) purchased five policies from Aetna Life Insurance Co. (P). Each policy provided for certain benefits in the event of D's total and permanent disability. With respect to four of the policies, P agreed to waive further premiums upon proof of disability, and to pay a specified monthly amount or keep the death benefits in force. P also agreed that, in the event of disability, D would be paid either 20 annual installments or a life annuity in full settlement of the fifth policy. In 1930 and 1931, D ceased paying premiums on all but the last policy, claiming disability. In 1934, payments on the last policy also stopped. P

Aetna Life
Insurance Co.
v. Haworth

at all times denied that D was permanently and totally disabled and claimed that the policies had lapsed for nonpayment of premiums (although P acknowledged that a $45 death benefit would be owed on one policy). P eventually sued in federal court for a judgment declaring the policies null and void except for the $45 obligation. The district court dismissed the suit on the ground that it presented no "controversy" in the constitutional sense and thus was not within the scope of the Federal Declaratory Judgment Act. P eventually sought relief in the Supreme Court.

b) **Issue.** Can a dispute concerning the status of insurance policies constitute a justiciable controversy of the type that the federal courts may decide?

c) **Held.** Yes. Judgment reversed.

(1) A definite and concrete dispute involving the legal interests of two adverse parties constitutes a controversy of the type that may be resolved by the federal courts. This definition of "controversy" is appropriate under both the Constitution and the Declaratory Judgment Act.

(2) This case involves a legitimate and present dispute between P and D. Each party has advanced legal arguments the resolution of which will result in significant consequences for both litigants.

(3) Whether D is disabled is a matter of controversy, notwithstanding that the rights and obligations of the parties may someday change if D's physical condition worsens or improves.

(4) Thus, this case presents a genuine controversy over which the federal courts may exercise jurisdiction. It follows that the suit was erroneously dismissed.

Golden v. Zwickler

2) **Moot controversy not certain to arise again--Golden v. Zwickler,** 394 U.S. 103 (1969).

a) **Facts.** A New York statute made it a crime to disseminate anonymous literature in connection with an election campaign. Zwickler (P) was charged with having violated this law during the 1964 campaign by distributing an anonymous leaflet criticizing a congressman for his opposition to two amendments to the 1964 Foreign Aid bill. P's conviction was later reversed by the New York Supreme Court and by that state's highest court which, in a memorandum opinion, specifically stated that the conviction had been reversed without resolving any constitutional issues. Several months later, P sued in federal court for a judgment declaring that the statute pursuant to which he had been prosecuted was unconstitutional. The federal district court in *Zwickler v. Koota* abstained from deciding whether P was entitled to such a declaration, but the United States Supreme Court ordered it to resolve the matter. The district court then ordered the relief sought, notwithstanding the fact that the 1964 election had passed and the congressman whom P had criticized had been named to the state supreme court and would therefore almost certainly not run for Congress in 1966. The Supreme Court noted probable jurisdiction. Now, before the United States Supreme Court, it is argued that this development had rendered the case moot, but P alleges that the congressman will be a candidate in 1966, and that P will again be distributing anonymous handbills opposing his election.

b) **Issue.** Should declaratory relief be granted to prevent prosecution for conduct that probably will never again be engaged in?

c) **Held.** No. Judgment reversed.

(1) A court should not issue a declaratory judgment unless confronted with a real and immediate controversy between parties having adverse legal interests. In the present case, no such controversy exists because the congressman's move to the state supreme court has rendered the entire matter moot.

(2) The district court reasoned that P's case was not moot because he was entitled to a general adjudication of the statute's constitutionality, but any judgment rendered under the circumstances of this case could amount to no more than an advisory opinion.

(3) The action presents only a hypothetical dispute, and clearly does not constitute a real and immediate controversy. Therefore, the district court should have dismissed the case.

C. CONSTITUTIONAL AND LEGISLATIVE COURTS

1. Congress Has Power to Establish Courts Other than Article III Courts.

a. **Introduction.** Pursuant to its Article I powers, Congress may create other courts and may delegate federal jurisdiction to those courts that it has established.

b. **Criminal court in District of Columbia--Palmore v. United States,** 411 U.S. 389 (1973).

Palmore v.
United States

1) **Facts.** Palmore (D) was arrested and charged with carrying an unregistered pistol in violation of the District of Columbia Code. Violations of the Code, which had been enacted by the Congress of the United States (P), were tried by judges of the Superior Court of the District of Columbia. D was found guilty in that court, and his conviction was affirmed by the District Court of Appeals, a local tribunal. D appealed the conviction to the Supreme Court. He argued that the District of Columbia Code, having been passed by Congress, was a law of the United States. Therefore, D contended that the Code was required to be administered by judges of the types specified by Article III of the Constitution; *i.e.*, judges with lifetime tenure and a guarantee against salary diminutions. The Supreme Court granted certiorari to review D's arguments.

2) **Issue.** Must the District of Columbia Criminal Code be administered by Article III courts whose judges have lifetime tenure and immunity against salary reduction?

3) **Held.** No. Judgment affirmed.

   a) The power to enact the Code and provide for its administration derives not from Article III, but from Article I, Section 8, clause 17, which empowers Congress to legislate for the District of Columbia.

   b) But laws passed pursuant to that authority need not be enforced only by Article III courts. In various contexts, laws passed by Congress have been carried out by courts not organized pursuant to Article III and whose judges do not enjoy lifetime tenure or immunity from salary reductions.

   c) For example, laws of Congress have in the past been carried out by territorial courts and by military tribunals. In fact, at one time almost all federal law was administered by state courts, and even today few states give their judges life tenure or protection from salary reduction.

   d) Congress was not required to create lower federal courts at all, and certainly was not obligated to provide that all its laws would be administered by them.

   e) Contrary to D's assertion that *O'Donoghue v. United States* compels the conclusion for which he contends, that case merely held that the judges of the District of Columbia Supreme Court and Court of Appeals were not subject to the salary reduction legislation that affected judges of legislative courts.

   f) Those courts resolved primarily federal questions of national scope and relevance, whereas the present day District of Columbia courts that administer the criminal code are almost entirely local in flavor and function.

   g) These courts were established solely to relieve the truly federal courts of the burden of administering the laws of the city. There is no basis for holding that the judges who administer the District of Columbia Code must have life tenure and protection from the threat of salary reductions.

4) **Dissent** (Douglas, J.). Because they lack lifetime tenure and other indicia of job security, the judges of the Superior Court of the District of Columbia are susceptible to pressure from a variety of factions, political and otherwise.

   a) Protection from such pressure is one of the touchstones of an incorruptible judiciary.

   b) When Congress resorts to its Article I powers as a basis for creating courts to administer its laws, it must clothe the judges with the protections that judges of Article III courts enjoy. Only in this way can the autonomy and integrity of the judiciary be preserved.

   c) Judges of Article III courts hold their offices during good behavior and their compensation cannot be diminished during their tenure in office.

   d) These same limitations do not apply to judges of the legislative courts. In addition, few states have afforded their judges the same privileges as Article III judges enjoy.

II. CASES ARISING UNDER THE CONSTITUTION, AND LAWS OF THE UNITED STATES

A. CONSTITUTIONAL AND STATUTORY BASES

1. **Source of Federal Question Jurisdiction—The Constitution.** Article III of the Constitution authorizes Congress to give the federal courts subject matter jurisdiction in "all Cases, in Law and Equity, arising under this Constitution, the Laws of the United States and Treaties made or which shall be made under this authority."

2. **Statutory Basis.** However, it was not until 1875 that Congress enacted 28 U.S.C. section 1331, the statute that gives the federal district courts original jurisdiction in federal question cases. The language of the statute is virtually identical to the language in Article III.

   a. The current statute states that the federal district courts shall have original jurisdiction in civil actions where the controversy "arises under the Constitution, laws or treaties of the United States."

   b. This statute is known as the general federal question or "arising under" statute.

3. **Federal Courts Have Enunciated Several Tests for Determining "Arising Under" Jurisdiction.**

   a. **The ingredient test.** The right or immunity created by federal law must be an ingredient of the plaintiff's claim for relief and the plaintiff's right or immunity must be supported or defeated by a construction of federal law.

      1) **Congressionally authorized suit--Osborn v. Bank of the United States,** 22 U.S. (9 Wheat.) 738 (1824).

         a) **Facts.** The state of Ohio passed a law levying a tax on all branches of the Bank of the United States (P) located within the state. Shortly thereafter, the case of *McCulloch v. Maryland* was decided, holding a similar tax void. P then sued to enjoin the state from enforcing its tax law. Hoping to collect the tax before the injunction could be issued, Osborn (D), the Ohio State Auditor, went to the bank and physically seized a portion of P's assets. The federal court entered a decree ordering D to repay to P the amount seized plus interest. D appeals, partly on the ground that the federal courts did not properly have jurisdiction over the action because the basic issues involved state, not federal, law.

         b) **Issue.** Does a suit "arise under" federal law by virtue of an act of Congress authorizing a bank to sue and be sued in federal courts?

         c) **Held.** Yes. Decree affirmed.

Osborn v. Bank of the United States

(1) Initially, it must be stated that the act of Congress that established P clearly authorized it to sue in federal court. Thus it is only the constitutionality of that provision that must be decided.

(2) Article III of the Constitution established the Supreme Court and defined cases in which the court shall exercise original jurisdiction. In all other federal cases, the Court has appellate jurisdiction only.

(3) However, this is not to say that inferior federal courts cannot exercise original jurisdiction in other federal cases, as D attempts to argue. Thus, if this case is found to arise under federal law, the circuit court may assume jurisdiction.

(4) P is totally a creature of federal statute. It cannot acquire the right to make a contract or bring a suit that is not ultimately authorized by federal law. As such, all of its actions must be seen as arising under federal law.

(5) Nonetheless, D contends that only those precise issues involving federal law may be presented to the federal courts. Other issues in the suit involving principles of state law may not be heard by the federal courts. This is not the law.

(6) If the powers of the federal court were to be so restricted, the federal courts would be rendered nearly powerless because virtually no case would be wholly devoid of nonfederal questions of law or fact. Instead, the Constitution must be read as permitting Congress to authorize the federal courts to exercise total jurisdiction over an action arising under federal law even though other nonfederal questions of law or fact may also be involved.

d) Dissent (Johnson, J.). Although it is true, as the majority states, that a federal court may assume jurisdiction over all questions involved in an action that principally arises under federal law, this principle does not permit federal jurisdiction in the action at hand. In this case, no federal question has arisen. Thus, federal jurisdiction is premature and not called for.

e) Comments.

(1) Commentators describe the basic premise of *Osborn* as being that every case in which a federal question might arise must be capable of being initiated in the federal courts because the issue of jurisdiction must be determined at the outset of the case. Despite the fact that the federal question might never actually be raised, the case, having been commenced in the federal court, may also be concluded there.

(2) The criticism is that there are numerous cases, actually involving only state law, about which it may be said that there are only remote connections to a federal question. It is suggested that Justice Marshall's holding in *Osborn* was greatly influenced by his belief that the bank would receive hostile treatment in state courts.

(3) In the *Pacific Railroad Removal Cases,* 115 U.S. 1 (1885), the Court held that any case involving a corporation chartered by an act of Congress fell within the ambit of "suits arising under the laws of the United States," thus allowing federal courts to assume jurisdiction. This ruling was limited by

the subsequent enactment of 28 U.S.C. section 1349, which provides for jurisdiction in the federal courts on the ground of federal incorporation only when the United States is the owner of more than 50% of the capital stock of the corporation.

b. Well-pleaded complaint rule. When it is the plaintiff who wishes a controversy litigated in federal court, his pleadings should always establish the existence of a federal question by showing that the claim arises under the Constitution, laws, or treaties of the United States. The allegation is a jurisdictional statement, and it is an essential element of his complaint, without which no federal court will take cognizance of his suit. If the defendant's pleadings reveal an issue of federal law, or if it is possible the defendant will raise an issue of federal law, federal jurisdiction ordinarily will not attach on that basis alone.

1) **Federal question not in pleadings but arising at trial--Albright v. Teas,** 106 U.S. 613 (1883).

Albright v. Teas

a) **Facts.** Teas (P) owned patents on certain improvements in coach pads, harness saddles, and saddle trees. By a written instrument, P assigned his letters patent to Albright and Cahoone (Ds), who agreed to use their best efforts to insure the manufacture of products utilizing the patented items and to pay royalties to P for the use of the patented improvements. After this agreement had been executed, Ds sold goods using the patented items, sometimes in conjunction with their business associate, Tompkins (D). Statements evidencing the sales were allegedly withheld from P, who also claimed that he was not receiving all the royalties due him under the contract. P sued in a New Jersey state court, seeking any amounts owed to him pursuant to the contract. Ds petitioned for removal to federal court, acknowledging that all parties were New Jersey citizens but arguing that the case arose under the patent laws, and thus presented a federal question. The petition for removal was granted, and a court-appointed master received testimony and other evidence. The federal court, on final hearing, granted P's motion to remand the case to the state court, holding that no federal question was present. On appeal, Ds argued that the evidence introduced at trial had raised a federal question, namely whether or not certain of the products sold actually incorporated the items invented by P or infringed his patents.

b) **Issue.** May the existence of a federal question be established by evidence offered at trial even if the pleadings did not reveal the presence of any federal question?

c) **Held.** No. Decree remanding to state court affirmed.

(1) The existence of a federal question should be established solely by the pleadings, unaided by any evidence adduced at trial, if a federal court is to exercise jurisdiction over a case. In this case, the pleadings reveal nothing more than a claim based on a written contract. Once P executed the assignment agreement, he retained no rights relating to the patents he had owned. Thus his suit could not have presented any questions arising under the patent laws. Therefore, the action was properly remanded to the state court.

4. **Federal Question Suits May Be Removed from State Court.** Ordinarily, a case that originally could have been filed in federal court is removable. If any portion of a case presents a federal question, the entire case generally may be removed to federal court. A case should be remanded to the state tribunal if it appears, at any stage of the proceedings, that no federal question is presented after all.

Feibelman
v. Packard

a. **State court proceeding involving federal statute--Feibelman v. Packard,** 109 U.S. 421 (1883).

1) **Facts.** Packard (D), a federal marshal, seized property that allegedly belonged to Feibelman (P). Packard acted pursuant to a writ or warrant issued by a federal judge in connection with bankruptcy proceedings instituted against E. Dreyfus & Co., but P argued that the writ did not justify the conduct engaged in by D. P sued Packard in state court and later amended his petition to name the sureties on Packard's bond as parties (Ds), alleging that Packard's acts were breaches of the conditions of the bond. Ds petitioned for removal to federal court, but their petition was denied. A removal petition was then filed in the federal circuit court, which held that the case presented a federal question because the bond was required by an act of Congress. Following removal, Ds won judgment. On appeal, an administrator who replaced Feibelman following his death argued that removal had been improper because the case presented no federal question.

2) **Issue.** May a state court proceeding be removed to federal court if it involves a federal statute?

3) **Held.** Yes. Judgment affirmed.

a) A state court civil action may be removed to federal court if it arises under an act of Congress and involves the requisite amount in controversy. In this case, the jurisdictional amount is met, and a federal statute is involved.

b) The action is more than a suit to recover damages for trespass. It is an action upon the bond itself, and therefore arises directly under the statute requiring that the bond be obtained.

c) Because the case arises under a statute of the United States, removal was appropriate. Therefore, the judgment against Ds must be affirmed.

5. **Federal Question Must Be the Essential Element of Plaintiff's Claims.** A plaintiff may not gain entry to the federal courts merely by padding his complaint with frivolous, nonessential references to matters of federal law.

Joy v.
St. Louis

a. **Extraneous references to federal law--Joy v. St. Louis,** 201 U.S. 332 (1906).

1) **Facts.** Joy (P), through a federal land patent, acquired title to land bordering the Mississippi River. Because of natural accretions and deposits, the area of the river bank expanded. P, claiming that the newly created land was part of his property, sued in federal court to eject the city of St. Louis (D) from the land. The complaint stated that

title had derived from the patent pursuant to an act of Congress, and P argued that the case thus involved a question of federal law and gave the federal courts jurisdiction over the matter. D contended that federal question jurisdiction should not attach because the reference to federal law was not essential to the complaint. The circuit court dismissed the complaint for lack of jurisdiction, and P appeals.

2) **Issue.** May a plaintiff, by including extraneous allegations relating to federal law in his complaint, require the federal courts to exercise jurisdiction over his case?

3) **Held.** No. Dismissal affirmed.

   a) The existence of a federal question must appear as a necessary element of the plaintiff's statement of his cause of action for federal jurisdiction to attach to a case. P needed to allege only that he was the owner of the land and entitled to possession of it, that D was wrongfully withholding that possession, and that P was damaged as a result.

   b) The allegation that title had been acquired was superfluous, and thus could not constitute a basis for the exercise of federal jurisdiction. It has been held that even a legitimate allegation that land derives from an act of Congress does not create an issue of federal law.

   c) In this case, whether the newly created land is within the original patent is merely a question of fact, and P's claim to this property may be resolved by reference to state and local law. Therefore, the circuit court properly dismissed the complaint on the ground that it asserted no valid basis for the exercise of federal jurisdiction.

4) **Comment.** Whether an allegation that title to land derives from the United States will be adequate to justify the exercise of federal jurisdiction may depend upon the nature of the action in which such an allegation is presented. Thus, federal jurisdiction will attach when the allegation is included in a bill to remove a cloud on title, but not when it is presented in a suit to quiet title. This is because only in the former action would such an allegation be a proper and necessary element of the claim for relief.

6. Plaintiff May Not Anticipate a Defense Based on a Federal Question to Form the Basis for Subject Matter Jurisdiction. The federal question involved in a case must arise from the plaintiff's complaint, unaided by potential defenses.

   a. **Federal statute creating defense--Louisville and Nashville R.R. v. Mottley,** 211 U.S. 149 (1908).

Louisville
and Nashville
R.R. v.
Mottley

     1) **Facts.** In 1871, the Mottleys (Ps) were injured when the Louisville and Nashville R.R. (D) train in which they were traveling collided with another train owned by D. Ps agreed to release D from all potential damage claims, in exchange for which D issued free passes, renewable annually, to Ps. D sent the passes each year until 1907, when the

passes were not renewed, apparently because Congress had enacted a law that precluded common carriers from granting free transportation. Ps sued D in federal court for specific performance of the agreement to provide lifetime passes and asserted that the act of Congress did not prevent the issuance of passes under the circumstances, or that, if construed as prohibiting their issuance, the statute was unconstitutional in that it deprived Ps of their property without due process of law. The court granted the relief sought, and D appeals directly to the Supreme Court.

2) **Issue.** May federal jurisdiction be exercised in a case if the only federal question involved will arise in connection with an anticipated defense or the response to that defense?

3) **Held.** No.

a) A federal court may not exercise jurisdiction over a case merely because an anticipated defense or the response thereto will involve a federal question.

b) There was no basis for diversity jurisdiction, and the federal law that Ps challenged need not be considered except as a defense offered by D.

c) Because the issue of federal law was not raised by the complaint itself, federal jurisdiction did not attach.

d) Thus, although D offered no objection, the court below had no basis for exercising jurisdiction over this case and should have dismissed the complaint.

4) **Comment.** The *Mottley* rule seems reasonable and desirable because a plaintiff could almost always imagine a plausible defense that might reasonably be interposed by his adversary and would involve an issue of federal law.

7. **Patent Suits.** Cases relating to the patent laws are within the jurisdiction of the federal courts. As a practical matter, state courts would lack the necessary experience and expertise to administer the patent laws as effectively as their federal counterparts.

American Well Works Co. v. Layne & Bowler Co.

a. **Peripheral patent issue--American Well Works Co. v. Layne & Bowler Co.,** 241 U.S. 257 (1916).

1) **Facts.** American Well Works Co. (P) produced and began selling a certain type of pump, allegedly the best on the market. Layne & Bowler Co. (D) claimed that the pump resembled parts of the pump sold by D, and threatened to sue both P and its customers. Suits were actually commenced against some customers. P then filed in state court seeking damages for the harm caused to its business by the litigation, threats, and accusations undertaken by D. The action was later removed to federal district court, whereupon P moved to have the case remanded to the state court. The federal court ruled that because the cause of action had arisen under the patent laws of the United

States, the state court had lacked jurisdiction over the case in the first place, and that the federal court was therefore not entitled to exercise removal jurisdiction. On appeal, it was contended that the cause of action was not based on the patent laws and thus presented no federal question.

2) **Issue.** May a federal court exercise jurisdiction over a suit alleging damage to a business as a result of a threat to sue for patent infringement?

3) **Held.** No. Judgment reversed.

   a) A suit for damages caused to one's business by a threat to sue for patent infringement is not a suit under the patent laws, and therefore may not be maintained in federal court.

   b) Such an action presented no federal question because it is not the patent, but the damage caused to the business, which is the basis for the cause of action.

   c) Whether the type of interference that has been alleged is actionable is purely a matter of state law. Therefore, this suit is not one to which federal jurisdiction attaches.

4) **Dissent** (McKenna, J.). The case clearly involves a controversy arising under the patent laws and thus presents a federal question.

8. **Source of the Right Creates a Federal Question.** In order for a suit to "arise under" federal law, the federal controversy must be basic to the dispute rather than of a collateral nature. Generally, it is the source of the right rather than the nature of that right that must raise the federal question. Merely because Congress creates a right does not mean that Congress has granted federal subject matter jurisdiction to enforce that right.

   a. **Suit challenging constitutionality of bank legislation--Smith v. Kansas City Title & Trust Co.,** 255 U.S. 180 (1921).

      1) **Facts.** A shareholder (P) in the Kansas City Title & Trust Company (D) sought to enjoin D from investing D's funds in farm loan bonds issued by federal land banks or joint-stock banks under authority of the Federal Farm Loan Act. P claimed that these acts were beyond the constitutional power of Congress. P alleged that D had been induced to make the investment by relying on provisions of the Farm Loan Acts that declare that farm loan bonds are instrumentalities of the United States government and, as such, the income from the bonds are exempt from federal, state, municipal, and local taxation. P sought to have these acts of Congress declared unconstitutional. The district court granted D's motion to dismiss, and P appeals.

      2) **Issue.** Does a suit challenging the constitutionality of banking legislation passed by Congress provide a basis for federal subject matter jurisdiction?

3) Held. Yes.

    a) The attack upon the proposed investment in the bonds is because of the alleged unconstitutionality of the acts of Congress undertaking to organize the banks and authorize the issue of the bonds.

    b) The general rule is that there is federal jurisdiction if it appears from the plaintiff's statement that the right to relief depends upon the construction or application of the Constitution or laws of the United States.

    c) D's directors were about to make investments based on their belief that the act authorizing the investments was constitutional and the investments were desirable. P alleges that the securities were issued under an unconstitutional law.

    d) Since the rights involved may be denied by one construction of the Constitution and sustained by another construction, federal subject matter does exist.

4) Dissent (Holmes, J.).

    a) This suit arises solely from the law of Missouri.

    b) The scope of D's duty depends on the charter of the corporation and the other laws of Missouri.

Moore v.
Cheasapeake
& Ohio
Railway Co.

b. Invocation of federal laws when the remedy is a creature of state law--Moore v. Chesapeake & Ohio Railway Co., 291 U.S. 205 (1934).

1) Facts. Moore (P) brought this action in the northern district of Indiana to recover for injuries sustained in the course of his employment with Chesapeake & Ohio Railway Company (D), an interstate carrier. There was diversity of citizenship between the parties, but venue was proper only if diversity was the only basis of jurisdiction for the second count in the complaint. In the second count, P alleged that he was employed in intrastate commerce and claimed under the Safety Appliance Acts, the rules of the Interstate Commerce Commission, and the Employers' Liability Act of Kentucky.

2) Issue. Does the mere invocation of a federal law give rise to federal question jurisdiction?

3) Held. No.

    a) While invoking the Safety Appliance Act, P relied upon the laws of Kentucky where the cause of action arose.

    b) The statute of Kentucky, in prescribing the liability of common carriers engaged in intrastate commerce corresponds almost exactly to the provisions of the Federal Employers' Liability Act as to injuries in interstate commerce.

    c) The Federal Safety Appliance Acts, while prescribing absolute duties and creating correlative rights, did not attempt to lay down rules governing actions for enforcing those rights.

d)   The second count of the complaint set forth a cause of action under the Kentucky statute, and the suit is not one arising under the Constitution or laws of the United States.

e)   In view of the diversity of citizenship and residence of P, the district court had jurisdiction.

c.   **Contract action with genesis in federal statute--Gully v. First National Bank in Meridian,** 299 U.S. 109 (1936).

1)   **Facts.** In 1931, assets of the First National Bank *of* Meridian were conveyed to the First National Bank *in* Meridian (D), which contractually assumed certain debts of the defunct bank. Gully (P), the state tax collector, sued D in a Mississippi state court, contending that one of the debts assumed was the bank's obligation to pay taxes owed by the shareholders on their shares of stock in the first bank. Pursuant to D's petition, the case was removed to federal court on the ground that it arose under a federal law that allowed the shares of national banks to be taxed. The district court denied P's motion to remand the case to state court, and his complaint was eventually dismissed. The circuit court of appeals affirmed the judgment of dismissal, but the Supreme Court granted certiorari to consider whether the case had properly been deemed to arise under federal law.

2)   **Issue.** May the federal courts exercise jurisdiction over an ordinary contract action that arguably has its genesis in a federal statute relating to the subject matter of the contract?

3)   **Held.** No. Judgment reversed.

a)   Federal question jurisdiction is established only if a right or immunity created by the Constitution or laws of the United States is an essential element of the plaintiff's cause of action. This test, necessarily an imprecise one, is the most reasonable one that can be derived from the legion of cases that have considered the concept of "arising under" federal law.

b)   The presence of an issue of federal law must appear from the complaint itself, unaided by any anticipated defenses or the responses thereto.

c)   This case is not primarily federal in character. It is based mainly on a contract that was a creation of Mississippi law.

d)   A federal enabling statute authorizes the states to impose taxes on shares in national banks. But, the statute is permissive rather than mandatory.

e)   The taxes P seeks to collect are actually levied pursuant to a state enactment.

f)   Although a federal question may lurk in the background of this case, it is basically a state law action and should not have been removed. Therefore, the judgment should be reversed, and the cause remanded to state court.

4) Comments. As *Gully* and the cases surveyed therein suggest, no single test of when a case arises under federal law has yet been satisfactorily formulated. Thus, most courts hesitate to articulate a fixed standard, preferring instead to evaluate the circumstances of each particular case to determine whether a federal question is presented.

9. The Court Cannot Consider Defenses to Establish Federal Question Jurisdiction. Federal issues that will be raised by the defendant may not be considered to establish subject matter jurisdiction.

Thurston
Motor Lines
v. Jordan K.
Rand, Ltd.

a. Character of action, not defense, determines jurisdiction--Thurston Motor Lines v. Jordan K. Rand, Ltd., 460 U.S. 533 (1983).

1) Facts. Thurston Motor Lines (P), a common carrier, brought suit in United States District Court against Rand (D) for failing to pay $660 in freight charges. The complaint alleged that the action arose under the Interstate Commerce Act. The district court granted D's motion to dismiss for lack of subject matter jurisdiction, and the Court of Appeals for the Ninth Circuit affirmed. D is petitioning for a writ of certiorari.

2) Issue. Can a common carrier, which is authorized by the Interstate Commerce Commission to transport commodities, bring a contract collection action in federal court?

3) Held. Yes. Petition for certiorari granted, judgment reversed, and case remanded.

a) The Interstate Commerce Act requires the carrier to collect and the consignee to pay all lawful charges duly prescribed by the tariff. The duties and obligations grow out of and depend upon that Act.

b) A carrier's claim is predicated on the tariff and not an understanding with the shipper.

c) The court of appeals was in error because it sought to decide federal jurisdiction based upon the defenses pleaded by the shipper, but it is the character of the action and not the defense that determines whether there is federal jurisdiction. As the action was brought pursuant to a federal act, federal jurisdiction exists.

10. Establishing Federal Question Jurisdiction. The plaintiff must establish any federal question that he anticipates the defendant will raise and on which he will predicate jurisdiction.

a. In general. Only matters essential to the plaintiff's bare cause of action may be considered for purposes of establishing federal question jurisdiction.

Merrell Dow
Pharmaceuti-
cals, Inc. v.
Thompson

b. Violation of federal statute as part of state cause of action--Merrell Dow Pharmaceuticals, Inc. v. Thompson, 478 U.S. 804 (1986).

1) Facts. The Thompsons and the MacTavishes (Ps) are residents of Canada and Scotland, respectively. They filed suit in state court against Merrell Dow Pharmaceuticals (D), the manufacturer and distributor of the drug Benedictin, alleging that the use of the drug during pregnancy by the respective mothers resulted in their giving birth to deformed children. The complaint stated six causes of action, five of them state-related: negligence, breach of warranty, strict liability, fraud, and gross negligence. The other was a federal cause of action alleging that the misbranding of the drug was a violation of the Federal Food, Drug, and Cosmetic Act ("FDCA"). D sought removal to federal court on the basis of this FDCA violation, which was granted. The district court then granted D's motion for dismissal on forum non conveniens. The Court of Appeals for the Sixth Circuit reversed, stating that the FDCA does not create or imply a private right of action for individuals injured as a result of the violation of the Act. The United States Supreme Court granted certiorari.

2) **Issue.** In a tort based on several state-related causes of action, is the inclusion of the violation of a federal standard sufficient to establish federal jurisdiction?

3) **Held.** No. Judgment affirmed.

a) Federal question jurisdiction exists only if Ps' right of relief depended on a substantial question of federal law. Ps' causes of action referred to the FDCA as merely one available criterion for determining whether D was negligent. A jury could find negligence on the part of D without finding a violation of FDCA, so Ps' causes of action did not depend necessarily upon a question of federal law.

b) D contends that federal question jurisdiction is appropriate when a substantial, disputed question of federal law is a necessary element of one of the well-pleaded state claims. However, there is a need for careful judgment about the exercise of federal judicial power in an area of uncertain jurisdiction. Given the significance of the assumed congressional determination to preclude federal private remedies, the presence of the federal issue, as an element of the state tort, is not the kind of adjudication for which jurisdiction would serve congressional purposes and the federal system.

c) While there is a powerful federal interest in having a uniform interpretation of a federal statute, granting federal jurisdiction is not the only way to achieve this review. The Supreme Court retains ultimate power to review the decision of a federal issue in a state cause of action. The complaint alleging a violation of a federal statute as an element of a state cause of action, when Congress has determined that there should be no private, federal cause of action for the violation, does not state a claim "arising under the Constitution, laws, or treaties of the United States."

4) **Dissent** (Brennan, White, Marshall, Blackmun, JJ.). It may be that a decision by Congress not to create a private remedy is intended to preclude all private enforcement. If that is so, then a state cause of action that makes relief available to private individuals for violations of the FDCA is preempted. But if Congress's decision not to provide a federal remedy does not preempt such a state remedy, then, in light of the FDCA's clear policy of relying on the federal courts for enforcement, it also should not foreclose federal jurisdiction over that state remedy.

B. PROTECTIVE JURISDICTION

1. **A Statute Passed by Congress Falls Under the 28 U.S.C. Section 1331 "Arising Under" Provision.** The theory of protective jurisdiction is that when Congress passes a statute that gives the federal courts jurisdiction to hear a category of claims, that jurisdictional statute is a law of the United States within the meaning of Article III. Even though Congress has not enacted any substantive rules to go along with the jurisdictional grant, the court would nevertheless have subject matter jurisdiction within the "arising under" provision of 28 U.S.C. section 1331, but the substantive rights would be decided according to state law.

2. **Where Federal Interest Exists, Federal Common Law Is Used.** In those areas where there is a significant federal interest in regulating the substantive rights of the parties, the courts will decide the case based on federal common law rather than state law.

E. Edelmann & Co. v. Triple-A Specialty Co.

3. **Declaratory Judgment as to Patent Infringement--E. Edelmann & Co. v. Triple-A Specialty Co.,** 88 F.2d 852 (7th Cir. 1937).

   a. **Facts.** Triple-A Specialty Co. (P) charged that E. Edelmann & Co. (D) had falsely accused it of infringing upon D's patent for a hydrometer. P therefore sued in federal district court, seeking a declaratory judgment concerning the validity of the patent and whether or not it had been infringed. P also asked the court to enjoin D from circulating the infringement charges among members of the trade. The court declared that P had not violated the patent and ordered an accounting to determine the amount of damages, if any, that had resulted from circulation of the wrongful infringement charges. On appeal, D argues that the federal court had lacked jurisdiction to consider the case.

   b. **Issue.** May a federal court exercise jurisdiction over a suit that seeks a declaratory judgment concerning the infringement of a patent and relief from allegedly unfounded allegations of infringement?

   c. **Held.** Yes. Decree affirmed.

      1) A federal court may exercise jurisdiction over a suit seeking a declaratory judgment that a patent has not been infringed. The Declaratory Judgment Act, pursuant to which P seeks relief, created no new substantive rights, but instead provided an additional remedy for the parties to a controversy.

      2) Prior to passage of the Act, a party had no right to sue for a declaration that a patent was not infringed, but that does not mean that P's suit is not one arising under the patent laws. Even though the alleged infringer could not previously have brought suit, the type of controversy involved before passage of the Act is the same as the present controversy.

      3) It is true that P's action for damages has no federal basis, but the facet of the case pertaining to the validity of the patent obviously is of a federal nature. Therefore, the district court properly assumed jurisdiction over this case.

4. **Anticipated Defense as Basis for Federal Question--Skelly Oil Co. v. Phillips Petroleum Co.,** 339 U.S. 667 (1950).

a. **Facts.** The Michigan-Wisconsin Pipe Line Company ("Michigan-Wisconsin"), anxious to construct a pipeline to carry natural gas from Texas to Michigan and Wisconsin, applied to the Federal Power Commission for a certificate of public convenience and necessity. To obtain the certificate, Michigan-Wisconsin had to prove that it had access to adequate reserves of gas. It therefore contracted with Phillips Petroleum Company (P), which agreed to make gas available from the Hugoton gas field, located in the southwestern United States. P contracted with Skelly Oil Company, Stanolind Oil and Gas Company, and Magnolia Petroleum Company (Ds). P agreed to purchase gas from these companies, but the contracts with each company provided that should Michigan-Wisconsin fail to obtain its certificate of public convenience and necessity by October 1, 1946, each D would have the right, after December 1, 1946 but before the issuance of a certificate, to terminate its contract with P. On November 30, 1946, the Federal Power Commission issued a certificate of public convenience and necessity to Michigan-Wisconsin. However, several burdensome conditions were attached to the issuance of that certificate, some of which were to be incorporated into a supplemental order. Michigan-Wisconsin was given 15 days from the issuance of the supplemental order to accept or refuse the certificate. The Commission's decision was made public on December 2, 1946, and on that date, Ds each gave notice terminating their contracts with P. All three Ds were then sued in federal district court by Michigan-Wisconsin and P, both of which sought relief under the Federal Declaratory Judgment Act. They claimed that, inasmuch as a certificate had been issued before Ds had sent termination notices, the contracts with the three companies should be declared to be in force. Michigan-Wisconsin was ultimately dropped from the case by the district court, but motions to dismiss the complaint for want of jurisdiction were denied. The district court ruled that the contested contracts were still in effect, and the appellate court affirmed. In seeking redress from the Supreme Court, Ds renew their claim that the district court had been without jurisdiction in the first place because the case did not present a federal question.

b. **Issue.** May the existence of a federal question be established by reference to an anticipated defense or the response to that defense?

c. **Held.** No. Judgment with respect to Magnolia vacated and remanded; judgment with respect to Skelly and Stanolind reversed.

   1) The existence of a federal question must be established by the plaintiff's own claim, and may not depend on an anticipated defense or on the response to a defense.

   2) Any federal claim that a plaintiff could possibly have raised had it not invoked the Declaratory Judgment Act could have arisen only as a defense by one of the other companies, or in response to such a defense. The action was brought pursuant to the Act only because P sought a predicate for federal jurisdiction.

3) The Declaratory Judgment Act does not expand the jurisdiction of federal courts. It merely empowers them to grant declaratory relief in cases over which they were already entitled to exercise jurisdiction.

4) Had P not invoked the Act, it could have sued for either damages or specific performance, but neither of these remedies would have required the consideration of questions of federal law.

5) If federal jurisdiction could be based on an anticipated defense, the docket of the federal tribunals would become dangerously overloaded. Therefore, the claims against Skelly and Stanolind should have been dismissed.

6) However, because Magnolia is a citizen of a different state than P, the suit against Magnolia was cognizable in the federal courts because of diversity jurisdiction.

7) Nevertheless, the judgment against Magnolia should be reversed, because the lower federal court erred in assuming that, because under the language of the Natural Gas Act a certificate was issued to Michigan-Wisconsin, a certificate was issued within the meaning of the contract between Phillips and Magnolia.

8) The words as used in the statute may have a different meaning than the parties intended them to have in the contract. Therefore, the judgments against Skelly and Stanolind should be reversed and the claims against them dismissed, while the case against Magnolia should be remanded for further proceedings.

d. **Dissent in part** (Vinson, C.J., Burton, J.). The judgments against Skelly and Stanolind should, as the majority decided, be dismissed. But the judgment against Magnolia should be affirmed, because Michigan-Wisconsin clearly was issued a certificate within the meaning of the contract.

Verlinden B.V. v. Central Bank of Nigeria

5. **Suit Between Foreign Parties--Verlinden B.V. v. Central Bank of Nigeria**, 461 U.S. 480 (1983).

a. **Facts.** Verlinden (P), a Dutch corporation, entered into a contract to sell cement to the Federal Republic of Nigeria. The contract provided that Nigeria was to establish a confirmed letter of credit for the purchase price. Subsequently, P sued the Central Bank of Nigeria (D), an agent of the Republic of Nigeria, in the United States District Court for the Southern District of New York for anticipatory breach of the letter of credit. P claimed jurisdiction under the provision of the Federal Sovereign Immunities Act granting district courts jurisdiction of "any non-jury civil action against a foreign state . . . as to any claim for relief in personam with respect to which the foreign state is not entitled to immunity." The district court dismissed the action on the basis that none of the exceptions to sovereign immunity specified in the statute were applicable. The Second Circuit affirmed the dismissal on the grounds that neither the Diversity Jurisdiction Clause nor the "Arising Under" Clause of Article III covered suits between foreign plaintiffs and sovereigns. The Supreme Court granted certiorari.

    b.   **Issue.** Does an act authorizing one foreign party to sue another in federal court violate the "Arising Under" Clause of Article III?

    c.   **Held.** No. Judgment reversed and remanded.

        1)   The "Arising Under" Clause of Article III provides an appropriate basis for the statutory grant of subject matter jurisdiction for actions by foreign plaintiffs.

        2)   By reason of its authority over foreign commerce and foreign relations, Congress has the undisputed power to decide, as a matter of federal law, whether and under what circumstances foreign nations should be amenable to suit in the United States.

        3)   To promote these federal interests, Congress exercised its Article I powers by enacting the Federal Sovereign Immunities Act, which must be applied by the district courts in every action against a foreign sovereign, since subject matter jurisdiction in any such action depends on the existence of one of the specified exceptions to foreign sovereign immunity.

        4)   The resulting jurisdictional grant is within the bounds of Article III since every action against a foreign sovereign necessarily involves application of a body of substantive federal law and, accordingly, "arises under" federal law within the meaning of Article III.

C. JURISDICTION DISTINGUISHED FROM MERITS

    1.   **Existence of Remedy.** If a plaintiff asserts a claim arising from or involving a substantial federal constitutional right, the objection that there is no federal remedy to enforce the right raises a question going to the merits of the claim, and therefore it has to be determined by the court. If no substantial federal question is raised in the complaint, the action should be dismissed on jurisdictional grounds.

    2.   **Jurisdiction over Violation of Constitutional Rights--Bell v. Hood,** 327 U.S. 678 (1946).   Bell v. Hood

        a.   **Facts.** Bell and others (Ps) claimed that their constitutional rights to be free from unreasonable searches and seizures and from deprivation of liberty without due process had been violated by Hood and other members of the FBI (Ds). Ps filed suit in federal court seeking damages in excess of the jurisdictional requirement. (Note that this case arose before the jurisdictional amount requirement in federal cases arising under section 1331 was abolished in 1980.) Ds moved to dismiss the complaint for failure to state a claim upon which relief could be granted and for summary judgment. The district court instead dismissed the suit for want of federal jurisdiction under section 1331 on the ground that the action did not arise under the Constitution and laws of the United States. The circuit court of appeals affirmed. Certiorari was granted because of the importance of the jurisdictional issue.

b. **Issue.** Must the district court take jurisdiction when a complaint seeks damages for violation of Fourth and Fifth Amendment rights?

c. **Held.** Yes. Judgment reversed.

1) If a complaint is drawn so as to seek recovery directly under the Constitution or laws of the United States, the federal courts must take jurisdiction unless the alleged claim appears to be immaterial or wholly insubstantial and frivolous.

2) Jurisdiction cannot be defeated by the possibility that the complaint might fail to state facts upon which P could actually recover damages.

3) This Court has never specifically decided whether federal courts can grant monetary recovery to plaintiffs whose constitutional rights under the Fourth and Fifth Amendments have been violated by federal officers. But such a question is a question of law and, like an issue of fact, must be decided after and not before the court has assumed jurisdiction.

4) If the complaint should fail to state a ground for relief, then the court could dismiss on the merits and further action on the transaction would be res judicata.

5) But such matters certainly do not preclude the court from taking jurisdiction when the cause of action is clearly based solely on the Fourth and Fifth Amendments to the Constitution. Therefore, the decision of the court of appeals must be reversed.

d. **Dissent** (Stone, C.J., Burton, J.). Where there is neither a constitutional provision nor an act of Congress authorizing money damages for violations of Fourth and Fifth Amendment rights, the mere assertion by the plaintiff that he is entitled to such recovery is not sufficient to meet jurisdictional requirements. The court below was correct in determining that the district court could not exercise jurisdiction because no cause of action arising under the Constitution or laws of the United States was stated.

e. **Comment.** In 1971, the Supreme Court held, in *Bivens v. Six Unknown Named Agents of the Bureau of Narcotics,* 403 U.S. 388 (1971), that there was a federal right to recover money damages against federal officers who violated the Fourth Amendment. Also, because the federal court has jurisdiction, it may exercise ancillary (supplemental) jurisdiction to reach related nonfederal claims.

D. PENDENT JURISDICTION

1. **Doctrine.** The basic doctrine of pendent jurisdiction arises when there is a claim over which the federal courts have subject matter jurisdiction that is linked to another claim not independently within their jurisdiction. In this situation, if the claims are closely enough related to be considered *arising out of a common nucleus of operative facts,* the court will exercise jurisdiction over both the federal and nonfederal claims.

2. **State Issue Closely Related to Federal Issue--United Mine Workers of America v. Gibbs,** 383 U.S. 715 (1966).

    a. **Facts.** There was a dispute between the United Mine Workers of America (D) and the Southern Labor Union over who should represent the coal miners in a particular area. Tennessee Consolidated Coal Company closed a mine where over 100 men belonging to the United Mine Workers were employed. Later, Grundy Company, a wholly owned subsidiary of Tennessee Consolidated Coal Company, hired Gibbs (P) to open a new mine using members of the Southern Labor Union. P was also given a contract to haul the mine's coal to the nearest railroad loading point. Members of D's Local 5881 forcibly prevented the opening of the mine. P lost his job and never entered into the performance of his haulage contract. He soon began to lose other trucking contracts and mine leases he held in the area. P claims this was a result of a concerted union plan against him. He filed suit in the United States District Court for the Eastern District of Tennessee for violation of section 303 of the Labor Management Relations Act and under a state law claim (based on the doctrine of pendent jurisdiction) that there was an unlawful conspiracy and boycott aimed at him to interfere with his employment and haulage contracts. The jury's verdict was that D had violated both section 303 and the state law. On motion, the trial court set aside the award of damages for the haulage contract and entered a verdict for D on the issue of violation of section 303, which was the federal claim. The award as to the state claim was sustained. The court of appeals affirmed. The Supreme Court granted certiorari.

    b. **Issue.** Can federal courts decide state issues that are closely related to the federal issues being litigated?

    c. **Held.** Yes. Judgment reversed.

        1)   When there are both state and federal claims involved in the same set of facts and the claims are such that the plaintiff would ordinarily be expected to try them all in one judicial proceeding, the federal court has the power to hear both the state and the federal claims.

        2)   The federal claims must have substance sufficient to confer subject matter jurisdiction on the court.

        3)   The court is not required to exercise pendent jurisdiction in every case. It has consistently been recognized that pendent jurisdiction is a doctrine of discretion, not of plaintiff's right. The court should look to judicial economy, convenience, and fairness to litigants in deciding whether to exercise jurisdiction over the state claims.

        4)   If the factual relationship between the state and federal claims is so close that they ought to be litigated at the same trial, the court ought to grant pendent jurisdiction to save an extra trial. If the issues are so complicated that they are confusing to the jury, the court probably should dismiss the state claim.

        5)   The issue of whether pendent jurisdiction has been properly assumed is one that remains open throughout the litigation. If, before the trial, the federal claim is dismissed, the state claim probably should also be

dismissed. If it appears that a state claim constitutes the real body of a case, the case may fairly be dismissed.

6) P may not recover damages for conspiracy under the state claim. To that effect, the judgment is reversed.

    d.   **Comment.** This case helped clarify the law that had been established by the case of *Hurn v. Oursler*, 289 U.S. 238 (1933).

3.   **Pendent Party Jurisdiction.** A pendent party is one involved in a case only with respect to a pendent claim, and for whom there is no independent basis for federal subject matter jurisdiction.

Finley v.
United States

    a.   **Supreme Court held pendent party jurisdiction unavailable--Finley v. United States,** 490 U.S. 545 (1989).

    1)   **Facts.** Finley's (P's) husband and two of her children were killed in a plane crash near an airport in San Diego. In state court, P sued an electric utility and the city of San Diego (Ds) for negligence. She later discovered that the Federal Aviation Administration was responsible for maintaining the runway lights, and thus sued the United States (D) in federal court pursuant to the Federal Tort Claims Act. A year later, P moved to amend the federal complaint to include claims against the original state court Ds, as to whom there was no independent basis (such as diversity of citizenship) for federal jurisdiction. The district court granted P's motion under the concept of pendent jurisdiction, citing judicial economy. In an interlocutory appeal, the ninth circuit reversed the grant of P's motion on grounds that it had previously disallowed such "pendent party" jurisdiction. The Supreme Court granted certiorari to resolve a split among the circuits.

    2)   **Issue.** May the federal courts exercise pendent party jurisdiction, *i.e.*, jurisdiction over parties not named in any claim that is independently cognizable by the federal court?

    3)   **Held.** No. Judgment affirmed.

    a)   *United Mine Workers of America v. Gibbs* specifies that for pendent claim jurisdiction, the required relationship between the federal and nonfederal claims is that they "derive from a common nucleus of operative fact," as do P's claims here. Analytically, however, pendent party jurisdiction is fundamentally different from pendent claim jurisdiction.

    b)   In our previous cases (*Zahn v. International Paper Co., Aldinger v. Howard, Owen Equipment & Erection Co. v. Kroger*), we have not assumed that full constitutional power has been congressionally authorized with respect to the addition of parties. When we have allowed the addition of parties, there has always been some other factor—such as the party having a claim on property within the court's exclusive control—in addition to the bare *Gibbs* relationship of the claims.

c)   P correctly asserts that the Federal Tort Claims Act requires that she sue the United States in federal court, and that disallowance of pendent party jurisdiction would require her to sue the state defendants separately in state court. This difficulty alone is not enough to confer pendent party jurisdiction. We previously held that suits under the Tucker Act similarly cannot include private defendants, presenting the same difficulty.

d)   The language of the Federal Tort Claims Act does not extend jurisdiction to pendent parties. P's assertion that the 1948 revision of the Act's language grants such jurisdiction is incorrect. That revision merely conformed the language of the Act to the then-recent Federal Rules of Civil Procedure. Also, P's reliance on the 1948 revision ignores the fact that pendent *party* jurisdiction was not considered even remotely viable until pendent *claim* jurisdiction was liberalized in *Gibbs* nearly 20 years later.

4)   **Dissent** (Blackmun, J.). In *Aldinger,* the Court found a congressional intent to exclude municipalities from the scope of section 1983 actions, and barred the use of pendent party jurisdiction to get around that limitation. Here, there is no such substantive limitation. The sensible result here, since the federal court is the only possible one for the defendant United States, would be to allow pendent party jurisdiction.

5)   **Dissent** (Stevens, Brennan, Marshall, JJ.). *Gibbs* highlighted the modern conception of a "civil action" and a "constitutional case." After *Gibbs,* the best federal appellate judges (*e.g.,* Henry Friendly) saw that its reasoning applied to pendent party situations, especially where Congress had vested the federal courts with exclusive jurisdiction over a matter. The absence of an affirmative grant of jurisdiction over pendent parties should not be taken as an implicit rejection of it. If this were the case, our careful reasoning in *Aldinger* would have been wholly unnecessary. Finally, denial of pendent party jurisdiction interferes with a court's ability to grant full relief.

6)   **Comment.** A year after *Finley* was decided, Congress effectively overruled it with the enactment of 28 U.S.C. section 1367, the supplemental jurisdiction statute discussed immediately below. Supplemental jurisdiction now allows pendent party jurisdiction of the type sought in *Finley.*

E.   SUPPLEMENTAL JURISDICTION

1.   **In General.** In late 1990, Congress codified the concepts of pendent and ancillary jurisdiction under the name supplemental jurisdiction. [28 U.S.C. §1367] Supplemental jurisdiction is available, with exceptions, over all claims so related to the claim over which there is original jurisdiction that they form part of the same case or controversy. The supplemental claims may specifically involve the joinder or intervention of additional parties.

2.   **Exceptions.** Exceptions to supplemental jurisdiction are for claims by plaintiffs against persons made parties by impleader, joinder, or intervention, or claims by persons proposed to be joined under Rule 19 or seeking to intervene under Rule 24, when any of these would be inconsistent with the requirements of diversity jurisdiction. Thus, for example, a plaintiff who wants to sue two defendants, only one of whom is diverse, cannot sue the diverse one and wait for the nondiverse one to be joined.

3.   **Discretionary Aspect.** The court may decline to exercise supplemental jurisdiction if the state law claim is novel or complex, if the state law claim predominates, if the federal claim has been dismissed, or for other compelling reasons.

Wasserman v. Potamkin Toyota, Inc.

4.   **Discretion to Hear State Law Claims--Wasserman v. Potamkin Toyota, Inc.,** 1998 WL 744090 (E.D. Pa. 1998)

a.   **Facts.** Rachel Wasserman (P) worked for almost two years at Potamkin Toyota, Inc. ("Potamkin") as an executive assistant for managers Weisen and Parrilla, and Vice President Hyman. P alleges that, during her employment, Weisen and Parrilla subjected her to a continuous pattern of sexually hostile and offensive conduct that created a hostile and offensive work environment. P brought her objections to Hyman who failed to intervene, subjected P to further harassment and thus added to the sexually offensive environment. P involuntarily resigned her position and filed suit against Potamkin, Weisen, Parrilla, and Hyman (Ds) alleging four causes of action. The first two counts were against Potamkin (Title VII and a claim under the Pennsylvania Human Relations Act ("PHRA")). The third count was against Weisen, Parrilla, and Hyman under the PHRA. The fourth count was for intentional infliction of emotional distress against all Ds. Ds now move to dismiss the third and fourth counts. The court dismissed the fourth count for failure to state a claim. This portion of the opinion deals with the third count. Ds are arguing that the court should decline supplemental jurisdiction over P's PHRA claim.

b.   **Issue.** Should the court exercise supplemental jurisdiction under 28 U.S.C. 1367 to hear P's state law claims along with her federal law claim?

c.   **Held.** Yes. Ds motion denied.

1)   Section 1367(a) states that the federal courts "shall have jurisdiction" over claims that are "part of the same case or controversy" as a claim over which the court exercises original jurisdiction.

2)   There are three requirements to satisfy supplemental jurisdiction. First, the federal claim must have substance sufficient to confer federal subject matter jurisdiction. Second, the federal and state claims must derive from a common nucleus of operative fact. Third, the plaintiff ordinarily must expect to try all claims in one judicial proceeding.

3)   P's claim satisfies the above three requirements. First, P's Title VII claim has substance. Second, the Title VII and PHRA claims are derived from the same set of facts concerning sexual harassment by

three supervisors. Third, P should have expected to try the claims together because these claims mirror one another and P would save on litigation.

4) Under 28 U.S.C. 1367(c), the district court may, in its discretion, decline to exercise jurisdiction if any one of the following conditions are met: (i) the claim raises a novel or complex issue of state law; (ii) the state claim substantially predominates over the claims over which the district court has original jurisdiction; (iii) the district court has dismissed all claims over which it has original jurisdiction; or (iv) in exceptional circumstances, there are other compelling reasons for declining jurisdiction.

5) This court declines to exercise its discretion to refuse jurisdiction over P's PHRA claim. This case is different from *Goodwin v. Seven-Up Bottling Co.*, where the court also dismissed that plaintiff's Title VII claim. In this case, P's Title VII claim is still viable. P would have to expend substantial effort, time, and money to prepare a claim that could be tried with the federal claim.

6) The PHRA claim no longer presents a novel or complex state issue. While the Supreme Court of Pennsylvania has yet to rule on the issue, this district court is confident that the supreme court would agree with the numerous courts that have concluded that individual employee liability is possible under section 955 of the PHRA.

III. DIVERSITY OF CITIZENSHIP

A. GENERAL

1. **Jurisdiction.** Under 28 U.S.C. section 1332, when the amount in controversy exceeds $75,000 exclusive of interest and costs, the federal district courts have ***concurrent jurisdiction*** in suits between citizens of different states, or between citizens of a state and citizens or subjects of foreign states, or between a foreign state as plaintiff and citizens of a state or different states. Permanent resident aliens are deemed citizens of the state where domiciled.

2. **Determination.** Jurisdiction in diversity cases depends on the character of the litigants and not on the nature of the controversy (except for a few types of cases the federal courts will not hear even if diversity is present).

3. **Rationale.** The historical reason for diversity jurisdiction was based on the distrust of the state courts and a desire to avoid bias against nonresident defendants.

B. REQUISITES FOR DIVERSITY

1. **Pleading.** The allegation of citizenship must be specially pleaded. The plaintiff must allege in the jurisdictional statement that the plaintiff is a citizen of a state different from the defendant.

2. **Multiple Parties.** Complete diversity of citizenship is required when there is a plurality of parties. If there are two or more joint plaintiffs and two or more joint defendants, each of the plaintiffs must, based on her respective citizenship, be capable of suing each of the defendants.

Strawbridge
v. Curtiss

    a. **Complete diversity requirement--Strawbridge v. Curtiss,** 7 U.S. (3 Cranch) 267 (1806).

        1) **Facts.** Strawbridge and others (Ps) were alleged to be citizens of Massachusetts. The defendants were citizens of Massachusetts, except Curtiss, who was averred to be a citizen of Vermont and was served with process. The circuit court dismissed the suit for want of diversity jurisdiction. P appeals.

        2) **Issue.** In a case brought in federal court based on diversity of citizenship, must there be complete diversity between the parties?

        3) **Held.** Yes. Decree affirmed.

            a) The words of the act of Congress are, "where an alien is a party, or the suit is between a citizen of a state where the suit is brought, and a citizen of another state." This means that each distinct interest should be represented by persons, all of whom are entitled to sue, or may be sued, in the federal courts.

            b) Because there is not complete diversity between the parties, the district court correctly dismissed the case.

4) Comment. It has been stated that Justice Marshall regretted the decision in *Strawbridge*. However, except for the interpleader cases, the rule of complete diversity enunciated in this case has been consistently upheld. In statutory interpleader cases, 28 U.S.C. section 1335 requires only that "two or more adverse claimants, of diverse citizenship" be parties. That is, this so-called minimal diversity requires only that one plaintiff and one defendant be from different states.

b. Modern application--Seyler v. Steuben Motors, Inc., 462 F.2d 181 (3d Cir. 1972).

Seyler v. Steuben Motors, Inc.

1) Facts. In this diversity action the district court found that Seyler (P) and Steuben Motors, Inc. (D), one of the two named defendants, were both citizens of Pennsylvania, thus destroying the requirement of complete diversity. The court dismissed the suit, and P appeals.

2) Issue. In a diversity action brought in the federal courts must there be complete diversity between the parties?

3) Held. Yes. Judgment affirmed.

a) Complete diversity between the parties is absolutely necessary in a diversity action brought in the federal courts and has been the accepted rule since it was first enunciated in *Strawbridge v. Curtiss*. Ancillary jurisdiction is not available on these facts.

3. Determining Domicile. When a person moves to another state before instituting a suit, with the intention of remaining in the new state indefinitely, the person acquires a new domicile. This is true even though the sole motive for moving was to create the right to bring a suit based on diversity. However, when the change of domicile is not real, there will be no diversity of jurisdiction based on the new domicile.

a. Changing domicile. To effect a change of domicile, two elements must exist: (i) the citizen must take up actual residence in the new domicile; and (ii) she must intend to remain there for an indefinite period of time. Neither factor by itself will be sufficient for the purposes of changing one's domicile.

b. No requirement of permanence. Although a citizen does not have to show an intention to remain in the new domicile permanently, she must have no present intention of removing herself elsewhere. If the aforementioned factors are met, a citizen's motive for setting up a new residence is immaterial.

c. Requirement of intention to remain in new domicile--Morris v. Gilmer, 129 U.S. 315 (1889).

Morris v. Gilmer

1) Facts. Gilmer (P), claiming to be a citizen of Tennessee, brought suit in federal district court against Morris (D), a citizen of Alabama, based solely on diversity of citizenship. Subsequently, D filed an affidavit of A.S. Gerald to the effect that in a conversation with P, P informed Gerald that he had returned to Alabama to reside permanently. D then filed a motion to dismiss on the ground that the action did not really and substantially involve a controversy within the jurisdiction of the federal court. The motion was based on depositions of P and his father both stating that P had moved to Tennessee for the sole purpose of acquiring jurisdiction in the federal courts. The district court denied the motion to dismiss. D appeals.

2) **Issue.** Must a district court dismiss a case for want of jurisdiction if the facts show the change of domicile was not actual and permanent but was solely for the purpose of creating diversity?

3) **Held.** Yes. Decree reversed and cause remanded with a direction to dismiss the suit.

    a) A citizen of the United States can instantly transfer his citizenship from one state to another. Furthermore, a citizen's right to sue in the courts of the United States is not lessened because his change of domicile was induced for the purpose of invoking the jurisdiction of a federal court.

    b) If the new citizenship is really and truly acquired, his right to sue is a legitimate, constitutional, and legal consequence, not to be impeached by the motive of his move to another state. But there must be an actual, not pretended, change of domicile that contemplates an absence from the former domicile for an indefinite and uncertain time with the intention that the new residence be permanent.

    c) However, in the case at bar, the evidence discloses that P had no purpose to acquire a domicile or settled home in Tennessee, and that his sole object was to place himself in a situation to invoke federal jurisdiction.

    d) P went to Tennessee without any present intention to remain there permanently or for an indefinite time. Rather, P's present intention was to return to Alabama as soon as he could without defeating federal jurisdiction. Therefore, it must be held that the district court erred in not dismissing the case.

4. **Citizenship Requirement.** The Fourteenth Amendment establishes that each citizen of the United States is also a citizen of the state wherein she resides.

    a. **Must have state domicile.** However, for the purposes of diversity, residence in a state is not enough; one must be domiciled in the state. A person can only have one domicile, but she can have several residences.

    b. **United States citizen without domicile may not be sued in federal courts.** A citizen of the United States who does not reside in any state and who is also not a citizen of a foreign state may not be sued in the federal courts based on diversity jurisdiction.

    c. **Personal relationships affect domicile.** Except in limited circumstances, a child takes on the domicile of his parents. Historically, a married woman's domicile was the domicile of her husband.

d. **United States citizen married to alien--Mas v. Perry,** 489 F.2d 1396 (5th Cir. 1974).

1) **Facts.** Mr. Mas, a citizen of France, and Mrs. Mas (Ps) were married at her home in Mississippi. Ps were graduate students at Louisiana State University for a year and nine months. Following their marriage, Ps returned to school in Louisiana for two more years. It was at this time that they rented an apartment from Perry (D). Later Ps moved to Illinois. At the time of trial, however, Ps intended to return to Louisiana to finish their studies. Ps brought suit against D, a citizen of Louisiana, in federal district court alleging injury as a result of the discovery that the apartment rented from D contained two-way mirrors, which D used to observe them. At the close of the case D made an oral motion to dismiss for lack of jurisdiction, contending that Ps failed to prove diversity of citizenship between the parties and that the requisite jurisdictional amount was lacking with respect to Mr. Mas, who was only awarded $5,000. The district court denied the motion, and D appeals.

2) **Issues.**

   a) For jurisdictional purposes in diversity cases in federal court, does one remain a domiciliary of a state until a new domicile is acquired?

   b) Does the monetary requisite (at the time of this case) of in excess of $10,000 govern the amount pleaded rather than the amount of recovery?

3) **Held.** a) Yes. b) Yes. Judgment affirmed.

   a) As to the issue of diversity, the federal judicial power extends to the claim of Mr. Mas, a citizen of France, against D, a citizen of Louisiana, pursuant to section 1332, which provides for original jurisdiction in federal district courts in actions between citizens of a state and citizens of foreign states.

      (1) We further conclude that Mrs. Mas is a citizen of Mississippi for diversity purposes. To be a citizen of a state within the meaning of section 1332, a natural person must be both a citizen of the United States and a domiciliary of that state.

      (2) A person's domicile is the place of her true, fixed, and permanent home to which she has the intention of returning whenever she is absent therefrom.

      (3) It is clear that at the time of her marriage, Mrs. Mas was a domiciliary of Mississippi. Although it is generally true that the domicile of the wife is deemed to be that of her husband, this is not the case when the husband is a citizen of a foreign state. To do otherwise would be to hold Mrs. Mas a domiciliary of France and, therefore, not a citizen of any state.

      (4) An American woman is not deemed to have lost her United States citizenship solely by reason of her marriage to an alien.

(5) Though Mrs. Mas did not intend to return to her parents' home in Mississippi, she did not effect a change of domicile because she and Mr. Mas were in Louisiana only as students and lacked the requisite intention to remain there.

b) As to the issue of jurisdictional amount, it is well settled that the amount in controversy is determined by the amount claimed by the plaintiff in good faith. Federal jurisdiction is not lost because a judgment of less than the jurisdictional amount is awarded. To justify dismissal, it must appear to a legal certainty that the claim is really for less than the jurisdictional amount.

5. **Unincorporated Associations.** A partnership, joint stock company, labor union, or other unincorporated association does not enjoy the same fiction applied to corporations. The citizenship of each member of an unincorporated association must be considered in determining whether diversity jurisdiction exists.

Carden v. Arkoma Associates

a. **Limited partnership--Carden v. Arkoma Associates,** 494 U.S. 185 (1990).

1) **Facts.** Arkoma Associates (P), a limited partnership under Arizona law, brought a contract action against Carden and Limes (Ds) in a United States district court in Louisiana, alleging diversity of citizenship as the basis of jurisdiction. Ds, citizens of Louisiana, moved to dismiss, claiming that one of Arkoma's limited partners was also a citizen of Louisiana. The district court denied the motion, and the fifth circuit declined to decide an interlocutory appeal on the issue. The district court found for P in the contract action, and Ds (with Magee Drilling Company, an intervening party) appeal.

2) **Issues.**

a) Should a limited partnership be considered in its own right a citizen of the state that created it?

b) For purposes of diversity of citizenship in an action involving a limited partnership, should the citizenship of only the general partners be considered?

3) **Held.** a) No. b) No. Judgment reversed and remanded.

a) While the rule treating corporations as citizens of their state of incorporation for diversity purposes has become firmly established, we have consistently resisted extending any similar rule to other entities. The one true exception pertained to a sociedad en comandita created under Puerto Rican civil law. We have since declined to use a similar analysis on other types of organizations.

b) P argues that only general partners manage assets, control litigation, and bear the risk of liability for a limited partnership's debts, and that the fifth circuit therefore correctly determined P's citizenship by considering only the general partners. Our precedents, however, have never held that an artificial entity suing in its own name may invoke diversity jurisdiction based on the citizenship of some but not all of its members.

   c)   While this opinion might validly be characterized as precedent-bound and unresponsive to the changing needs of business organizations, the issue is properly a matter for legislative consideration. Congress has in fact acted in this general area previously: in 1958 it revised section 1332 to make corporations citizens of the state where they have their principal place of business.

4)   Dissent (O'Connor, Brennan, Marshall, Blackmun, JJ.). Complete diversity is not constitutionally mandated. For example, in a Rule 23 class action only the citizenship of the named class representatives is considered. In *Steelworkers v. R.H. Bouligny Inc.*, the labor union case, the Court did not consider the issue that is relevant here: whether some members have more power than others over the litigation and other affairs of the association. In *Navarro Savings Association v. Lee,* which the majority attempts to distinguish, the Court properly considered who the real parties in interest were, as we should here.

b.   Alien partners--China Nuclear Energy Industry Corporation v. Arthur Andersen, LLP, 11 F. Supp. 2d 1256 (D. Colo. 1998).

> China Nuclear Energy Industry Corporation v. Arthur Andersen

1)   Facts. China Nuclear (P) brought this action against Arthur Andersen (D) alleging that D issued a false and misleading report upon which P relied and ultimately suffered damages. D claims that the court lacks subject matter jurisdiction because P is an alien and some partners of D are aliens.

2)   Issue. Does the 1998 amendment to 28 U.S.C. section 1332(a) permit diversity jurisdiction in suits by an alien permanently residing in one state against an alien permanently residing in another state?

3)   Held. No. Complaint dismissed for lack of jurisdiction.

   a)   The diversity requirement also applies to corporations and partnerships. Unlike corporations, however, partnerships are not for diversity purposes artificial citizens by virtue of their place of inception or principal place of business. Rather, a partnership's citizenship is determined by the citizenship of each of its partners. Since a partnership such as D has partners from every state as well as partners who are citizens of foreign countries, only rarely will the diversity requirement be satisfied.

   b)   P invokes the alienage provision claiming that it is an alien and that the partners of D are all citizens of the United States. However, this is not the case because D has over a dozen equity partners that are foreign citizens but are permanent resident aliens living in the United States.

   c)   The 1998 amendment to section 1332(a) deems permanent resident aliens to be citizens of the state in which they are domiciled. The plain meaning of the amendment would deem all of the permanent resident alien partners of D to be citizens of the state in which they live, thereby preserving complete diversity jurisdiction.

d) The plain meaning of the amendment would lead to anomalous results. It would authorize diversity jurisdiction when neither party is a citizen of the United States. The judicial power of the United States does not extend to such an action under Article III.

e) Congress passed the amendment as part of a comprehensive effort to reduce the federal court's diversity jurisdiction caseload. Despite the plain language of the alienage amendment of section 1332(a), it would be illogical to conclude that Congress intended to eliminate diversity jurisdiction in cases between a citizen and an alien permanently residing in the same state but simultaneously intended to expand jurisdiction in cases between an alien permanently residing in one state and an alien permanently residing in another state.

f) Because P is an alien and D has partners who are aliens, the requirement of complete diversity does not exist.

6. **Corporations.** Originally, the law was that a corporation was not a citizen for determining diversity jurisdiction. Instead, the citizenship of each of the stockholders was considered.

a. **Citizenship.** However, 28 U.S.C. 1332 was amended so that for purposes of diversity, a corporation is treated as a citizen of each state in which it is incorporated and the state in which it has its principal place of business.

b. **Court may determine principal place of business.** Under the statute, the corporation can have only one principal place of business and the court must often examine the facts to determine the state that constitutes the place of the corporation's principal activities.

c. **Tests for principal place of business.** The *total activity test* combines two other tests that had previously been utilized to determine a corporation's principal place of business. Under the *nerve center test,* general emphasis is placed on the locus of the managerial and policy-making functions of the corporation. The *place of activity test* focuses on production or sales activities.

Tubbs v. Southwestern Bell Telephone Company

d. **"Total activity" test--Tubbs v. Southwestern Bell Telephone Company,** 846 F. Supp. 551 (S.D. Tex. 1994).

1) **Facts.** Tubbs (P), a citizen of Texas, was injured by one of Southwestern Bell Telephone Company's (D's) cables. D is a telecommunication public utility that is incorporated in Missouri and operates in Texas, Arkansas, Kansas, Missouri, and Oklahoma. At the time the suit was filed, 56% of D's total operating revenue was generated in Texas and about 57% of D's customer bills were bills of Texas customers. Wages paid to Texas employees comprised over 50% of the total wages paid by D. On the other hand, Missouri operations generated only 17% of customer bills, 17% of total operating revenue, and 27% of total wages paid by D. D had two operating divisions. The Texas division had 31 officers and directors including the chairman of the board, chief executive officer, and secretary. The Texas division was responsible for Texas operations, and sales, installation, and maintenance of activities

related to Texas customers. The Missouri division was the overall headquarters for D with 18 officers and directors based in Missouri. Corporate books and records were kept in Missouri, and the Missouri office was responsible for company-wide information services and data processing, which engaged a staff of 1500 to 2000 employees. Missouri operations were responsible for all customer billing and accounting, company-wide legal affairs, primary banking relationships, federal regulatory affairs, and overall accounting, including payroll. Missouri activities also included the design of new technology and all technical planning. About 59% of D's equipment and cable and 57% of its total assets were located in Texas. Three of D's area purchasing managers resided in Texas, two in Missouri, and one in Kansas. These purchasing agents were responsible for the purchase of equipment and cable of the type that allegedly injured P. About 57% of D's equipment purchases were for Texas. Alternatively, Missouri contained about 15% of D's equipment and cable and about 17% of D's total assets. Contracting managers in Missouri were responsible for negotiating contracts with company-wide supplies and also promulgated company-wide practices and procedures for purchasing. P brings a motion to remand the case to state court based on lack of subject matter jurisdiction. P contends that D's principal place of business is Texas and thus there is no diversity jurisdiction. D contends its principal place of business is Missouri.

2) **Issue.** Is D's principal place of business Texas?

3) **Held.** Yes. P's motion granted and case remanded to state court.

   a) The fifth circuit has stated that, in determining a corporation's principal place of business, a court must apply the "total activity" test, which incorporates both the "nerve center" test, and the "place of activity" test. Under the "nerve center" test, the state in which the corporation has its nerve center or "brain" is its principal place of business. Under the "place of activity" test, the state in which the corporation carries out its operations is its principal place of business. Although these two tests seem to conflict, they are actually harmonious because they are applied in different factual situations depending on the organization of the business entity under consideration.

   b) The nerve center test is most appropriately applied when the corporation is engaged in far-flung and varied activities that are carried on in different states. The state that hosts the nerve center is the principal place of business because no place in which the corporation conducts operations or activities can be denoted "principal."

   c) The place of activity test is applied when the corporation has a collection of nerve cells serving the common function of making the corporate enterprise go.

   d) Based on the present factual situation, D's organizational structure is more closely analogous to corporations who are principally analyzed under the place of activity test.

   e) Consequently, D's principal place of business will most likely not be Missouri, the state with significant administrative authority and some activity, but will likely be Texas, the state with lesser executive offices but principal operations.

f) D operated uniformly throughout five states. Texas accounted for over 55% of all of D's activities and assets while Missouri accounted for less than 20%. Additionally, both of these states contained nerve centers.

g) D is not engaged in far-flung and varied activities that would render its principal nerve center Missouri because D is a public utility that provides one uniform service over a five-state area. However, the location of D's nerve center is an important consideration, which favors Missouri. Although Missouri contained most of D's nerve center, Texas contained a significant portion of the nerve center that had substantial autonomy over Texas operations.

h) Texas accounts for a clear majority of D's revenues, employees, assets, and customers.

i) Under the total activity test, Texas is D's principal place of business. Texas contained almost one-third of D's top executives and Texas activities accounted for a majority (two times more than Missouri) of D's total operating revenue, customers and their bills, employees and their wages, and total assets. Furthermore, the officers, executives, and other managers in Texas had significant autonomy to oversee and control Texas operations.

j) Since about 59% of D's equipment and cable and 57% of its total assets are in Texas, more people in Texas are susceptible to the type of injury suffered by P than the combined number of individuals in the four other states served by D.

k) It is anomalous to think that D would not be treated fairly in a Texas state court considering its virtual universal visibility.

l) Since Texas is D's principal place of business, there is no diversity jurisdiction under 28 U.S.C. section 1332(c).

C. MANUFACTURING DIVERSITY

When diversity of citizenship jurisdiction is invoked, the citizenship of the party who is the real party in interest must be considered rather than the citizenship of a purely formal or nominal party.

1. **Real Parties in Interest.** Real parties in interest are "citizens" of a particular state for diversity purposes. A "citizen" may be a person, a corporation, or the individuals in an association.

Tank v.
Chronister

    a. **Wrongful death action--Tank v. Chronister,** 160 F.3d 597 (10th Cir. 1998).

      1) **Facts.** Tank (P) filed a wrongful death action in the Kansas district court asserting that the negligent conduct of Chronister (Ds) contributed to the death of his mother. P is a resident of

Wisconsin. At the time of her death, P's mother was a resident of Kansas. Her husband and adult daughter were also residents of Kansas at the time of her death and at the time the action was filed. Ds are residents of Kansas. Ds filed a motion to dismiss asserting complete diversity of jurisdiction was not present because, pursuant to 28 U.S.C. section 1332(c)(2), a wrongful death plaintiff in Kansas is deemed to be a citizen of the same state as the decedent. In initially granting Ds' motion, the district court concluded that one who brings a wrongful death action under Kansas law is a legal representative of the decedent's estate for purposes of section 1332(c)(2) and therefore is deemed to be a citizen of the same state as the decedent. P moved for reconsideration of the motion to dismiss and the district court reversed its ruling, holding that section 1332(c)(2) did not apply to individuals who are authorized by state statute to pursue a wrongful death claim in their individual capacities and not on behalf or for the benefit of the decedent's estate. The district court granted P's motion for reconsideration and certified its decision for interlocutory appeal pursuant to 28 U.S.C. section 1292(b).

2) **Issue.** Is an individual bringing a wrongful death action under Kansas law a legal representative of the estate of the decedent under section 1332(c)(2) and therefore deemed to be a resident of the same state as the decedent for diversity of jurisdiction purposes?

3) **Held.** No. Judgment affirmed.

  a) There are two types of actions that may arise out of a person's death caused by the negligence of another. A survival action may be brought only by the estate administrator and only for the purpose of recovering damages suffered by the decedent prior to death. In contrast, a wrongful death action may be brought only by the decedent's heirs-at-law and only for their exclusive benefit for damages suffered by them as a result of the wrongful death.

  b) Section 1332 was added to the diversity statute as part of the Judicial Improvements Act of 1988 to reduce substantially the diversity jurisdiction in the federal courts. Section 1332(c)(2) was written to discourage the appointment of out-of-state personal representatives solely to create diversity where it would not otherwise exist.

  c) By its plain terms, section 1332(c)(2) excludes from its coverage those who are not representing the estate of a decedent, even if the individual is appointed pursuant to statute with authority to bring an action for wrongful death. Section 1332(c)(2) therefore is not triggered, as Ds suggest, by the fact that under Kansas law a wrongful death plaintiff acts in a representative capacity. Although the named plaintiff does serve as a representative, the plaintiff represents only the other heirs and not the estate itself. Ds' proposed interpretation ignores that part of section 1332(c) requiring that representation be on behalf "of the estate of the decedent."

  d) We hold that an individual bringing a wrongful death action under Kansas Statutes Annotated section 60-1902 is not a legal representative of the estate of the decedent under Section 1332(c)(2) and is therefore not deemed to be a resident of the same state of the decedent for diversity purposes.

  e) P has a real, beneficial interest in the lawsuit and is entitled to a share of any eventual recovery. It is irrelevant that a local, non-diverse heir may more easily or logically serve as the plaintiff. A party with a real substantive stake in the litigation may not be subjected to a collusive jurisdiction argument under section 1359 even if the party was appointed simply to create diversity jurisdiction.

United States
Fidelity and
Guaranty
Co. v. A & S
Manufacturing
Co.

b.   Realignment of parties to reflect their actual interest--United States Fidelity and Guaranty Co. v. A & S Manufacturing Co., 48 F.3d 131 (4th Cir. 1995).

1)   **Facts.** A & S Manufacturing Company ("A & S") separately contracted with United States Fidelity and Guaranty Company, ("USF&G"), Federal Insurance Company ("Federal"), and Hartford Accident and Indemnity Company ("Hartford") for primary liability insurance. Environmental contamination allegedly occurred at A & S's sites that were covered by the contracts. The Environmental Protection Agency sued A & S for the contamination and A & S called upon the insurers for defense and indemnity. USF&G filed this action seeking a declaratory judgment that it is not liable to A & S and, even if liable, the other insurers would be liable for reimbursement. As aligned in USF&G's complaint, complete diversity existed. One month later A & S filed a virtually identical declaratory judgment action against USF&G and the other insurers. A & S then moved to realign the parties in USF&G's suit. The district court applied the "principal purpose" standard and aligned the three insurers as plaintiffs and A & S as the sole defendant. Both A & S and Federal have their principal place of business in New Jersey; thus complete diversity was destroyed by the realignment. The district court dismissed the action for lack of jurisdiction, and USF&G appeals.

2)   **Issue.** Should the "principal purpose" test be used to determine the proper alignment of the parties?

3)   **Held.** Yes. Dismissal affirmed.

a)   The "substantial controversy" test asks whether any actual and substantial conflict exists between the opposing parties. The substantial controversy test allows diversity limited only by the creative pleading of the plaintiff.

b)   The "principal purpose" test entails two steps: (i) the court must determine the primary issue in controversy; and (ii) the court should align the parties according to their positions with respect to the primary issue.

c)   The insurers share the primary goal of avoiding obligations to A & S and the court properly realigned them as plaintiffs opposite A & S.

2.   **Direct Action Suits.** Some states recognize a tortfeasor's right to proceed directly against an insurance company for injuries caused by the insured. The tortfeasor in such a situation must establish not only the insured's liability but also that the acts of the insured fall within the terms of the policy.

a. **Diversity in direct action suit--Lumbermen's Mutual Casualty v. Elbert**, 348 U.S. 48 (1954).

1) **Facts.** Pursuant to the Louisiana Direct Action Statute, Elbert (P), a Louisiana citizen, brought a personal injury action against Lumbermen's Mutual Casualty (D), an Illinois insurance company that insured a citizen of Louisiana who allegedly had harmed P in a Louisiana accident. D argued that because both parties to the accident were citizens of Louisiana, no diversity of citizenship existed.

2) **Issue.** For the purposes of diversity in a direct action suit, is the insurance company considered only a citizen of its state of incorporation and principal place of business regardless of the citizenship of the insured?

3) **Held.** Yes.

4) **Concurrence** (Frankfurter, J.). The availability of federal tribunals for controversies of matters that are outside federal power and exclusively within state power is the essence of diversity jurisdiction. The power of Congress to confer such jurisdiction was based on the desire of the Framers to assure out-of-state litigants courts free from potential local bias. However, instead of protecting out-of-state litigants against discrimination by state courts, the effect of diversity jurisdiction was discrimination against citizens of the state in favor of litigants from outside the state. Such a device offers constant temptation to new abuses. This case is an example.

   a) Here we have a Louisiana citizen resorting to the federal court in Louisiana to avoid the consequences of the Louisiana law by which every Louisiana citizen is bound when suing another Louisiana citizen.

   b) But by the fortuitous circumstance that this Louisiana litigant could directly sue an out-of-state insurance company, she can avoid her amenability to Louisiana law.

5) **Comment.** The result of this case was changed by a 1965 amendment to section 1332(c). It provides "that in any direct action against the insurer of a policy or contract of liability insurance to which action the insured is not joined as a party-defendant, such insurer shall be deemed a citizen of the state of which the insured is a citizen, as well as of any state by which the insurer has been incorporated and of the state where it has its principal place of business."

IV. JURISDICTIONAL AMOUNT

A. GENERAL CONSIDERATIONS

Congress has imposed a jurisdictional amount requirement in certain statutes that confer subject matter jurisdiction on the district courts. For example, 28 U.S.C. section 1332 requires that, in addition to diversity of citizenship, the amount in controversy must exceed $75,000 exclusive of interest and costs.

1. **How the Amount Is Determined.** The sum claimed by the plaintiff controls if the claim is apparently made in good faith. It must appear to a legal certainty that the claim is for less than the jurisdictional amount to justify dismissal.

   a. **Plaintiff's burden.** Because the jurisdictional amount is an aspect of subject matter jurisdiction, the burden is on the plaintiff to establish the requisite amount in controversy.

Vance v.
W.A. Van-
dercook Co.

2. **Where Complaint Shows Amount Not Met--Vance v. W.A. Vandercook Co.,** 170 U.S. 468 (1898).

   a. **Facts.** W.A. Vandercook Company (P), a California corporation, began this action against the present plaintiffs in error, including Vance (D), averring the alleged wrongful seizure by Bahr and Scott of packages of wines and brandies, the property of P. P averred that D had, subsequent to the seizure and with knowledge of its wrongful nature, received the packages into his custody and that upon demand for the return of the seized property D still retained it. P sought the recovery of the packages alleged to be worth $1,000. P also prayed for consequential damages in the sum of $10,000. D appeals the circuit court finding of jurisdiction.

   b. **Issue.** Does a federal trial court acquire jurisdiction if, on the face of the plaintiff's complaint, recovery is limited as a matter of law to less than the jurisdictional amount?

   c. **Held.** No. Judgment reversed.

      1) It is clear that the amount of recovery to which P was entitled, on the construction put upon the complaint, could not equal the sum of $2,000, the requisite jurisdictional amount.

      2) In an action of trover, consequential damages are not recoverable. Further, the action for delivery damages for detention must relate to the property and to a direct injury from the detention. Destruction of business is not a direct injury; therefore, the special damages of $10,000 prayed for by P were not recoverable.

      3) Therefore, because P's action was solely one for claim and delivery of property alleged to have been unlawfully detained and for damages for the detention thereof, the amount of recovery depended first on the alleged value of the property, which in the present case was $1,000, and such damages as it was by operation of law allowed to recover.

4) However, the law allows recovery only for the actual damage caused by the detention. Such recovery is confined to interest on the value of the property. This, when added to the value of the property, does not amount to $2,000. Upon the face of the complaint the circuit court was without jurisdiction.

3. **Effect of Uncertainty of Recovery.** Even though it may appear highly unlikely that a plaintiff can recover the amount prayed for, unless it can be shown to a legal certainty that the plaintiff will be unable to recover the requisite jurisdictional amount, jurisdiction will be upheld.

a. **Good faith claim--Burns v. Anderson,** 502 F.2d 970 (5th Cir. 1974).

Burns v. Anderson

1) **Facts.** Burns's (P's) automobile was struck by Anderson's (D's) automobile. P's principal injury from the accident was a broken thumb. P brought the action in the Louisiana district court claiming $1,026 in lost wages and medical expenses and another $60,000 for pain and suffering. After a pretrial conference and considerable discovery, the district court dismissed for want of jurisdiction. P appealed.

2) **Issue.** May a district court dismiss a diversity suit when it appears to a legal certainty that the claim was really for less than the jurisdictional amount?

3) **Held.** Yes. Dismissal affirmed.

a) The test for jurisdictional amount is a plaintiff's good faith claim. To justify dismissal it must appear to a legal certainty that the claim is really for less than the jurisdictional amount.

b) The test is an objective one and once it is clear that as a matter of law the claim is for less than $10,000, the trial judge is required to dismiss.

c) In the instant case, the district judge dismissed only after examination of an extensive record. The record shows that P was back working only a month after the accident, doing heavy manual labor. P admitted that after three months there was no pain whatsoever. P's total medical bills were less than $250. It really does appear to a legal certainty that the amount in controversy is less than $10,000.

4. **Valuing Actions for Declaratory Relief.** Valuation of the matter in controversy in suits for declaratory or injunctive relief is a complex task. The court must not only undertake to evaluate intangible rights as opposed to objects commonly found in the marketplace, but it must decide what rights are involved in the controversy and from whose viewpoint their value is to be measured.

a. **Flexible approach--Hoffman v. Volcanic Materials Company,** 19 F. Supp. 2d 475 (M.D.N.C. 1998)

Hoffman v. Volcanic Materials Company

1) **Facts.** Some homeowners (Ps) filed a nuisance and trespass action in state court against Volcanic Materials Company (D) for operation of a

quarry near the homes of Ps. Ps each sought in excess of $10,000 for damages to their homes and property from the blasting rocks and in excess of $10,000 in punitive damages. Ps also sought an injunction to prevent D's continuing trespass and nuisance. D removed the case to district court. Ps are seeking a remand to state court. Ps claim that the cases should be remanded because D failed to show the jurisdictional amount in excess of $75,000 because Ps only seek damages in excess of $30,000 each. D claims that in determining the jurisdictional amount, the court may look beyond the dollar amount of damages sought by Ps and may consider as well the amount that Ps' injunction request, if granted, would cost D. Ps claim that the amount in controversy should be determined from the plaintiffs' perspective and the court should not consider the economic impact on D.

2) **Issue.** Should the amount in controversy be determined solely from the face of the plaintiffs' complaint?

3) **Held.** No. Ps' motion to remand denied.

   a) The amount in controversy is normally determined from the plaintiff's perspective.

   b) When federal jurisdiction is not plain from the face of the plaintiff's complaint, the defendant must offer evidence (pleadings, affidavits, or other matters in the record) in support of its claim that the controversy satisfies the federal jurisdictional amount.

   c) In an action such as this one where the plaintiffs seek injunctive or declaratory relief, the amount in controversy is measured by the value of the object of the litigation.

   d) There is basic agreement among the courts concerning *what* must be valued but there is confusion as to *how* to value it.

   e) Under the "plaintiff-viewpoint" rule, the court looks only to the benefit to be gained by the plaintiff.

   f) The "either-viewpoint" rule has been adopted by a number of circuits and appears to be the more recent trend.

   g) Neither fourth circuit law nor the Supreme Court commands this court to follow the "viewpoint" terminology. Instead, a case may be legitimately valued in a number of different ways, no one of which may be said to inherently represent true value in every case. A flexible approach better reflects the Supreme Court's mandate to consider the pecuniary consequence to those involved in the litigation.

   h) In a lawsuit for declaratory and injunctive relief, the relief will have both a cost and benefit to the parties, depending on whether the relief is granted or denied.

   i) In the present case, the losses that would be sustained if the quarry operations were curtailed is better evidence of the value of the injunction to D. Since D will sustain this loss even if only one P were to obtain the injunction, Ps have an individual interest in the injunction.

j) The value of the injunction exceeds the federal jurisdictional amount.

5. **Jurisdictional Amount on Removal.** Because the device of removal is restricted to the defendant, if a plaintiff's complaint is for less than the requisite jurisdictional amount, and the defendant's counterclaim is an amount over $75,000, the plaintiff cannot remove the case to a federal court. If the defendant's counterclaim is a permissive one under state law, the courts look to the amount prayed for in the plaintiff's complaint. However, the courts are split in their approach to removal based on compulsory counterclaims.

a. **Amounts sought in counterclaims--Barnes v. Parker,** 126 F. Supp. 649 (W.D. Mo. 1954).

Barnes v. Parker

1) **Facts.** Parker (D) sought to remove two cases from Missouri state court to the federal district court. The first case (no. 1255) had been brought for $4,063.62 against Parker and Cron jointly. Cron did not join in the removal petition. In the second case (no. 1256), Barnes had brought a breach of contract action against D for $2,161.30. D counterclaimed for $4,876.84 in this action, allegedly for the sole purpose of establishing the minimum amount in controversy necessary for removal to federal court.

2) **Issues.**

a) When an action is brought against defendants jointly, must all defendants join in the removal petition?

b) In determining the amount in controversy in actions sought to be removed, do federal courts look to the amount in good faith prayed for in the complaint?

3) **Held.** a) Yes. b) Yes. Cases remanded.

a) Since the cause of action asserts a joint liability, the petition for removal in case no. 1255 must, under the relevant case law, be joined in by all of the defendants.

b) In determining the amount in controversy in actions sought to be removed, the federal court to which removal is sought determines the question solely by looking to the amount in good faith prayed for in the complaint.

c) Accordingly, if the amount therein claimed was less than the jurisdictional requirement, amounts claimed by way of counterclaim could not be considered as increasing the amount of the required sum.

d) Furthermore, this court rejects a line of decisions by other district courts that creates an exception to the above rule when a counterclaim is classified as compulsory under the local state practice. To recognize such an exception is to make the federal removal practice dependent on state court procedure. This court concludes that removal herein was improvident and without jurisdiction and remands these causes to the state court.

6. **Future Interest Due on Judgment.** The amount of interest that may accrue on a judgment may not be used to determine jurisdictional amount. The face value of bonds or notes constitutes the amount in controversy.

Elgin v. Marshall

    a. **Value of res judicata effects--Elgin v. Marshall,** 106 U.S. 578 (1882).

        1) **Facts.** Marshall (P) held 15 bonds of $500 each ($7,500 total) issued by the town of Elgin, Minnesota (D) to finance construction. P brought an action in federal court on the basis of diversity of citizenship for unpaid interest of $1,660 on the bonds. D argued that it was not liable and could not pay because the bonds were issued under an unconstitutional statute. A decision would have res judicata effects on further interest payments and the cashing in of the bonds at their maturity date. Thus, the real value of the decision in this case exceeded the jurisdictional minimum of $5,000, even though only $1,660 was immediately in issue. The court found for P. D appealed. The federal appeals court held that the jurisdictional amount in this case was under $5,000. D brings a writ of error and argues that its potential liability based on the decision far exceeded this amount.

        2) **Issue.** May a federal court consider only the amount actually in controversy in the instant suit in determining whether it meets jurisdictional requirements?

        3) **Held.** Yes. Writ of error dismissed for want of jurisdiction.

           a) The federal jurisdictional requirements must be satisfied by the actual case in controversy. The court may not consider, for jurisdictional purposes, the larger ramifications of the case.

           b) While a decision on the case herein involved a potentially greater amount as further interest payments become due and the bonds reached their maturity date, these factors are not currently at issue. They cannot be utilized to satisfy the jurisdictional requirement.

7. **Installment Payments.**

    a. **Future payments.** Future installment payments may be used to meet amount in controversy requirements even though the payments would terminate if certain events occur.

Aetna Casualty & Surety Co. v. Flowers

    b. **Installment payments contingent on survival--Aetna Casualty & Surety Co. v. Flowers,** 330 U.S. 464 (1947).

        1) **Facts.** Flowers (P) instituted a workers' compensation claim in state court for maximum benefits and burial expenses for her deceased husband. Aetna Casualty & Surety Company (D), the insurer of the employer, removed to federal court based on diversity of citizenship and the fact that the maximum award claimed by P met jurisdictional amount requirements. P challenged the presence of the jurisdictional

amount because installment payments depended on her survival. If she died early, the jurisdictional amount might never be met. State law required all of P's workers' compensation claims to be adjudicated in a single action and that a specific amount should be awarded even though it was to be paid in installments. The court dismissed for want of jurisdictional amount since P might die before the jurisdictional amount was paid. The Supreme Court granted certiorari.

2) **Issue.** Is the jurisdictional amount satisfied even if the award is based on installment payments that end at death?

3) **Held.** Yes. Judgment reversed.

a) It is the amount in controversy that must meet jurisdictional requirements. The amount herein exceeds jurisdictional requirements. The fact that payment is to be made in installments, terminable at the death of P, is immaterial for jurisdictional purposes.

b) State law prescribes that all of P's rights must be adjudicated in a single proceeding. The award is to be specified in the decree.

c) The fact that P may never receive that amount is not relevant. Absolute certainty is not required to establish the presence of jurisdiction.

c. **Anticipatory breach of contract.** A plaintiff cannot anticipate the future breach of a contract and base the amount in controversy on the future installment payments that would become due.

1) **Insurance benefits--Beaman v. Pacific Mutual Life Insurance Co.,** 369 F.2d 653 (4th Cir. 1966).

Beaman
v. Pacific
Mutual Life
Insurance Co.

a) **Facts.** Beaman (P) owned a disability income insurance policy. Under the policy, Pacific Mutual Life Insurance Company (D) promised to pay P $200 per month if he were totally disabled and $100 per month if he were only partially disabled. P became totally disabled and D paid him $200 a month for 24 months. P's doctor reported to D that P could perform light work. D ceased its payments. P brought suit in federal court based on diversity of citizenship. P alleged that he met the jurisdictional amount requirement because the payments due under the policy based on his actuarial life expectancy of 25.7 years exceeded jurisdictional amounts. P's suit was for a declaratory judgment that he was permanently disabled. D alleged that only the past-due payments could be considered for jurisdictional purposes because the validity of the policy was not in question. The district court held for D, and P appeals.

b) **Issue.** If the basic validity of an insurance policy contract is not in question, should the court consider only the past-due payments to determine whether the jurisdictional amount has been met?

c) **Held.** Yes. Judgment affirmed and case dismissed.

(1) Only the amount actually owed may be considered in determining the presence of the requisite jurisdictional amount.

(2) Here, the only thing due to P is six months of past-due payments. Prospective payments can be claimed only if the validity of the policy itself is in doubt.

(3) There is absolutely no certainty that the jurisdictional amount will ever be met. P may die prematurely or his disability may end well before payments meet the jurisdictional limit. P's claim of anticipatory breach cannot be maintained.

(4) Payments under this type of policy cannot be claimed until due. If the validity of the policy itself is not in question, only the amounts past due may be considered for jurisdictional purposes.

    d) **Comment.** In *New York Life Insurance Co. v. Viglas*, 297 U.S. 672 (1936), the Supreme Court stated that only the amount that could actually be recovered if the plaintiff prevailed could be used to satisfy the jurisdictional amount requirement. Of course, if the plaintiff had several claims against the insurer, (*e.g.*, for intentional infliction of emotional distress in addition to policy benefits), she could aggregate the claims to meet the jurisdictional amount.

8. **Aggregation of Claims.** Generally, a single plaintiff may aggregate as many claims as she has against a single defendant to meet the jurisdictional amount even though the claims are unrelated.

    a. **Difficulty with multiple parties.** The courts are reluctant to allow aggregation when there are multiple parties. Aggregation in multiple party suits is allowed only when the parties claim a common undivided interest or a single right or title.

Pinel v. Pinel

    b. **Pretermitted heirs' undivided interest--Pinel v. Pinel,** 240 U.S. 594 (1916).

        1) **Facts.** Pinel died leaving a will. The will left an undivided interest in real property to several of his children (Ds). Three of the children were not provided for in the will. Two of these children (Ps) brought suit in federal district court based on diversity. Slyfield (P) alleged a 2/8 interest in the property due to an assignment by the third child of his interest to her. Pinel (P) alleged a 1/8 interest. They claimed that their combined interest was in excess of $4,500. The district court found that Ps' actions were separate and neither one met the jurisdictional amount of $3,000 in damages. It dismissed for want of jurisdiction.

        2) **Issue.** May two plaintiffs join their separate actions to meet the jurisdictional amount requirement?

        3) **Held.** No. Decree affirmed.

            a) As a general rule, each plaintiff must individually meet the jurisdictional amount requirement to maintain an action.

b)   An exception is made when several plaintiffs unite to enforce a single title or right in which they have a common and undivided interest.

c)   Here, the question is whether they are pretermitted heirs entitled to a forced share of their father's estate. These are separate and distinct claims because one of them may establish he was unintentionally pretermitted while the other may not.

d)   Therefore they cannot unite unless each meets the jurisdictional amount. Pinel obviously fails. Slyfield's interest might mathematically be deemed sufficient to meet her jurisdictional amount requirement (*i.e.*, 2/3 of $4,500 is $3,000), but she failed to allege it and the costs associated with partition must reduce this amount.

c.   **Separate and independent claims--Meritcare Inc. v. St. Paul Mercury Insurance Co.,** 166 F.3d 214 (3rd Cir. 1999).

1)   **Facts.** Meritcare, Inc. and Meritcare Ventures, Inc. (Ps) operate a nursing home that they lease from its owner, Caring I, Ltd. Quinlan Medical, Inc. (P) is a subsidiary of Meritcare and furnishes liquified food and other products to the residents. St. Paul Mercury Insurance Company (D) had issued policies to Ps that provided property damage and business interruption insurance. Because the roof on the nursing home was unsound, the facility was closed and all residents were temporarily moved to other institutions. D denied coverage on the ground that the policies covered loss from a roof "collapse" and that in this instance the roof was only unsound and did not fall in. Ps filed suit in state court claiming damages in excess of $25,000. D removed the case to federal district court alleging that the amount in controversy exceeded $50,000, the then-applicable amount. Both sides agreed that Quinlan's claim amounted to no more than $50,000. The district court granted summary judgment to D. Ps appeal.

2)   **Issue.** In a diversity case, can the separate and distinct claims by several plaintiffs be aggregated to meet the jurisdictional amount?

3)   **Held.** No. Judgment against Meritcare affirmed; Quinlan's claim remanded to state court.

a)   The claims of several plaintiffs, if they are separate and distinct, cannot be aggregated for purposes of determining the jurisdictional amount.

b)   Supplemental jurisdiction under section 1367(b) applies in cases brought solely under the diversity statute.

c)   The limitations placed on diversity cases in subsection (b) as contrasted with the broad scope of supplemental jurisdiction granted in other instances of federal jurisdiction in subsection (a), means that section 1367 was not intended to substantially expand diversity jurisdiction.

d)   The legislative history and origins of section 1367 preserve the prohibition against aggregation outlined in *Zahn v. International Paper Co.* and *Clark v. Paul Gray, Inc.*, and thus maintain the traditional rules governing diversity of citizenship and the amount in controversy under 1332.

    e)   Quinlan's claim did not meet the jurisdictional amount and must be remanded.

9.   Interest and Costs. Interest and costs are specifically excluded from the amount in controversy by 28 U.S.C. section 1332. However, if interest on a penalty is an integral part of the claim or if attorneys' fees and costs are statutorily imposed, then these items are not deemed to be "interest and costs" within the meaning of 28 U.S.C. section 1332, and therefore can be used to calculate the jurisdictional amount.

Brainin v.
Melikian

a.   Interest prior to maturity may be counted--Brainin v. Melikian, 396 F.2d 153 (3d Cir. 1968).

    1)   **Facts.** Melikian (D) and Rudd personally guaranteed a loan granted by Brainin (P) to their company. The company subsequently went bankrupt. One term of the loan was that it was payable in 10 months with interest of 8% per annum. The note contained an acceleration clause in the event of bankruptcy. P brought suit against D, who later moved to vacate the judgment for lack of jurisdictional amount because the face of the note, exclusive of interest and costs, was only $10,000. P argued that the interest exacted prior to maturity of the note could be added to the principal to satisfy the jurisdictional amount requirement.

    2)   **Issue.** May interest before the maturity of a note be added to the principal to meet jurisdictional amount requirements?

    3)   **Held.** Yes. Motion denied.

        a)   The amount in controversy must exceed $10,000 exclusive of costs and interest. However, the interest referred to in section 1332 is penalty interest for nonpayment of the debt. It does not refer to interest prior to maturity, which is a charge for the use of the funds.

        b)   Such an amount is a proper measure of damages for determining the jurisdictional amount. Interest arising after maturity must be excluded.

        c)   Here, the amount in controversy is $10,300, which meets the jurisdictional requirement.

V. REMOVAL JURISDICTION AND PROCEDURE

A. GENERAL DEFINITION

Removal is a procedure that allows federal district courts to acquire jurisdiction of cases originally filed in state courts. Removal merely provides the defendant with an option to have the case tried in the federal district court in those instances where the plaintiff could have brought the action in either state or federal court.

1. **Requirements.** Removal may be accomplished only if the subject matter jurisdiction requirement is satisfied by the plaintiff's claim. A defendant's defense is not grounds for removal to a federal court if the plaintiff's claim presents no federal question. [Tennessee v. Union & Planters' Bank, 152 U.S. 454 (1894)]

B. REMOVAL IN FEDERAL QUESTION SUITS

The cases in which the issue of federal question removal jurisdiction arises generally fall into one of three categories. The first category includes cases where the federal statute is enforceable exclusively in the federal courts and Congress has preempted the subject matter of the statute, barring state legislation. The second category involves actions where the federal statute is enforceable exclusively in the federal courts but Congress has not preempted the subject matter, leaving states free to enact and enforce their own legislation. The third category involves cases where the federal statute is enforceable in both state and federal courts. In any event, however, it is the nature of the plaintiff's claim that determines removability.

1. **Defense That Action Is Preempted--Metropolitan Life Insurance Co. v. Taylor,** 481 U.S. 58 (1987).

   Metropolitan Life Insurance Co. v. Taylor

   a. **Facts.** The United States Supreme Court ruled in *Pilot Life Insurance Co. v. Dedeaux,* 481 U.S. 41 (1987), that the Employee Retirement Income Security Act ("ERISA") preempts anyone from bringing an action in a state court in which they allege improper process of claims for benefits under any employee benefit plan regulated by ERISA. General Motors (D), whose principal place of business is Michigan, had such an employee benefit plan for its salaried employees disabled by sickness or accident. Metropolitan Life (D) is General Motors' insurance carrier. Taylor (P) was an employee of General Motors from 1959-86. P was involved in a job-related automobile accident and sustained an injury. He filed a workers' compensation claim for his injury and eventually returned to work. In May 1980, P took a leave of absence on account of severe emotional distress. D began paying benefits to P and had him examined by a psychiatrist, who found him unable to work. Six weeks later, however, another psychiatrist determined that P was fit to work. P filed a claim for benefits, alleging that his back injuries prevented him from working. An orthopedist, however, found that P could work, and D denied the supplemental disability claim that P had filed. P still refused to work and was fired. P filed suit against General Motors and Metropolitan in state court for wrongful termination and for all benefits and insurance coverage that he was denied. Ds removed the case to federal court, alleging federal question jurisdiction over the disability benefit claims by virtue of ERISA and pendent jurisdiction over the remaining claims. The district court found the case properly removable and granted Ds summary judgment on the merits. The court of appeals reversed on the grounds that P's complaint stated only state law causes of action subject to the federal defense of ERISA preemption, and that the well-pleaded complaint rule of *Louisville and Nashville Railroad v. Mottley* precluded removal on the basis of a federal defense. The Supreme Court granted certiorari.

    b.   **Issue.** Can a civil suit based on a state law cause of action that is subject to a federal question defense be removed to federal court?

    c.   **Held.** Yes. Judgment reversed.

        1)   A claim based on a state cause of action but which warrants a federal question defense can be removed to federal court to satisfy the objective of the federal statute.

        2)   While it is a long settled law that a cause of action arises under federal law only when the plaintiff's well-pleaded complaint raises an issue of federal law, there are instances where Congress may so completely preempt a particular area of the law that any civil complaint raising this select group of claims is necessarily federal in character.

        3)   To deny removal here would be to undermine the intent of Congress when it passed ERISA. The policy choices of the inclusion of certain remedies and the exclusion of others under the federal scheme should be decided pursuant to ERISA, and plan participants and beneficiaries should not be free to obtain remedies under state law that Congress rejected in ERISA.

Rivet v.
Regions Bank
of Louisiana

2.   **Claim Preclusion No Basis for Removal--Rivet v. Regions Bank of Louisiana,** 522 U.S. 470 (1998).

    a.   **Facts.** A partnership holding the Louisiana equivalent of a leasehold estate mortgaged that interest to Regions Bank of Louisiana ("Bank"). One year later, the partnership granted a secured mortgage to Rivet and others (Ps). The partnership thereafter filed for bankruptcy and the bankruptcy trustee sought court permission to sell the leasehold estate free and clear of all claims. In 1986, the bankruptcy court first granted the sale application and later approved sale of the leasehold estate to the Bank. The court also directed the recorder of mortgages to cancel all liens, mortgages, and encumbrances including the mortgages held by Ps and the Bank. Nonetheless, Ps' mortgage remained inscribed on the mortgage rolls. Subsequently, in 1993, the Bank acquired the underlying land. The Bank then sold the entire property to its current owner, Fountainbleau Storage Associates ("FSA"). Ps filed this action in state court against the Bank, FSA, and others (Ds) alleging that the 1993 transactions violated Louisiana law. Ds removed the action to district court claiming that federal question jurisdiction existed because the prior bankruptcy court orders extinguished Ps' rights under the second mortgage. Ps filed a motion to remand, which was denied on the ground that removal was properly predicated on the preclusive effect of the 1986 bankruptcy court orders. The fifth circuit affirmed. The Supreme Court granted certiorari.

b. **Issue.** May removal be predicated on a defendant's assertion that a prior federal judgment has disposed of the entire matter and thus bars plaintiffs from later pursuing a state-law-based case?

c. **Held.** No. Judgment reversed.

    1) Federal question jurisdiction is governed by the "well-pleaded complaint rule" and the federal question must be presented on the face of the plaintiff's properly pleaded complaint.

    2) An "independent corollary" is that a plaintiff may not defeat removal by omitting to plead necessary federal questions.

    3) The decision in *Federated Department Stores v. Moitie* did not create a preclusion exception to the rule that a defendant cannot remove on the basis of a federal defense. Claim preclusion by reason of a prior federal judgment is a defensive plea that provides no basis for removal.

    4) Ps' complaint sought recognition and enforcement of a mortgage. The dispute involved Louisiana parties only and Ps relied exclusively on Louisiana law. The fact that Ps' action was precluded, as a matter of federal law by the earlier bankruptcy court orders, does not provide a basis for removal.

3. **To Be Removable, the Claim Must Meet Jurisdictional Standards.** If there is only a single cause of action against several defendants who are not jointly and severally liable, and at least one defendant shares citizenship with the plaintiff, there can be no removal under section 1441(c) of a claim lacking a federal subject matter jurisdiction basis.

    a. **Diverse defendants' attempt to remove--American Fire & Casualty Co. v. Finn,** 341 U.S. 6 (1951).

        1) **Facts.** A home belonging to Finn (P), a Texas resident, was destroyed by fire. Supposedly, Reiss, an insurance broker and also a resident of Texas, had agreed to procure fire insurance on the property from either American Fire & Casualty Company ("American") or Indiana Lumbermen's Insurance Company ("Indiana"), both of which were corporations based outside of Texas. P therefore sued American, Indiana, and Reiss (Ds) in state court to recover for her losses, pleading alternative allegations against American and Indiana separately, and against the two companies jointly with Reiss. American and Indiana had the case removed to federal court, where a judgment was eventually rendered against American but in favor of Indiana and Reiss. The court of appeals affirmed. The Supreme Court granted certiorari. American asks that the Supreme Court vacate the judgment below, arguing that removal of the case to federal court had been inappropriate because the case involved no federal claim or cause of action that was sufficiently separate and independent from the state law claim.

        2) **Issue.** May a state court case be removed to federal court even if it involves no federal claim or cause of action separate and independent from the state law controversy?

3) **Held.** No. Judgment reversed.

    a)   A state court action may not be removed to federal court unless, in addition to the state law controversy, the case involves a wholly separate and independent claim or cause of action that would be removable to federal court if sued on alone.

    b)   The present removal statute, 28 U.S.C. section 1441(c), imposes the "separate and independent" requirement because Congress has determined that removal should be permitted in fewer types of cases than formerly.

    c)   It cannot be said, consistent with the congressional policy restricting removal, that the claims against American and Indiana were separate and independent from those presented in the portion of the complaint which pertained to Reiss, a Texas resident. The suit against Reiss was not removable because P and Reiss are citizens of the same state. And the case was not removable by American or Indiana because the claims against those companies were not distinct from those involving Reiss.

    d)   Because the federal district court could not have exercised original jurisdiction over this suit due to the fact that P and Reiss are both Texas citizens, American cannot even now be estopped from challenging the propriety of the removal of the case.

    e)   Therefore, the judgment below must be reversed with instructions to remand the matter to the state court unless some other federal jurisdictional predicate is established.

4) **Dissent** (Douglas, Black, Minton, JJ.). Once a federal court has decided the removal issue, the plaintiff should be estopped from pleading removal irregularities. Such irregularities may be waived if the action could have originally been brought in federal court. Here there was diversity of citizenship and the amount in controversy exceeded jurisdictional requirements. Because the only judgment that has been rendered is between two parties who have diversity of citizenship, the parties destroying original diversity having been dismissed, I would affirm.

C. REMOVAL OF SEPARATE AND INDEPENDENT CLAIMS

Title 28 U.S.C. section 1441(c) replaced 28 U.S.C. section 71 in 1948 because Congress had concluded by then that removal was too liberally permitted. Limitations on removal were accomplished primarily through inclusion of the "separate and independent" language of section 1441(c). Thus, when a separate and independent claim over which the court would lack subject matter jurisdiction is joined with a claim that meets jurisdiction requirements, both claims can be removed. Under a 1990 amendment to section 1441(c), the claim that meets jurisdictional requirements must be based on a federal question.

1. **Requirements of Remand Under the Federal Rules--Borough of West Mifflin v. Lancaster,** 45 F.3d 780 (3d Cir. 1995).

   a. **Facts.** Lindsey and Coughanour (Ps) allege they were harassed, threatened, and assaulted by security guards at an indoor shopping mall owned by the DeBartolo organization. A police officer came to the mall in response to a call from Ps. The officer refused to arrest or admonish the guards but told Ps to leave the mall and never return. Over the next few weeks Lindsey repeatedly tried, without success, to contact mall management to find out why he had been accosted. He then consulted a lawyer, who advised him that the law did not prohibit his entrance to the mall. Ps then returned to the mall to shop and were accosted and handcuffed in the men's room and dragged through the corridor to the mall office. They were cited for disorderly conduct and trespass. They were convicted in common pleas court, but the convictions were vacated by an appellate court. Ps then filed a complaint in state court against the Borough of West Mifflin and the police officer involved ("the municipal Ds") and the owners, supervisors, and security guards of the mall ("the DeBartolo Ds") asserting various state law claims and a federal civil rights claim under 42 U.S.C. section 1983. Relying on the federal claim, the municipal Ds filed a notice of removal to the district court. On Ps' motion the case was remanded under section 1441(c) based on the finding that issues of state law predominated both the state and federal law claims. The municipal Ds are asking for a writ of mandamus to require the district court to accept jurisdiction.

   b. **Issue.** Is it within the court's discretion under section 1441(c) to remand a case that has been properly removed from state court under sections 1441(a) and (b) when the federal and nonfederal claims are not "separate and independent" of each other?

   c. **Held.** No. Petition for writ of mandamus granted.

      1) The state court action included a claim under 42 U.S.C. section 1983 over which the court has jurisdiction under 28 U.S.C. sections 1331 and 1343 plus a variety of state law claims arising out of the same events and circumstances over which the court has supplemental jurisdiction under 28 U.S.C. section 1367. Because the district court had subject matter jurisdiction, the action was properly removed under 28 U.S.C. section 1441(a).

      2) Under section 1441(b), diversity cases have an additional obstacle because a resident defendant is banned from removal. If jurisdiction is based on a federal question, there is no residency restriction. This shows an added concern by Congress that cases such as this one, involving civil rights claims raising federal questions, should be permitted in the federal courts.

      3) The dispute on this mandamus application focuses on section 1441(c), which was amended in 1990. In amending this section, Congress altered two provisions. First, it replaced the phrase "separate and independent claim or cause of action, *which would have been removable if sued upon alone*" with "a separate and independent claim or cause of action *within the jurisdiction of 1331 of this title*." Second, it replaced the phrase "the district court may . . . remand all matters *not*

otherwise in its original jurisdiction" with "the district court may . . . remand all matters *in which State law predominates*."

4) A fair reading of Congressional intent in enacting the amendment is that it was designed to restrict removal to only those cases falling within the court's federal question jurisdiction and to bring the remand provisions into harmony with section 1367, thereby possibly avoiding piecemeal litigation.

5) In the present case, the district court relied upon the addition that reads, "may . . . remand all matters in which State law predominates" to remand the entire case, including the section 1983 claim. It did so without regard for the requirement, which Congress left unchanged, that the federal cause of action removed by Ds had to be "separate and independent" from the state causes of action.

6) If there is a single injury to the plaintiff arising from an interrelated series of events or transactions, there is no separate and independent cause of action under section 1441(c) and the district court must retain the federal claim.

7) In the present case, Ps rely on the same series of events for all counts of their complaint, including the federal count. Therefore, the federal claim is not separate and independent under 1441(c) and the district court had no authority to remand the case under that section.

8) Nothing in section 1367(c) authorizes a district court to decline to hear a claim over which it has original jurisdiction. Furthermore, while the discretion bestowed by 1367(c) exists with respect to removed claims as well as claims filed initially in the district court, it is apparent that the district court has not exercised that discretion in this case. The magistrate's opinion, adopted by the district court, refers only to 1441(c).

9) A district court may be called upon to exercise its discretion at any time during the course of a proceeding and the following guidance is offered:

   a) While 1367(c) does not specify what disposition the district court is to make of state claims it decides not to hear, we believe that in a case that has been removed from a state court, a remand to that court is a viable alternative to a dismissal without prejudice.

   b) Section 1367(a)'s grant of "supplemental" jurisdiction was intended to broaden what had previously been termed "pendent" jurisdiction to include cases involving the addition of parties. Section 1367(c), on the other hand, was intended simply to codify the preexisting pendent jurisdiction law enunciated in *Gibbs* concerning those instances in which a district court is authorized to decline to hear a state claim it would have the power to hear because of its relationship to an original federal jurisdiction claim.

   c) Under *Gibbs*, if the claim over which the district court has original jurisdiction is dismissed before trial, the district court must decline to decide the pendent claims unless considerations of judicial economy, convenience, and fairness to the parties provide an affirmative justification for doing so. If the original federal jurisdiction claim is proceeding to trial, however, such considerations will normally counsel an exercise of district court jurisdiction over state claims based on the same nucleus of operative facts unless the district court can point to some substantial countervailing consideration.

     d)   The "substantially predominate" standard of 1367(c) comes from *Gibbs*. The authority of 1367(c)(2) should be invoked only when there is a countervailing interest to be served. This will normally be the case only when a state claim constitutes the real body of the case to which the federal claim is only an appendage.

     e)   This case involves several substantial claims that Ps' constitutional rights have been infringed. The addition of negligence claims based on the same facts as the constitutional claim will not likely cause the state issues to predominate.

D. FRAUDULENT JOINDER TO PREVENT REMOVAL

A joinder is fraudulent even if the plaintiff has no actual knowledge of the lack of a bona fide claim against the defendant joined, if she purposely closes her eyes to information readily obtainable. A plaintiff may not join defendants solely for the purpose of destroying federal subject matter jurisdiction.

1.   Subsequent Case with Identical Facts--Dodd v. Fawcett Publications, Inc., 329 F.2d 82 (10th Cir. 1964).

Dodd v. Fawcett Publications, Inc.

    a.   Facts. Fawcett Publications published in its magazine *True* an article in which reference was made to the University of Oklahoma football team. Alleging the article to be libelous, 13 members of the team (Ps), each a citizen of Oklahoma, filed separate actions for damages in the Oklahoma state court naming Fawcett (D), a foreign corporation, and Mid-Continent, a Delaware corporation with its principal place of business in Oklahoma, as co-defendants. Mid-Continent is a distributor of *True* and other magazines. D moved to remove the case to federal court, but it was denied on the ground that Ps and Mid-Continent were citizens of Oklahoma. The action by one plaintiff, Morris, proceeded to trial in the state court and a verdict was entered against D and in favor of Mid-Continent. The Oklahoma Supreme Court affirmed the judgment. Thereafter, D petitioned for removal to the federal court with respect to the other suits. The petition was granted. Another plaintiff, Dodd, attempted to have the case remanded back to state court, but the federal court denied remand on the ground that the Oklahoma Supreme Court decision was final as to Mid-Continent and, therefore, there existed complete diversity between Ps and the defendant. Dodd appealed on the basis that res judicata did not apply because there were different parties than in the earlier action. D stated that the only reason Mid-Continent had been made a party was to prevent removal.

    b.   Issue. Upon specific allegations of fraudulent joinder may a court pierce the pleadings, consider the entire record, and determine the basis of joinder by any means available?

    c.   Held. Yes. Judgment affirmed.

      1)   In many cases, removability can be determined by the original pleadings, and normally the statement of a cause of action against the resident defendant will suffice to prevent removal.

2) Upon specific allegations of fraudulent joinder, the court may pierce the pleadings, consider the entire record, and determine the basis of joinder by any means available.

3) The joinder of a resident defendant against whom no cause of action is stated is a patent sham, and though a cause of action may be stated, the joinder is similarly fraudulent if in fact no cause of action exists. In the case at bar the trial court properly refused to remand.

4) The Oklahoma Supreme Court has judicially determined that unrecited but specific proof occurring in the *Morris* case was insufficient to impose liability on Mid-Continent.

5) Without material addition, that same proof appears with complete certainty to be the sole basis of the plaintiff's claim against the same defendant in a case having identical origin.

6) Mid-Continent's nonliability is thus established as both a matter of fact and law, and its continued joinder serves only to frustrate federal jurisdiction. In such cases joinder is fraudulent.

E. PROCEDURE FOR REMOVAL

A defendant accomplishes removal by filing a notice of removal in the district court geographically encompassing the state court in which the case is pending. The notice must contain a statement of the grounds for removal together with copies of all process, pleadings, and orders served on the defendant. The notice must be filed within 30 days after receipt by the defendant of the initial pleading or summons, or, if the case is not initially removable, within 30 days after receipt by the defendant of an amendment or other paper indicating that the case has now become removable (*e.g.*, through dismissal of a nondiverse party). An action may not be removed on the basis of diversity more than one year after it was commenced.

F. ASSIGNMENTS

A complete assignment of a claim will be sufficient to create diversity jurisdiction and thus permit removability. A partial assignment, however, will be insufficient to create diversity jurisdiction. A federal court may pierce the form of any assignment to determine whether there is in substance a complete assignment.

Gentle v.
Lamb-
Weston, Inc.

1. **Assignment to Defeat Removal--Gentle v. Lamb-Weston, Inc.,** 302 F. Supp. 161 (D. Me. 1969).

   a. **Facts.** Gentle (P) and several other farmers brought suit against Lamb-Weston, Inc. (D) for breach of contract. Because diversity of citizenship existed and P's attorney wanted to try the matter in state court, a small portion of the claim was assigned to Tamblyn (P), a resident of Oregon. D attempted to remove to federal court. P raised the assignment as a bar to diversity jurisdiction.

   b. **Issue.** May a party partially assign his claim to defeat diversity jurisdiction?

c. Held. No. P's motion for remand denied.

  1) A complete assignment of a claim, even for the purpose of defeating jurisdiction, will be honored, based on prior decisions.

  2) However, for anything less than a total assignment, a federal court need not submit to devices that are solely designed to defeat jurisdiction. Federal courts may jealously guard their own jurisdiction.

  3) The existence of federal jurisdiction is a matter of federal law. It need not submit to a state court proceeding to determine whether an assignment made to defeat jurisdiction is valid.

  4) Because we have jurisdiction already, we decide that partial assignments to defeat jurisdiction need not be honored by federal courts.

2. When Removal Is Effective--Burroughs v. Palumbo, 871 F. Supp. 870 (E.D. Va. 1994).

Burroughs v. Palumbo

  a. Facts. Burroughs (P), an attorney in Virginia, brought this action for unpaid legal fees against his former client, Palumbo (D). The case was filed in a Virginia circuit court and D, a citizen of Florida, was served in accordance with the Virginia long-arm statute. D filed a notice of removal, which was filed within the 30-day requirement of 28 U.S.C. section 1446(b) but was out of time for filing an answer under the 21-day state court rule. The state court entered a default judgment against D, who later on the same day filed the notice of removal with the state court. D now seeks to have this court set aside the default judgment.

  b. Issue. During the period between the filing of the notice of removal in federal court and the filing in state court, which court had jurisdiction?

  c. Held. There is concurrent jurisdiction. The case was properly removed with the default judgment intact.

  1) There is a two-step procedure for removal. First, the defendant must file a notice of removal in the district court for the district and division in which the state action is pending. Second, promptly after filing the notice of removal, the defendant must file a copy of the notice with the clerk of the state court.

  2) A finding that the state court had exclusive jurisdiction until the two-step process is completed would undermine the federal rules.

  3) Federal jurisdiction attached when the notice of removal was filed in the federal court and the state court had concurrent jurisdiction until the notice was filed in the state court.

  4) During the period of concurrent jurisdiction, the default judgment was properly entered.

  5) The federal court takes removal cases as though everything done in the state court had been done in the federal court.

6) Therefore, this court may vacate the default judgment based on an adequate showing by D as to why he did not make a timely answer to the complaint.

Matthews v. County of Fremont, Wyoming

3. **Unanimity Among Defendants Required for Removal--Matthews v. County of Fremont, Wyoming,** 826 F. Supp. 1315 (D. Wyo, 1993).

a. **Facts.** Matthews (P), a former county deputy sheriff, brought an action for wrongful termination of employment against Lucero, the elected county sheriff, and the county of Fremont (Ds). The basis of P's claim was 42 U.S.C. section 1983. Lucero filed a notice of removal. The county did not join in or consent to the petition for removal, and together with P seeks remand.

b. **Issue.** Does an exception to the general rule requiring unanimity among defendants for the purposes of removal apply in this case?

c. **Held.** No. Remand granted.

1) The general rule is that all defendants must join in or consent to removal.

2) One exception to the general rule is when a nonconsenting defendant is merely nominal. It is clear that the county is more than a nominal party because the public purse is exposed.

3) A second exception is when jurisdiction of a party is based on a separate and independent jurisdictional grant. In the instant case, there is no party with an independent, party-based jurisdictional grant.

4) There is no requirement that section 1983 actions should be treated differently to allow removal even if there are nonconsenting defendants.

5) Because there are no specific allegations asserting claims in terms of racial equity, removal under section 1443 is not appropriate.

G. **REMAND OF REMOVAL CASES**

A judge may not remand a properly removed case for any reasons except those authorized by statute, and a writ of mandamus will lie to challenge the judge's action.

Bloom v. Barry

1. **No "Remand" to Different Court--Bloom v. Barry,** 755 F.2d 356 (3d Cir. 1985).

a. **Facts.** Bloom (P) filed suit in a Florida state court against American Honda Motor Company (D) for breach of warranty. The claim also sought relief pursuant to the Magnuson-Moss Warranty Act. Under this statute there is no federal question jurisdiction unless the amount in controversy exceeds $50,000. D filed a petition alleging that there was diversity of citizenship between the parties and that the amount in controversy exceeded $10,000, thereby removing the case to the federal district court in Florida. Simultaneously, D moved the federal court to transfer the case to the District of New Jersey, and this was granted. After the transfer, D moved to dismiss the complaint on the ground that the federal court lacked subject matter jurisdiction because the claim under the Magnuson-Moss Warranty Act was less than $50,000 and the state law warranty claim to a legal certainty could not result in a judgment in excess of $10,000. The district court did not dismiss the action but issued an order remanding the case to New Jersey's state court. P petitions for a writ of mandamus to have the order vacated.

b.   **Issue.** Can a case that was first filed in state court, then removed to a federal court, and then transferred to another jurisdiction, be remanded by the federal court to the state court in the new jurisdiction?

c.   **Held.** No. Petition granted.

1)   Remand means send back, it does not mean send elsewhere. The federal court in New Jersey lacks authority to remand to a New Jersey court. Following the change of venue, the federal court in New Jersey had the same authority with respect to the disposition of the case as the federal court in Florida. It was even obliged to apply the same law as that court must have applied. [Van Dusen v. Barrack, 376 U.S. 612 (1964)]

2)   The federal court in Florida had the power to remand the case to a state court in Florida and so the federal court in New Jersey inherited this authority with respect to Florida, not with respect to New Jersey. Because the order remanding to a New Jersey court was entered without legal authority, it must be vacated.

VI. VENUE

A. IN GENERAL

Jurisdiction is the *power to adjudicate* a particular controversy on the merits. *Venue* relates to the *geographic locality* for the exercise of jurisdiction. Unlike subject matter jurisdiction, venue is always waivable by the parties. Venue in the federal courts is governed by statute.

1. **General Rules—Venue in Federal Courts.** Venue in civil actions in the federal courts is proper in:

   (i)   A judicial district where *any defendant resides,* if all defendants reside in the same state;

   (ii) A judicial district in which *a substantial part of the events or omissions giving rise to the claim occurred,* or *a substantial part of property that is the subject of the action is situated;* or

   (iii) If there is no district in which the action may otherwise be brought,

        i.   For actions based *solely on diversity,* a judicial district in which *the defendants are subject to personal jurisdiction at the time the action is commenced;* or

        ii. For actions *not based solely on diversity,* a judicial district in which *any defendant may be found.*

   [28 U.S.C. §1391(a), (b)]

2. **Corporations.** Venue for corporate defendants is proper in any judicial district in which the corporation is subject to personal jurisdiction. [28 U.S.C. §1391(c)]

3. **Unincorporated Associations.** Unlike a corporation, the residence of an unincorporated association is not prescribed by statute. An unincorporated association is regarded as an indivisible unit for the purpose of diversity jurisdiction. Therefore, an unincorporated association may be sued under the venue statute in any district where it is doing business or where the claim arises.

Gregory v. Pocono Grow Fertilizer Corp.

4. **Venue Based on Where the Claim Arose--Gregory v. Pocono Grow Fertilizer Corp.,** 35 F. Supp. 2d 295 (W.D.N.Y. 1999).

   a.   **Facts.** The shareholders of Waste Stream, a New York corporation (Ps) and Pocono Grow Fertilizer Corp., a Pennsylvania corporation (Ds) began discussing a potential business relationship. All of the stock of Waste Stream was purchased by U.S. Liquids, Inc. and U.S. Liquids, Inc. informed Ps that it did not wish to enter into the business relationship. When Ds advised Ps that Ds were prepared to commence litigation for breach of the letter of intent, Ps brought this action for a declaratory judgment that there is no enforceable agreement between the parties. Ds now move to dismiss Ps' complaint for improper venue, or in the alternative, to transfer this action to Pennsylvania.

b. **Issue.** Do the two subsections of the venue statute provide two independent and alternative bases for venue?

c. **Held.** Yes. Ds' motions to dismiss or transfer denied.

1) Prior to 1966, the statute provided that venue would be proper only in the judicial district where all the plaintiffs or all the defendants reside. If there was no such district, then a "venue gap" resulted and the case could not be brought in federal court.

2) In 1966, the statute was amended to add the district in which the claim arose. In 1990, the statute was again amended to eliminate the plaintiff's residence as a proper place for venue.

3) Some courts have concluded that suit may be brought in the district where a substantial part of the events occurred only if all the defendants do not reside in the same state. However, in my opinion, this conclusion is incorrect. The plain language of the statute clearly provides alternative bases for jurisdiction.

4) Ps have alleged sufficient facts to establish that a substantial part of the events giving rise to their claim occurred in New York. There were telephone calls, facsimile transactions, and correspondence between New York and Pennsylvania. The letter of intent was also prepared and executed in New York for transmittal to Pennsylvania.

5) Ds also have failed to make out a strong case for transfer.

B. CHANGE OF VENUE

1. **Court May Determine Convenient Forum.** Even when jurisdiction is proper under the general venue statute, a district court may refuse to exercise its jurisdiction if the court determines, in its discretion, that litigation in another forum would be more convenient.

2. **Factors.** Under 28 U.S.C. section 1404(a) a district court may, in the interest of justice and for the convenience of the parties, transfer a case to a more convenient district court where the suit may have been brought.

3. **Law Applicable on Transfer--Ferens v. John Deere Co.,** 494 U.S. 516 (1990).

Ferens
v. John
Deere Co.

a. **Facts.** Albert Ferens, a resident of Pennsylvania, lost his right hand while working with a combine manufactured by John Deere Co. (D). More than two years later, Ferens and his wife (Ps) brought a diversity suit raising contract and warranty claims against D in the United States district court in Pennsylvania. Ps could not bring a tort action in Pennsylvania because Pennsylvania's two-year tort statute of limitations had expired. Ps then filed another diversity suit in federal court in Mississippi, where D was a corporate resident, alleging tort claims. The six-year Mississippi tort statute of limitations had not yet expired. Under *Klaxon v. Stentor Electric Manufacturing Co.,* the federal court in Mississippi would apply the same choice of law rule that a Mississippi state court would; *i.e.,* Pennsylvania substantive law would control the substantive claim and Mississippi's limitations period would apply. Ps then moved in the Mississippi federal court to transfer the case under 28 U.S.C. section 1404(a) to the Pennsylvania federal court on the ground that Pennsylvania was a more convenient forum. The motion was granted, and the Pennsylvania federal court consolidated the transferred tort action with the contract and warranty action already pending there. The court then dismissed the tort action on the basis that the two-year Pennsylvania tort statute of limitations applied rather than the six-year Mississippi statute. The third circuit affirmed, and the Supreme Court granted certiorari.

b.   **Issue.** When a plaintiff initiates a transfer for convenience under section 1404(a), should the transferee court apply the choice of law rules of the transferor court?

c.   **Held.** Yes. Judgment reversed and remanded.

1)   Section 1404(a) itself does not answer the question presented here. In *Van Dusen v. Barrack,* we held that when a defendant initiates the transfer under section 1404(a), the transferee court must apply the law of the transferor court.

2)   The legislative history of section 1404(a) shows that it was enacted because broad venue provisions in federal acts often resulted in inconvenient forums. Transfers for convenience were intended to remedy this problem, not to narrow a plaintiff's venue privilege or defeat state law advantages that might accrue from the plaintiff's selection of a particular venue.

3)   Applying the transferor court's law deprives Ps of no state law advantages. In one sense, D also loses no legal advantage, except that D cannot force Ps to litigate in either the inconvenient forum Ps have chosen or not at all. That is, if Ps were forced to litigate in the Mississippi federal court, Mississippi state law would apply anyway. If Ps had known that their motion to transfer to Pennsylvania would result in dismissal, they would no doubt have litigated in Mississippi.

4)   Applying the transferee law would undermine *Erie* in a serious way. In general, section 1404(a) has been seen as a housekeeping measure that should not alter the state law applicable in a case under *Erie.*

5)   *Van Dusen v. Barrack* sought to fashion a rule that would not create opportunities for forum shopping by defendants. No interpretation of section 1404(a) will create comparable forum shopping opportunities for plaintiffs, because plaintiffs already have the opportunity to shop among the available forums for the one with the most favorable law.

6)   The federal courts should be able to evaluate section 1404(a) motions by considering only convenience factors; they should not have to conduct elaborate surveys of the possible prejudicial effects of different states' laws on the outcome of the case.

d. **Dissent** (Scalia, Brennan, Marshall, Blackmun, JJ.). It is unlikely that Congress, in enacting section 1404(a), meant to provide a plaintiff with a vehicle by which to appropriate the law of a distant and inconvenient forum in which he does not intend to litigate, and to carry that prize back to the state in which he intends to try the case. Also, application of the transferor court's law encourages forum shopping between state and federal courts in the same jurisdiction. The Court's decision will cost the federal courts more time than it will save them; the Court's calculation of the "systemic costs" is incorrect.

VII. JURISDICTION TO DETERMINE JURISDICTION

A. IN GENERAL

If a court lacks the jurisdiction to determine its own subject matter jurisdiction, no lawsuit can proceed if objected to on the ground that the court lacks subject matter jurisdiction.

1. **Interim Actions.** Any court may protect the res before it in an in rem action by enjoining another action affecting the res. In an in rem action, the first court to attach the res maintains jurisdiction over the res until such jurisdiction is relinquished.

2. **In Personam Actions.** Two courts may exercise in personam jurisdiction simultaneously unless the second court is willing to dismiss or stay its proceeding because a prior action is pending in another court.

3. **Protecting Jurisdiction.** A court has jurisdiction to issue a temporary restraining order until it has the opportunity to determine the issue of its subject matter jurisdiction.

United States
v. United
Mine Workers
of America

    a. **Disobedience of restraining order--United States v. United Mine Workers of America,** 330 U.S. 258 (1947).

        1) **Facts.** In October 1946, all bituminous coal mines were in the possession of and operated by the United States. They were controlled by an agreement between Krug, the Secretary of the Interior, and Lewis, President of the United Mine Workers Union (D). Under section 14 of the National Bituminous Coal Wage Agreement of April 11, 1945, either Krug or Lewis could give 10 days notice, in writing, of a desire to negotiate, and the other party was required to attend; 15 days after the beginning of the negotiation conference either party could give written notice of termination of the agreement, effective five days thereafter. After writing a request for a conference, Lewis, within the required time limits, sent notice of termination of the agreement; Krug notified Lewis that Lewis had no power under law or the agreement to unilaterally terminate the agreement. Lewis thereafter circulated the termination notice to mine workers. The United States (P) then filed an action for declaratory relief seeking a judgment that Lewis could not unilaterally terminate the agreement, and, claiming the circulation of the termination notice was in fact a strike notice. P also requested a temporary restraining order restraining D from continuing to circulate the termination notice or from encouraging strikes or cessation of work. The order was granted by the district court. However, a general walkout occurred, followed by a full strike. P sought an order to show cause why Lewis and D should not be punished for contempt. D contended that the court lacked jurisdiction to issue the restraining order, and that the Norris-LaGuardia Act prohibited the issuance of an injunction or restraining order. The court found Lewis and D in both civil and criminal contempt, and fined Lewis $10,000 and D $3.5 million, from which order D appeals.

2) **Issue.** Does a court have jurisdiction to issue a restraining order, punishable by contempt, when the court's jurisdiction over the subject matter has not yet been determined?

3) **Held.** Yes. Judgment affirmed in part.

   a) D first contends that the Norris-LaGuardia Act prohibits the issuance of this restraining order. The Act applies only to cases involving employers, and the United States is not an "employer" within the Act.

   b) Even assuming the Act applies, the restraining order was properly issued by the district court. The notice of termination amounted to a strike call, and the district court had the power to issue a restraining order for the purpose of preserving the status quo pending a determination of the issue of whether the court had jurisdiction.

   c) Rather than obeying the order and challenging it properly, the defendants ignored it. As stated in *United States v. Shipp,* 203 U.S. 563 (1906), although it has been held that orders made by a court having no jurisdiction may be disregarded, only the court has the power to determine if it does have jurisdiction, and until such determination is made, the court has power to preserve existing conditions by way of orders.

   d) Here, the restraining order was issued to preserve the status quo, and violation of it was punishable as criminal contempt. If a court has jurisdiction over the person and the subject matter, its order must be obeyed until reversed by orderly and proper proceedings. This is true even if the act under which the order was issued was unconstitutional.

   e) Insofar as the fines imposed are concerned, Lewis's fine of $10,000 is affirmed; as to D, $700,000 is a proper fine on the condition that if D does not, within five days, show compliance with the restraining order, it is to be fined an additional $2.8 million.

4) **Dissent** (Murphy, J.). Congress specifically prohibited the use of restraining orders to break strikes and we are not free to disregard that prohibition.

5) **Dissent** (Rutledge, J.). The Norris-LaGuardia Act applies here, and thus the restraining order was improperly issued. Congress has the power to limit the lower court's jurisdiction, and has done so here. To hold otherwise would place a party in peril of certain punishment regardless of the validity of the order violated. Such action would, in effect, put an end to some litigation, as for example, First Amendment cases where the opportunity to speak could be simply denied by the issuance of such an order. Thus, there must be raised a substantial doubt sufficient to bring the *Shipp* case into effect; and that has not been shown here.

6) **Comment.** An important distinction drawn by the Court involves those orders of a court to preserve its jurisdiction and those orders that are made when the court has no jurisdiction. The latter may be disregarded, because an order of a court having no jurisdiction is void. But, in order to make a jurisdictional determina-

tion, a court may issue orders preserving the status quo until it does so. As here, such orders are valid and their violation is punishable by contempt.

B. APPEARANCE

The defendant does not waive the right to raise a jurisdictional defense because it is joined with other defenses. [*See* Fed. R. Civ. P. 12(g)]

1. **Effect of Decision upon Objection.** If a defendant appears to contest jurisdiction and is successful, then the case is dismissed. If the defendant loses the jurisdictional challenge, then the defendant must litigate the case on the merits. If the defendant defaults on the merits, the judgment is valid because the jurisdiction issue has been litigated. The only basis for the defendant to challenge the court's ruling on the jurisdiction issue is to appeal. The defendant may not collaterally attack the court's ruling.

Baldwin v.
Iowa State
Traveling
Men's
Association

2. **Opportunity to Litigate Jurisdiction--Baldwin v. Iowa State Traveling Men's Association,** 283 U.S. 522 (1931).

   a. **Facts.** The Iowa State Traveling Men's Association (D) originally moved to quash and dismiss, for want of service, an action instituted by Baldwin (P) in Missouri state court and removed to federal district court. The court quashed service but refused to dismiss, whereupon an alias summons was issued and served. D again appeared specially, moving to set aside the service on the basis that D was not sufficiently present in Missouri to support jurisdiction. After a hearing, the motion was overruled, but D did not file a response and judgment was entered against it. The present action was brought in federal court in Iowa to enforce this judgment, and D again raised the lack of jurisdiction over its person. The court sustained D's contention. The Supreme Court granted certiorari. P is claiming that the second judgment is invalid on the basis of full faith and credit and res judicata.

   b. **Issue.** Is a judgment, rendered against a defendant who appeared specially and tried the issue of jurisdiction over his person, res judicata on that issue in an action brought to enforce the judgment?

   c. **Held.** Yes. Judgment reversed.

      1) Contrary to P's claim, the Full Faith and Credit Clause does not apply here because neither of the courts involved was a state court.

      2) The real issue, then, is whether the first judgment amounted to res judicata on the issue of jurisdiction.

      3) The fact that D appeared specially is immaterial here, and is important only when an appeal from the judgment is taken. Had D never appeared to litigate the issue of jurisdiction, it could have, in an action to enforce the judgment, raised the question of the first court's jurisdiction.

4) However, having litigated the issue, public policy requires an end to litigation, and thus the first judgment was res judicata on the issue of jurisdiction.

d. **Comment.** The distinction drawn between a special and a general appearance was established to permit a defendant to contest the issue of jurisdiction without consenting to it.

1) Once having had a chance to argue the question, the defendant should and is estopped from further contesting the judgment other than to take a direct appeal.

2) The only time a party can collaterally attack a judgment for lack of jurisdiction is when the judgment is entered on default and the issue never litigated. While this forces a defendant to risk default judgment, he may decide to do so if the state where the judgment is to be enforced is less likely to find jurisdiction than the first state.

3. **Res Judicata Even If Based on Unconstitutional Statute--Chicot County Drainage District v. Baxter State Bank,** 308 U.S. 371 (1940).

a. **Facts.** The Chicot County Drainage District (D) issued numerous bonds, 14 of which were purchased by the Baxter State Bank (P). After D defaulted, P brought an action to recover. D alleged in its answer that it had effected a plan of readjustment of its indebtedness under a "Municipal-Debt Readjustment Act" and that the plan had been approved by the bankruptcy court. Under the plan, all obligations held by D's creditors had to be prosecuted within one year. Unless so presented, they would be forever barred from collection under the plan, and creditors were enjoined from asserting any claim on the bonds. P had notice of the plan and participated in the proceedings. No question was raised as to the constitutionality of the Act under which the court acted. After a final decree was entered, the United States Supreme Court, in another case, declared the Act unconstitutional. D contended that the bankruptcy judgment is res judicata on P's claim. The district court ruled in favor of P, and the court of appeals affirmed. The Supreme Court granted certiorari.

b. **Issue.** Is the determination by a federal court on questions of jurisdiction open to direct review so that, if collaterally attacked, the judgment would be res judicata even if the statute under which the court acted is unconstitutional?

c. **Held.** Yes. Judgment reversed.

1) The courts below acted on the premise that once the Act was found unconstitutional it had no effect, and thus could not afford the basis for the court's decree. However, there can be no rule of absolute retroactive invalidity.

2) In this case, two reasons justify the application of res judicata. First, the bankruptcy proceedings were conducted in conformity with the statute. P appeared, but did not challenge the validity of the statute. P cannot claim not to be bound to the decree because it failed to raise the issue. Second, although the district court sitting in bankruptcy is a

court of limited jurisdiction, it still has the power to determine whether or not it has jurisdiction to hear the case and thus to construe the statute under which it is asked to act.

3) The court's determination on this matter is open only to direct review and cannot be collaterally attacked. The court's finding of jurisdiction is thus res judicata on collateral attack.

4) There is no question that had the issue of the statute's constitutionality been raised in the bankruptcy court, that court's decision would be subject only to direct review on appeal.

d. **Comment.** By holding that there could be no collateral attack of a federal court decision pertaining to jurisdiction, the Court was able to solidify the basic tenet of federalism that state courts do not have the power or jurisdiction to define or limit the jurisdiction of federal courts. The decision avoids the problem of having a state court later find that a federal court did not have jurisdiction over federal matters. Of course, there is nothing to preclude a party from directly attacking the decision of the federal court.

Ruhrgas AG v. Marathon Oil Company

4. **Sequence for Determining Jurisdictional Issues--Ruhrgas AG v. Marathon Oil Company,** 119 S. Ct. 1563 (1999).

a. **Facts.** Marathon Oil Company (P) filed suit against Ruhrgas AG (D) in Texas state court asserting state law claims of fraud, tortious interference with prospective business relations, breach of fiduciary duty, and civil conspiracy. D removed the case to federal district court. D moved to dismiss the case for lack of personal jurisdiction. P moved to remand the case to state court for lack of federal subject matter jurisdiction. After permitting jurisdictional discovery, the district court dismissed the case for lack of personal jurisdiction. The court of appeals held that in removed cases district courts must decide issues of subject matter jurisdiction first. The Supreme Court granted certiorari.

b. **Issue.** In removal cases, must the federal court first decide the issue of subject matter jurisdiction before reaching issues of personal jurisdiction?

c. **Held.** No. Judgment reversed.

1) In cases removed from state court to federal, as in cases originating in federal court, there is no unyielding jurisdictional hierarchy.

2) Customarily, a federal court first resolves jurisdiction over the subject matter but there are circumstances where a district court could first decide the issue of personal jurisdiction.

3) While *Steel Co. v. Citizens for Better Environment*, reasoned that subject matter jurisdiction necessarily precedes a decision on the merits, the same reasoning does not dictate a sequencing of jurisdictional issues.

4) Where, as here, the district court has before it a straightforward personal jurisdiction issue presenting no complex question of state law, and the alleged subject matter jurisdiction defect raises a difficult and

novel question, the court does not abuse its discretion by turning directly to the personal jurisdiction issue.

C. EFFECT OF LACK OF SUBJECT MATTER JURISDICTION

A judgment rendered by a court that lacks subject matter jurisdiction is void. This rule applies even though the defect in subject matter jurisdiction is not discovered until after the final judgment has been entered.

1. **Federal Court Judgments.** Under Federal Rule 60(b)(4), a district court is authorized to give relief against a void judgment and there is no time limitation within which such relief must be requested. The jurisdictional defect may also be raised on appeal even if the defect had not been raised in trial court.

2. **State Court Judgments.** In cases appealed from state courts, where there has been an assertion of federal policy that outweighs the policy of res judicata, there may be a collateral attack on an otherwise valid state court judgment.

   a. **State court acting in exclusive federal area--Kalb v. Feuerstein, 308 U.S. 433 (1940).**

      Kalb v. Feuerstein

      1) **Facts.** Mr. and Mrs. Kalb (Ps) were farmers and mortgaged their property to Feuerstein (D), who obtained a judgment of foreclosure on the property and had the county sheriff sell the property after Ps had filed a petition in bankruptcy. The county court confirmed the sheriff's sale. No stay of the foreclosure action or of the action to enforce it was sought in a state or bankruptcy court. After Ps had been ejected they brought an action both to recover the property and for damages. The applicable bankruptcy statute provided that the filing of a petition in bankruptcy subjected the debtor to the exclusive jurisdiction of the court in all cases. At the time of filing the petition, the sale had not yet been confirmed. The act further provided that if a petition had been filed, a proceeding for foreclosure or for recovery of possession of land could not be maintained in any court. This prohibition applied to all the property of the debtor. Such property should be in the sole and exclusive jurisdiction of the bankruptcy court. Ps' action was dismissed, and Ps appeal.

      2) **Issue.** Is a state court judgment, rendered with respect to a debtor who has filed a petition in bankruptcy, void and subject to collateral attack because Congress provided bankruptcy courts with exclusive jurisdiction over debtor's property in bankruptcy?

      3) **Held.** Yes. Judgment reversed.

         a) The questions presented are whether the state court had jurisdiction to confirm the sheriff's sale while the bankruptcy petition was pending, and if not, whether it was, absent direct appeal, subject to collateral attack.

b) It is clear that if the filing of the bankruptcy petition ousted the state court of jurisdiction, the state court judgment was void and subject to collateral attack. This is a federal question.

c) Congress, by having plenary power over bankruptcy, could by legislation create an exception to the principle that a judgment of a court of competent jurisdiction bears a presumption of regularity, and Congress could thus render any such judgment a nullity and subject to collateral attack.

d) Because the Constitution vests Congress with exclusive jurisdiction over bankruptcy, and because Congress, under this power, vested exclusive jurisdiction over bankruptcy matters to a bankruptcy court, a state court cannot also exercise jurisdiction over such matters. To do so would violate the supreme law of the land.

e) The wisdom of providing automatic stays was and is left to Congress alone. The statute here makes clear Congress's intent that only the bankruptcy court shall have jurisdiction over these matters to the exclusion of state courts.

f) It therefore follows that the judgment of the state court was void and subject to collateral attack.

4) Comment. It is clear that a determination of whether the bankruptcy statute gave bankruptcy courts exclusive jurisdiction is a federal question, and cannot be decided by a state court. To suggest otherwise would be to permit state courts to resolve the meaning of the United States Constitution and an Act of Congress. Although a court judgment is usually not subject to collateral attack in the absence of a direct appeal, where that judgment is void as being in excess of jurisdiction, then it is subject to collateral attack.

VIII. CONFLICTS BETWEEN STATE AND NATIONAL JUDICIAL SYSTEMS

A. STATE ENFORCEMENT OF FEDERAL LAW

A state court must entertain a cause of action created under federal law providing concurrent jurisdiction in state courts. States may not discriminate against rights that arise under federal laws. The Supremacy Clause requires state courts to apply federal law if the federal law governs the cause of action.

1. **State's Assertion of Sovereign Immunity Against Federal Cause of Action--Howlett by Howlett v. Rose,** 496 U.S. 356 (1990).

Howlett
by Howlett
v. Rose

   a. **Facts.** A former high school student (P) sued a school board and three school officials (Ds) in state court. P claimed that the high school principal had illegally searched his car, thus violating P's rights under the Fourth and Fourteenth Amendments of the United States Constitution. P alleged civil rights violations under 42 U.S.C. section 1983. The state court dismissed the case against the school board. In explaining the dismissal, the court stated that sovereign immunity existed for state governmental entities, and that as a consequence, the school board was immune from suits alleging federal civil rights statute violations when sued in state court. The Florida Court of Appeals affirmed the decision and the state supreme court denied review. P appeals.

   b. **Issue.** Can a school board assert a state law defense of sovereign immunity to a suit brought in state court that alleges federal civil rights violations when the same defense could not be asserted if the suit was brought in federal court?

   c. **Held.** No. Judgment reversed.

      1) Federal law is enforceable in state courts because of the Supremacy Clause of the Constitution. This clause makes federal law the "supreme law of the land and charges state courts with a coordinate responsibility to enforce that law according to their regular modes of procedure." From this proposition comes three principles.

      2) First, a state court may not deny a federal right, if properly brought to the state court, in the absence of a valid excuse. Second, an excuse that violates federal law is not a valid excuse. Third, if a state refuses jurisdiction because of a neutral state rule concerning judicial administration, a federal court must examine the circumstances carefully before forcing the state court to hear the case.

      3) In the facts before the court, a federal right was properly presented in state court and dismissed without a valid excuse. Federal law, not state law, defines the scope of a section 1983 action. No sovereign immunity defense exists in the statute to protect municipal corporations from suit. Indeed, this court has held otherwise in prior cases.

4) Nor can it be said that section 1983 claims are excluded from the types of tort claims that state law permits to be heard against a school board. The court in which P filed has heard similar cases against school boards prior to this. P is not asking Florida to establish a new forum to enforce federal rights. P seeks only to have the same access to Florida defendants that other plaintiffs have had.

5) In addition, no valid excuse exists for the circuit court's refusal to hear P's section 1983 action. The Florida court would have adjudicated a case against an individual school official under section 1983 or if P's action was based on state statutory or common law. Denial of access because P brings a federal law violation to a state court is contra to the Supremacy Clause and cannot be allowed.

B. FEDERAL INJUNCTIONS AGAINST STATE COURT PROCEEDINGS

1. **In General.** Title 28 U.S.C. section 2283, the anti-injunction statute, states: "A court of the United States may not grant an injunction to stay proceedings in a State court except as expressly authorized by Act of Congress, or where necessary in aid of its jurisdiction, or to protect or effectuate its judgments."

    a. **Language changed.** A previously recognized exception as to acts of Congress relating to bankruptcy was omitted and the general exception was substituted to cover all exceptions. The phrase "in aid of its jurisdiction" was added to further clarify the recognized power of the federal courts to stay proceedings in state cases removed to the district courts.

    b. **Implication.** The words "to protect or effectuate its judgments" conferred upon the federal courts jurisdiction to enjoin relitigation of cases and controversies fully adjudicated in the federal system.

2. **Enjoining State Court Proceeding Under the Anti-Injunction Statute.** A state or federal court, in which an in rem action is commenced, may enjoin subsequent actions involving the same res.

    a. **In personam action.** However, where the action is in personam, suit must be allowed to proceed in two courts simultaneously until one court renders a judgment.

    b. **Effect.** The first judgment in time will be res judicata in all other courts. If the judgment is one that is rendered by a federal court, it can be protected by injunctive relief under the anti-injunction statute.

3. **The "Except as Expressly Authorized" Exception to the Anti-Injunction Statute.** Title 28 U.S.C. section 2283, which normally operates as an absolute ban to an injunction of state court proceedings, permits the issuance of injunctions where Congress has expressly authorized injunctive relief.

a. Requirement of specific federal remedy--Vendo Co. v. Lektro-Vend Corp., 433 U.S. 623 (1977).

1) Facts. Vendo Co. (P) acquired most of the assets of Stoner Manufacturing. Harry Stoner (D) was employed by P in the business of manufacturing vending machines. Later P sued D and others in Illinois state court for breach of certain noncompetition covenants. Shortly thereafter, D sued P in federal district court alleging that P had violated the Sherman Act with the covenants. After nine years of litigation in the state courts, the Supreme Court of Illinois affirmed a judgment in favor of P in the amount of $7,363,500. The aforementioned federal suit, which remained dormant for nine years, was reactivated by D and the others, who moved for a preliminary injunction against collection of the Illinois judgment. The district court granted the injunction, holding that the injunctive relief provision of the Clayton Act constituted an express exception to the Anti-Injunction Act. The court of appeals affirmed. The Supreme Court granted certiorari.

2) Issue. In order to qualify as an exception to the anti-injunction statute, must an Act of Congress have created a specific federal right or remedy that could be frustrated if the federal court was not empowered to enjoin a state court proceeding?

3) Held. Yes. Judgment reversed.

    a) On its face, the language of section 16 of the Clayton Act merely authorizes private injunctive relief for antitrust violations. It does not mention the anti-injunction statute or the enjoining of state court proceedings.

    b) In order to qualify as an expressly authorized exception to the anti-injunction statute, an Act of Congress must have created a specific and uniquely federal right or remedy, enforceable in a federal court of equity, which could be frustrated if the federal court were not empowered to enjoin a state court.

    c) The private action for damages conferred by the Clayton Act is uniquely a federal right or remedy in that actions based upon it may be brought only in the federal courts.

    d) However, it is not an Act of Congress that could be given its intended scope only by the stay of a state court proceeding. The injunction was not absolutely necessary.

4) Concurrence (Blackmun, J., Burger, C.J.). Section 16 is an exception to the Anti-Injunction Act if the state proceedings are part of a pattern of baseless, repetitive claims that are being used as an anticompetitive device.

5) Dissent (Stevens, Brennan, White, Marshall, JJ.). Because section 16 of the Clayton Act is an Act of Congress that expressly authorizes an injunction against a state court proceeding that violates the antitrust laws, the plain language of the anti-injunction statute excepts this kind of injunction from its coverage.

6)   Comment. Any doubts as to the propriety of a federal injunction against state court proceedings should be resolved in favor of permitting the state courts to proceed in an orderly fashion to finally determine the controversy. *Atlantic Coast Line R. Co. v. Brotherhood of Locomotive Engineers*, 398 U.S. 281 (1970). This cautious approach is mandated by the explicit wording of section 2283, the Anti-Injunction Act, and the fundamental principle of a dual system of courts.

C.   STATE INJUNCTIONS AGAINST FEDERAL COURT PROCEEDINGS OR FEDERAL OFFICERS

1.   In General. A state court cannot enjoin a plaintiff from bringing or appealing an action in a federal court that has jurisdiction over the parties in an in personam cause of action. If the basis of the action is in rem or quasi in rem, the state court may protect the jurisdiction of the state court over property in its custody or control.

Donovan v.
City of Dallas

a.   State court injunction not allowed--Donovan v. City of Dallas, 377 U.S. 408 (1964).

1)   Facts. Forty-six Dallas citizens (Ps) filed a class action suit in Texas state court seeking to restrain Dallas (D) from issuing bonds to enlarge its airport. Summary judgment was granted for D and upheld on appeal. Some of the original Ps and others then filed suit in United States District Court seeking similar relief. D answered, simultaneously applying to the Texas Court of Civil Appeals to enjoin the federal district court action. The Court of Civil Appeals refused, but the Texas Supreme Court granted mandamus ordering the Court of Civil Appeals to prohibit Ps from further prosecuting the district court action. The district court case was dismissed. Attorney Donovan appealed the dismissal in the United States Court of Appeals for the Fifth Circuit, whereupon he and 87 other Ps were cited for contempt by the Texas Court of Civil Appeals and fined a total of $17,200. Donovan then moved "under duress" for dismissal of his appeal before the fifth circuit. The United States Supreme Court granted certiorari not to review the federal court dismissals, but to review the Texas Supreme Court's upholding of the injunction against Ps' prosecution of the federal court suit.

2)   Issue. Can a state court validly enjoin a person from prosecuting an in personam action in a district or appellate court of the United States that has jurisdiction both over the parties and the subject matter?

3)   Held. No. Judgment reversed and remanded.

a)   Early in the history of our country a general rule was established that state and federal courts would not interfere with or try to restrain each other's proceedings. That rule has continued substantially unchanged to this time.

b) While Congress has seen fit to authorize courts of the United States to restrain state court proceedings in some special circumstances, it has in no way relaxed the old and well-established judicially declared rule that some courts are completely without power to restrain federal court proceedings in in personam actions like the one here.

c) The Texas courts were without power to take away D's federal rights by contempt proceedings or otherwise.

4) **Dissent** (Harlan, Clark, Stewart, JJ.). The question presented in this case is not the general one stated by the Court at the outset of its opinion, but a much narrower one: May a state court enjoin resident state court suitors from prosecuting in the federal courts vexatious, duplicative litigation, which has the effect of thwarting a state court judgment already rendered against them? I consider both the state injunction and the ensuing contempt adjudication to have been perfectly proper.

5) **Comment.** "Despite the broad language setting forth the state ban, state court injunctions against the prosecution of federal suits have been upheld in a number of state cases. In many the ban on state injunctions was simply ignored, while in others the authority of cases . . . was evaded or distinguished. . . . Thus, historically, the conclusion is far from inescapable that state courts are absolutely without power to enjoin the prosecution of federal court actions." [32 U. of Chicago L. Rev. 497-8 (1964)] The instant case is therefore important because the court in effect rejected this position based on "comity" and "the prevention of inequities" and reaffirmed the state court prohibition in broad terms.

D. FEDERAL ACTIONS TO RESTRAIN STATE OFFICERS

1. **In General.** The Eleventh Amendment to the United States Constitution prohibits suits against a state by citizens of another state or an alien. A suit against the state by one of its own citizens is also beyond the federal judicial power.

2. **Suit Proper When Interference with a Federal Right.** Despite the Eleventh Amendment immunity, a state officer or agency may be sued in federal court if it is claimed that the state officer acted beyond his power and thus interfered with a federal right.

a. **Federal injunction against state officer's enforcement of unconstitutional act--*Ex Parte* Young, 209 U.S. 123 (1908).**   *Ex Parte* Young

1) **Facts.** In 1907, Minnesota passed a law reducing railroad rates that was unpopular with stockholders of railroad companies. They sought to enjoin their railroads from complying with the law, claiming a violation of due process. The state attorney general, Young (D), was joined in the suit, and the plaintiffs prayed that he be restrained from enforcing the law. The federal

court granted a preliminary injunction; D subsequently sued in state court for a writ of mandamus against the railroads, and the district court adjudged D guilty of contempt until he dismissed the state court proceeding. D, from jail, petitioned for writs of habeas corpus and certiorari to the United States Supreme Court.

2) Issue. Does a federal court have jurisdiction to enjoin state officers?

3) Held. Yes. Petitions dismissed.

a) When a state officer threatens or is about to commence proceedings, either of a civil or criminal nature, to enforce an unconstitutional act against parties affected by it, he may be enjoined by a federal court of equity from such action.

b) The officer's general discretion regarding the enforcement of the laws when and as he deems appropriate is not interfered with by an injunction that restrains him from taking any steps toward the enforcement of an unconstitutional enactment to the injury of the complainant.

c) In such case no affirmative action of any nature is directed, and the officer is simply prohibited from doing an act that he has no legal right to do.

d) An injunction to prevent an officer from doing that which he has no legal right to do is not an interference with his discretion. If the act that the state attorney general seeks to enforce is a violation of the federal Constitution, the officer in proceeding under such enactment comes into conflict with the superior authority of the Constitution, and he is stripped of his official or representative character and is subjected to the consequences of his individual conduct.

e) The State has no power to give him an immunity from responsibility to the supreme authority of the United States.

4) Dissent (Harlan, J.). I cannot suppose that the great men who framed the Constitution ever thought the time would come when a subordinate federal court, having no power to compel a State in its corporate capacity to appear before it as a litigant, would yet assume to deprive a State of the right to be represented in its own courts by its regular officer.

5) Comment. Contrasting the instant decision with *Pennsylvania Turnpike Commission v. McGinnes,* 179 F. Supp. 578 (E.D. Pa. 1959), federal decisions have all but dispelled the notions of equality and due deference between federal and state equity jurisdiction. In *McGinnes,* a state injunction against a federal official in the performance of his statutory duty was disallowed. Here, a federal injunction and contempt citation of a state official was allowed, because the activities of the attorney general came "into conflict with the superior authority of the Constitution." [*See* Hutcheson, A Case for Three Judges, 47 Harvard L. Rev. 795, 779 n.9 (1934)—"The authority and finality of *Ex Parte Young* can hardly be overestimated"]

b. Suits pursuant to the Indian Commerce Clause--Seminole Tribe of Florida v. Florida, 517 U.S. 44 (1996).

1) **Facts.** The Seminole Tribe of Indians (P) sued the state of Florida and its governor (Ds) for refusing to enter into any negotiations for inclusion of certain gaming activities in a compact between that tribe and the state. Jurisdiction was based on 28 U.S.C. section 2710 (d)(1)(C), which imposes a duty on the states to negotiate in good faith with an Indian tribe toward formation of such a compact. Ds moved to dismiss. The district court denied the motion. The circuit court reversed the district court, ruling that the Eleventh Amendment barred the suit. The Supreme Court granted certiorari.

2) **Issues.**

   a) Does the Eleventh Amendment prevent Congress from authorizing suits by Indian tribes against the states for injunctive relief to enforce legislation enacted pursuant to the Indian Commerce Clause?

   b) Does *Ex Parte Young* permit suits against a state's governor for injunctive relief to enforce the good faith bargaining requirement of the Act?

3) **Held.** a) Yes. b) No. Dismissal affirmed.

   a) Congress provided a clear statement of its intent to abrogate state sovereign immunity when it passed the Indian Commerce Clause.

   b) The remedy sought, prospective injunctive relief rather than retroactive monetary relief, is irrelevant to whether a suit is barred by the Eleventh Amendment.

   c) The plurality decision in *Pennsylvania v. Union Gas Co.*, 491 U.S. 1 (1989), has proven to be a solitary departure from established law. In overruling *Union Gas*, we reconfirm that the Eleventh Amendment does not dissipate when the subject of the suit is in an area, like regulation of Indian commerce, that is under the exclusive control of the federal government. The Eleventh Amendment restricts the judicial power under Article III and Article I and cannot be used to circumvent the constitutional limitations placed upon federal jurisdiction.

   d) Where Congress has prescribed a detailed remedial scheme for the enforcement against a state of a statutorily created right, a court should hesitate before casting aside those limitations and permitting an action against a state officer based upon *Ex Parte Young*.

4) **Dissent** (Stevens, J.).

   a) This decision prevents Congress from providing a federal forum for a broad range of actions against states, including copyright and patent law, bankruptcy, environmental law, and the regulation of the national economy.

   b) While there may be debate over whether, in light of the Eleventh Amendment, Congress has the power to ensure that a cause of action be enforced in federal court by a citizen of another state or a foreign citizen, there is no debate as to such a cause of action by a citizen of the same state.

5) **Dissent** (Souter, Ginsburg, Breyer, JJ.).

a) The adoption of the Eleventh Amendment did not affect federal question jurisdiction.

b) When judging legislation passed under unmistakable Article I powers, no further restriction could be required.

3. **Suits Against State Officers for Money Damages.** A private party may not sue a state officer for money damages in federal court, if the damages are to be paid from public funds in the state treasury. Such a suit is barred by the Eleventh Amendment because a payment of damages out of public funds constitutes a suit against the state.

E. THE ABSTENTION DOCTRINE

1. **In General.** Abstention is a self-imposed judicial limitation on the exercise of jurisdiction.

a. **Rationale.** A federal court will abstain not because of a lack of subject matter jurisdiction but rather because of the federal policy of promoting intergovernmental harmony.

b. **Rule.** The abstention doctrine compels federal courts to refrain, at least temporarily, from deciding cases that may be resolved by reference to state law or that require a preliminary consideration of state law issues. The state court determination may thus avoid the need for the federal court to resolve the case as a matter of federal constitutional law.

c. **Purpose: Consistency between state and federal courts.** The purpose of the doctrine is to insure that federal courts will not interfere with their state counterparts by rendering decisions that are inconsistent with ultimate state court resolutions of identical issues.

2. **Relevance.** Abstention is proper when federal intervention in one case may have the effect of interfering with a pattern of state administrative regulations.

Railroad Commission of Texas v. Pullman Co.

a. **Issues could be decided by state court--Railroad Commission of Texas v. Pullman Co.,** 312 U.S. 496 (1941).

1) **Facts.** When passenger traffic was light, certain trains operating in Texas were served by only one sleeping car. On these occasions, the cars were supervised by the porters (Ps), most of whom were black, instead of by the conductors, who were white. In response to this situation, the Railroad Commission of Texas (D) promulgated an order that forbade the operation of sleeping cars unless they were continuously in the charge of a conductor.

Pullman Co. (P), which manufactured sleeping cars, together with the railroads (Ps) affected, brought suit in federal district court to enjoin D's order, and the porters were permitted to intervene in the action. The railroads and Pullman contended that the order contravened Texas law as well as the federal Constitution. The porters argued that the discriminatory effects of the order violated the Fourteenth Amendment. A three-judge panel enjoined enforcement of the order, denying that the applicable Texas statutes sustained the Commission's order.

2) **Issue.** Should federal courts resolve issues of state law that could be decided by state courts?

3) **Held.** No. Judgment reversed and remanded.

    a) The porters have raised a significant constitutional issue, but they have also touched upon a sensitive social question.

    b) It is preferable that the case be resolved by resort to state law, rather than by determining the merits of the constitutional issue.

    c) The outcome can turn on whether the contested order is consistent with D's authority to prevent discrimination and other abuses. A state court may determine whether the order is within the ambit of D's authority, thus precluding the necessity for a federal court to decide the case in a manner that might ultimately create friction between state and federal law.

    d) Because Texas law facilitates a state court resolution of this dispute, the federal action should not be given effect until the appropriate Texas court has had a chance to consider the merits of this controversy.

b. **Federal decision would interfere with state policy--Burford v. Sun Oil Co.,** 319 U.S. 315 (1943).

    Burford v. Sun Oil Co.

1) **Facts.** Sun Oil Co. (P) brought an action in a federal district court attacking the validity of an order of the Texas Railroad Commission. The Texas Railroad Commission had granted Burford (D) a permit to drill four wells on a small plot of land in the East Texas oil field. P seeks to enjoin the execution of this order. Jurisdiction of the federal court was invoked because of the diversity of citizenship of the parties and because P contended that the order denied it due process of law. The district court dismissed P's complaint. The court of appeals reversed the judgment and granted P's injunction. D appealed to the Supreme Court.

2) **Issue.** Assuming that the federal district court had jurisdiction, should it have declined to exercise that jurisdiction as a matter of sound equitable discretion?

3) **Held.** Yes. Dismissal by district court affirmed.

    a) The order under consideration is part of the general regulatory system devised for the conservation of oil and gas in Texas.

b) The federal government has chosen to leave the principal regulatory responsibilities of these large oil fields with the states. The standards applied by the Commission in a given case necessarily affect the entire state conservation system.

c) The overall plan of regulation is of vital interest to the general public, which must be assured that the speculative interests of individual owners will be put aside when necessary to prevent the irretrievable loss of oil in other parts of the field.

d) With full knowledge of the importance of the decisions of the Railroad Commission both to the state and to oil operators, the Texas legislature has established a system of thorough judicial review by its own state courts. Texas courts can give the same relief, including temporary restraining orders, as the federal courts.

e) Delay, misunderstanding of local law, and needless federal conflict with the state policy are the inevitable products of a double system of review.

f) Furthermore, if P follows the state procedure from the Commission to the state supreme court, ultimate review of the federal question of due process is fully preserved in this court. Past cases reflect a doctrine of abstention whereby federal courts, exercising a wise discretion, restrain their authority, leaving problems of state law to state courts.

g) This case, involving as it does basic problems of Texas conservation and regulation of natural resources, is intricately bound up with state policy and requires the exercise of the district court's equitable discretion, so that Texas courts have the first opportunity to consider these important questions. Therefore, the decision of the court of appeals is reversed and the judgment of the district court dismissing the complaint is affirmed.

4) Concurrence (Douglas, Murphy, JJ.). The Texas courts do not sit merely to enforce rights based on orders of the state administrative agency. They sit in judgment of that agency. If the federal courts undertook to sit in review of this state agency, they would in effect actively participate in the fashioning of the state's domestic policy.

5) Dissent (Frankfurter, Roberts, Reed, JJ., Stone, C.J.). To deny a suitor access to a federal district court under the circumstances of this case is to disregard a duty enjoined by Congress based on diversity of citizenship between parties. Furthermore, it has never been questioned that a right created by state law and enforceable in state courts can also be enforced in the federal courts if the parties to the controversy are citizens of different states. The duty of the judiciary is to exercise the jurisdiction that Congress has conferred.

6) Comment. In cases such as *Burford*, the usual course followed is for a court to dismiss the case rather than retaining jurisdiction pending a determination by the state courts.

3. **The Court Will Abstain If the State Law Is Unsettled.** Under what has come to be known as the "*Pullman* type" of abstention, from the case of *Railroad Commission of Texas v. Pullman Co., supra*, a court will abstain if the state law is unsettled. In cases of this type a state action is challenged as being in violation of the federal Constitution and is brought in federal court, but there are questions of state law that may also determine the course of the case. Nonetheless, it must always be kept in mind that abstention of the *Pullman* type is not ordered when the state law has been settled or the state law is patently unconstitutional no matter how the state courts construe it.

a. **State constitutional provision not yet interpreted by state--Reetz v. Bozanich,** 397 U.S. 82 (1970).

Reetz v.
Bozanich

1) **Facts.** Bozanich and others (Ps) were denied commercial salmon net gear licenses because they did not qualify under the laws and regulations of Alaska. These laws provide that, except in cases of extreme hardship, salmon net gear licenses for commercial fishing may be issued only to persons who have previously held such a license for a specific area or have for three years held a commercial fishing license and engaged in commercial fishing in a specific area. Ps brought this action in a federal district court seeking a declaration that these fishing laws are unconstitutional under the Equal Protection Clause of the Fourteenth Amendment and the Alaska Constitution. Ps also sought an injunction against enforcement. Ps moved for summary judgment on the ground that the Act and regulations, limiting as they do licensees to a defined group of people, deprive Ps of their rights under the Equal Protection Clause and the Alaska Constitution. That constitution provides that the fish and waters are reserved to the people for common use and that no exclusive right or special privilege of fishery may be created. Reetz (D) filed a motion to dismiss or alternatively to stay the proceedings in the district court pending the determination of the Alaska constitutional question by an Alaska court. The district court denied D's motion to dismiss or to stay and granted Ps' motion for summary judgment. The three-judge district court held that the Act and regulations in question were unconstitutional both under the Equal Protection Clause of the Fourteenth Amendment and under the Alaska Constitution.

2) **Issue.** Does the proper exercise of federal jurisdiction require that controversies involving unsettled questions of state law be decided in the state tribunals preliminary to a federal court's consideration of the underlying federal constitutional questions?

3) **Held.** Yes. Judgment of district court vacated and remanded.

a) In the case at bar, when the state court's interpretation of the statute or evaluation of its validity under the state constitution may obviate any need to consider its validity under the federal Constitution, the federal court should wait, so that it does not render a constitutional decision unnecessarily.

b) Furthermore, this Court is advised that the provisions of the Alaska Constitution at issue have never been interpreted. Given these two considerations, the instant case is a classic example of the circumstances under which the abstention doctrine should be applied.

c) The district court held, however, that this was not a proper case for abstention, saying that if the question had been presented to an Alaska court, it would have shared our conviction that the challenged gear licensing scheme is not supportable. In doing so, the district court overlooks the basis of the abstention doctrine, namely the avoidance of needless friction between federal pronouncements and state policies.

d) This case is the classic case in that tradition, for here the nub of the whole controversy may be the state constitution. The constitutional provisions relate to fish resources, an asset unique in its abundance in Alaska. The statute and regulations relate to that same unique resource, the management of which is a matter of great state concern.

e) This Court concludes that the first judicial application of these constitutional provisions should properly be by an Alaska court. The federal court should have abstained while the parties repaired to the state courts for a resolution of their state constitutional questions. The judgment is vacated and the case remanded to the district court for proceedings consistent with this opinion.

4. Abstention Is Improper If There Is No Prospect for State Court Resolution. The federal court will abstain when the state court will be presented with primarily state law claims under the state constitution which, if decided, will render moot any federal constitutional claims.

Wilton
v. Seven
Falls Co.

a. **Decision by federal appeals court while action is pending--Wilton v. Seven Falls Co., 515 U.S. 277 (1995).**

1) **Facts.** A dispute between the Hill Group (D) and other parties over the ownership and operation of oil and gas properties appeared likely to culminate in litigation. London Underwriters (P) was asked by D to provide coverage under several commercial insurance policies. P refused to defend or indemnify D. A state court entered a verdict against D on various state law claims. P filed a declaratory judgment action in district court claiming that its policies did not cover D's liability for the state court judgment. After negotiations, P voluntarily dismissed the district court action upon condition that D give P two weeks' notice if it decided to bring suit on the policy. D notified P of its intention to file a suit in state court and P refiled its declaratory judgment in district court. On the same day that D filed its state court suit, it moved to dismiss, or in the alternative, to stay the declaratory judgment action. The district court granted the stay on the ground that the issues in the two cases were the same and a stay would avoid piecemeal litigation and forum shopping by P. The court of appeals affirmed. The Supreme Court granted certiorari.

2) **Issue.** Does the discretionary standard in *Brillhart v. Excess Insurance Co.*, rather than the "exceptional circumstances" test, govern a district court's decision to stay a declaratory judgment action during the pendency of a parallel state court proceeding?

3) **Held.** Yes. Judgment affirmed.

    a) In *Brillhart v. Excess Insurance Co.*, the Court addressed circumstances that are virtually identical to the present case. *Brillhart* makes it clear that district courts possess discretion in determining whether and when to entertain a declaratory judgment action even when the suit otherwise satisfies subject matter jurisdiction requirements.

    b) If another suit involving the same parties and same state law issues is pending in state court, a district court might be indulging in gratuitous interference if it permitted the federal declaratory judgment action to proceed.

    c) We do not agree that the federal court must hear declaratory judgment actions except in exceptional circumstances.

    d) If a district court, in its sound discretion, determines after a complaint is filed that a declaratory judgment will serve no useful purpose, it cannot be incumbent upon that court to proceed to the merits before staying or dismissing the action.

b. **Certification of questions to state courts.** Where the state procedures provide, a federal court may certify questions to the state for resolution by the state court. The federal court will defer any decision in the case pending the outcome of the state case.

1) **Where state law provides for certification--Lehman Brothers v. Schein,** 416 U.S. 386 (1974).

    a) **Facts.** These are shareholders' derivative suits consolidated and brought in the District Court of New York. Lum's, one of the defendants (D) in the Lehman Brothers' (P's) petition, is a Florida corporation. The basis of federal jurisdiction is diversity of citizenship. The complaints allege that Chasen, president of Lum's, called Simon, a representative of P, and informed him about disappointing projections of Lum's earnings, estimates that were confidential. Simon (D) is alleged to have told an employee of IDS (D) and on the next day IDS sold shares of Lum's on the New York Stock Exchange for $17.50. Later that day the exchanges halted trading in Lum's stock, and on the next day trading opened at $14 per share, the public being told that the projected earnings would be substantially lower than anticipated. The theory of the complaint was that Chasen was a fiduciary but used inside information for profit and that the defendants are liable to P for their unlawful profits. Lehman and Simon defended on the ground that the IDS sale was not made through them and that neither one benefited from the sale. The district court held that the law of the place of incorporation governed and found that under Florida law Ds would not be liable. The court of appeals reversed, holding that while Florida law was controlling, there was no state law that was decisive. The court looked to the law of other jurisdictions and held that Ds had misused corporate property. The dissenter on the court of appeals urged that the court certify the state law question to the Florida Supreme Court as provided under Florida certification law.

b) **Issue.** May a federal court certify to a state court the controlling issue of state law?

c) **Held.** Yes. Judgment of court of appeals vacated and remanded.

    (1) The Florida statutes provide that a state law question can be certified to the Florida Supreme Court. Furthermore, the path of certification is open to this court and to any court of appeals of the United States in order that the highest state court may resolve the controlling state law on which the federal rule may turn.

    (2) This Court is not suggesting that where there is doubt as to local law and where the certification procedure is available, resort to it is obligatory. It does of course in the long run save time, energy, and resources. However, its use in a given case rests in the sound discretion of the federal court. Here, resort to it would seem particularly appropriate in view of the novelty of the question and unsettled Florida law.

    (3) When federal judges in New York attempt to predict uncertain Florida law, they act in matters of state law as outsiders lacking the common exposure to local law that comes from sitting in the jurisdiction. The judgment of the court of appeals is vacated and the cases are remanded so that the court of appeals may reconsider whether the controlling issue of Florida law should be certified to the Florida Supreme Court.

d) **Concurrence** (Rehnquist, J.). The question of whether certification on the facts of this case, particularly in view of the lateness of its suggestion by petitioner, would have advanced the goals of correctly disposing of this litigation is one to be left to the sound discretion of the court making the initial choice. However, as this is the first time the Court has expressed its views on the use of certification, it is appropriate to vacate and remand.

F. "OUR FEDERALISM"

1. **In General.** In *Dombrowski v. Pfister*, 380 U.S. 479 (1965), the Supreme Court held that the anti-injunction statute permitted an injunction of a state proceeding when no criminal prosecution was pending if, based on the facts of the case, the party could demonstrate that the threat of the prosecution would have a chilling effect on First Amendment rights.

2. **Injunctions Limited to Unusual Circumstances.** In a subsequent case, the Court limited *Dombrowski* by holding that the concept of federalism does not permit federal injunctive relief upon the mere allegation of the unconstitutionality of a state statute on its face. The party must also show bad faith, harassment, or some other unusual circumstances that justify relief in the federal courts.

3. **Rationale Is Comity with the States.** The doctrine of "Our Federalism" is based on comity with the states and comprehends forcing a party to litigate any state and federal constitutional defenses to the prosecution in the state court.

   a. **Type of unusual circumstances required--Younger v. Harris,** 401 U.S. 37 (1971).

Younger v. Harris

1) **Facts.** Harris (P) was indicted in a state court for violation of the California Criminal Syndicalism Act. P then filed a complaint in the federal district court seeking an injunction against Younger (D), the district attorney in charge of the state prosecution, to restrain him from prosecuting P further. P alleged that the prosecution and even the presence of the Act violated his First and Fourteenth Amendment rights. A three-judge district court held that the Act was void for vagueness, was overbroad, and was in violation of the First and Fourteenth Amendments. It granted the injunction. D appeals on the ground that national policy forbids federal courts from enjoining pending state proceedings.

2) **Issue.** Can federal courts stay or enjoin pending state court proceedings absent special circumstances showing irreparable injury?

3) **Held.** No. Judgment reversed.

   a) There is a national policy forbidding federal courts from staying or enjoining pending state court proceedings except under special circumstances where a person about to be prosecuted in a state court can show that he will suffer irreparable injury.

   b) In the instant case a proceeding was already pending in the state court, affording Harris an opportunity to raise his constitutional claims. Furthermore, there is no suggestion that this single prosecution against Harris is brought in bad faith or is meant to be one of a series of repeated prosecutions designed to harass him.

   c) The existence of a chilling effect, even in the area of First Amendment rights, has never been considered a sufficient basis, in and of itself, for prohibiting state action. First, the chilling effect cannot be satisfactorily eliminated by federal injunctive relief. Second, if a statute does not directly abridge free speech, but tends to have an incidental effect, it is well established that the statute can be upheld if the effect is minor in relation to the need for control of the conduct.

   d) Therefore, this court holds that the possible unconstitutionality of a statute on its face does not in itself justify an injunction against good faith attempts to enforce it. Harris has failed to make any showing of bad faith, harassment, or any other unusual circumstance that would result in irreparable injury and call for equitable relief.

4) **Concurrence** (Stewart, Harlan, JJ.). It is important to recognize the areas into which this decision does not necessarily extend. Because this decision is based on policy grounds, it does not, for example, reach the independent force of the anti-injunction statute, deal with the considerations that should govern federal court intervention in a state civil proceeding, or resolve problems involved when a federal court is asked to grant relief against future state criminal prosecutions.

5) **Concurrence** (Brennan, White, Marshall, JJ.). P has failed to make an adequate showing of need for federal interference. He did not allege that the prosecution was in bad faith. He has an adequate opportunity to assert his constitutional defense in state court.

6) **Dissent** (Douglas, J.). This case should fall within the scope of *Dombrowski v. Pfister*. That case represents an exception to the general rule that federal courts should not interfere with state criminal prosecutions. The exception does not arise merely because prosecutions are threatened to which the First Amendment will be the proffered defense. *Dombrowski* governs statutes that have an overbroad sweep. The special circumstances where federal intervention in a state criminal proceeding is permissible are not restricted to bad faith on the part of state officials or the threat of multiple prosecutions. They also exist where for any reason the state statute being enforced is unconstitutional on its face. In *Younger* there is a prosecution under an unconstitutional statute and relief is denied. A federal injunction should issue under 42 U.S.C. section 1983.

7) **Comment.** In state criminal prosecutions unrelated to freedom of expression, defendants have been unable to obtain *Dombrowski*-type relief. However, in cases where state action has been found to have a chilling effect on First Amendment rights, lower courts have granted *Dombrowski*-sanctioned relief in a wide range of cases. These cases have usually involved prosecutions against civil rights workers or protest demonstrators under statutes unconstitutional on their face or under statutes applied in an unconstitutional manner.

4. **Suits for Declaratory Relief If State Action Is Pending.** A declaratory judgment of the unconstitutionality of a statute is not permitted if a state prosecution is pending absent a showing of bad faith, harassment, or other unusual circumstances.

Samuels v.
Mackell

a. **Declaratory judgment not available when prosecution is pending-- Samuels v. Mackell**, 401 U.S. 66 (1971).

1) **Facts.** Samuels and others (Ps) were indicted on charges of violating the New York state criminal anarchy statute. Prior to their state court trials, Ps filed actions in federal court against Mackell (D). Each action claimed that the anarchy statute was void for vagueness and violated the First and Fourteenth Amendments, that the statute had been preempted by federal law, and that the New York laws pertaining

to the drawing of grand juries were unconstitutional. Ps argued that their indictments would harass them and cause irreparable damage. Therefore, Ps prayed for either injunctive or declaratory relief. A three-judge panel dismissed the federal court actions, but Ps appeal.

2) **Issue.** Should a federal court grant declaratory relief during the pendency of a state criminal prosecution?

3) **Held.** No. Judgment affirmed.

   a)   Once a state criminal prosecution has commenced, a federal court should not issue a declaratory judgment in the case unless, under the circumstances, injunctive relief would be appropriate.

   b)   A pending state court prosecution should be enjoined by a federal tribunal only when necessary to prevent irreparable injury. And, according to *Great Lakes Dredge & Dock Co. v. Huffman,* 319 U.S. 293 (1943), declaratory relief should be granted only under the same circumstances.

   c)   Principles of federalism militate against federal court interference with pending state court actions. Because Ps have not demonstrated that their indictments will cause them irreparable injury, their federal actions for injunctive and declaratory relief were properly dismissed.

4) **Concurrence** (Douglas, J.). The case against Ps is not palpably unconstitutional, since the state courts may preserve First Amendment rights by sifting the chaff from the charges through motions to strike, jury instructions, and other procedural devices.

5) **Comment.** The Constitution establishes a system of federal courts, but also limits their jurisdiction. Crucial to the federal scheme is the notion that the state courts must be autonomous, *i.e.,* free to operate without interference by the federal courts. Congress has reinforced the constitutional blueprint by enacting statutes that limit the power of federal courts to meddle in the affairs of their state counterparts. And, of course, cases such as *Samuels v. Mackell* and *Younger v. Harris* have further affirmed the proposition that state courts are to be protected from federal intervention.

b. **Declaratory judgment may be available if prosecution not yet pending--Steffel v. Thompson,** 415 U.S. 452 (1974). Steffel v. Thompson

   1) **Facts.** Steffel (P) was twice threatened with arrest if he did not stop distributing handbills protesting the Vietnam War on the sidewalk of a shopping center. P brought this action seeking a declaratory judgment that the Georgia criminal trespass law was being applied in violation of his First and Fourteenth Amendment rights, and seeking an injunction restraining Thompson (D) and others from enforcing the state statute. The district court denied all relief and dismissed the action. P appealed only from the denial of declaratory relief. The court of appeals affirmed the lower court's judgment refusing declaratory relief, stating that because declaratory relief would normally disrupt the state criminal justice system in the manner of injunctive relief, it follows that the same test of bad faith harassment is a prerequisite

for declaratory relief. A petition for rehearing was denied, and P appeals to the Supreme Court.

2) **Issue.** Can declaratory relief act as an alternative to an injunction and be used to test the constitutionality of state criminal statutes in cases where injunctive relief would be unavailable?

3) **Held.** Yes. Judgment reversed and remanded.

a) Although it is true that federal courts should ordinarily refrain from enjoining ongoing state criminal prosecutions when no state proceeding is pending, the propriety of granting federal declaratory relief may properly be considered independently from a request for injunctive relief.

b) In the case at bar, the court of appeals held that because injunctive relief would not be appropriate because Steffel failed to demonstrate irreparable injury, it followed that declaratory relief was also inappropriate. The court erred in treating the two requests as a single issue.

c) Declaratory relief is expressly authorized to be used because it is a less harsh and abrasive remedy than the injunction. Further, when no state criminal proceeding is pending at the time the federal complaint is filed, federal intervention does not result in duplicative legal proceedings, nor can it be interpreted as infringing upon the state court's ability to enforce constitutional principles.

d) Declaratory relief does not necessarily bar prosecutions under a state statute, as a broad injunction would. A state prosecutor, after the federal court decision, may still bring a prosecution under the state statute, if he reasonably believes that the defendant's conduct is not constitutionally protected.

e) What is clear, however, is that even though a declaratory judgment has the force and effect of a final judgment, it is a much milder form of relief than an injunction. Though it may be persuasive, it is not ultimately coercive; noncompliance with it may be inappropriate, but is not contempt.

f) This court therefore holds that, regardless of whether injunctive relief may be appropriate, federal declaratory relief is not precluded when there is no state prosecution pending and a federal plaintiff demonstrates, as P has done, a genuine threat of enforcement of a disputed state criminal statute. The judgment of the court of appeals is reversed and the case remanded.

4) **Concurrence** (Stewart, J., Burger, C.J.). Our decision today must not be understood as authorizing the invocation of federal declaratory judgment jurisdiction by a person who thinks a state criminal statute is unconstitutional, unless he can demonstrate a genuine threat of enforcement of the disputed statute. Cases where such a genuine threat can be demonstrated are exceedingly rare.

5) **Concurrence** (Rehnquist, J., Burger, C.J.). Any arrest prior to resolution of the federal action would constitute a pending prosecution and bar declaratory relief.

5. **Federal Injunction of State Civil Actions.** The doctrine of "Our Federalism" also applies to certain civil proceedings where the civil proceeding is used to enforce the state's criminal laws. A party cannot avoid the state appellate machinery by resort to the federal court unless the *Younger* standard of bad faith, harassment, or other unusual circumstances is satisfied.

a. **State appellate procedures must be completed--Huffman v. Pursue, Ltd.,** 420 U.S. 592 (1975).

   1) **Facts.** Huffman (D), the sheriff and prosecuting attorney of an Ohio county, sued Pursue (P) in state court under statutes declaring a place in which lewd or obscene films are shown to be a public nuisance and to be closed down. The state court rendered a judgment that there had been a course of conduct of displaying obscene movies, and ordered the theater closed for a period of one year. Rather than appealing that judgment, P sued in federal district court, alleging that this use of the Ohio nuisance statute deprived the theater of constitutional rights under the color of state law. A three-judge district court found that the Ohio statute was not vague but did constitute an overly broad prior restraint on First Amendment rights insofar as it prevented the showing of films that had not been adjudged obscene in prior adversary hearings. The court enjoined the execution of that portion of the state court's judgment that closed the theater to films that had not been adjudged obscene.

   2) **Issue.** Is a federal district court barred, except in extraordinary circumstances of immediate irreparable injury, from intervening in a state civil proceeding prior to completion of state appellate procedures, when the proceeding is based on a state statute believed by the district court to be unconstitutional?

   3) **Held.** Yes. Judgment reversed and remanded.

      a) The seriousness of federal judicial interference with state civil functions has long been recognized by this Court. It has been consistently required that when federal courts are confronted with requests for such relief, they should abide by standards of restraint unless intervention is necessary to prevent great and irreparable injury.

      b) Interference with a state judicial proceeding prevents the state not only from effectuating its substantive policies, but also from continuing to perform the separate function of providing a forum competent to vindicate any constitutional objections interposed against those policies. Such interference also results in duplicative legal proceedings.

      c) A civil litigant may, of course, seek review in this Court of any federal claim properly asserted in and rejected by state courts. Moreover, when a final decision of a state court has sustained the validity of a state statute challenged on federal constitutional grounds, an appeal to this Court lies as a matter of right. Thus, P in this case was assured of eventual consideration of its claim by this Court.

d)   It must be noted that federal court intervention should be restrained until the completion of state appellate proceedings. Intervention prior to exhaustion of state remedies, is, if anything, more highly duplicative, since the entire trial has taken place. It is also a direct aspersion on the capabilities and good faith of state appellate courts.

e)   In the case at bar, at the time P filed its action in the federal district court, it had available the remedy of appeal to the appellate courts.

f)   The district court should not have entertained this action seeking preappeal interference with a state judicial proceeding, unless P established that each intervention was justified by bad-faith harassment or the pattern was in violation of constitutional rights that would result in immediate and irreparable injury.

g)   Because the district court did not consider the issue of whether intervention was justified, the case is appropriate for remand to that court so that it can be decided whether irreparable injury can be shown.

4)   **Dissent** (Brennan, Douglas, Marshall, JJ.). Today's holding that the plaintiff in an action under 42 U.S.C. section 1983 may not maintain it without first exhausting state appellate procedures for review of an adverse state trial codecision is but an obvious first step toward the discard of settled law that such actions may be maintained without exhausting state remedies. Unlike the long tradition culminating with the *Younger* case that federal courts will not interfere with pending state criminal prosecutions, the result has been quite opposite in respect to federal injunctive interference with pending state civil proceedings. Thus, in today's extension, *Younger v. Harris* turns the clock back to a time when state courts were free from interference by federal injunction altogether. This theory is not supported by congressional law or case law.

5)   **Comment.** It should be noted that, in the case at bar, the Court attempts to draw a strong corollary between the *Younger* criminal prosecution and the close relation of nuisance litigation to criminal statutes. Similarly, while the district court injunction did not directly disrupt Ohio's criminal justice system, it did disrupt the state's efforts to protect the very interests that underlie its criminal laws. It is difficult to grasp exactly how far the Court expects restraint on federal judicial interference in civil litigation to extend.

6.   **Federal Equitable Relief When No State Prosecution Is Pending.** The *Younger* standard is not a bar to federal equitable relief when there is no pending state prosecution. In this situation, there is no danger of duplicating or disrupting state court proceedings.

a.   **Alternate situation.** In the situation where there is a pending state prosecution, a party can raise the constitutional claims in the state court.

b. **Avoid violating state law.** However, when there is no pending state prosecution but there is a threat of prosecution unless the federal court intervenes, the party would have to either violate the state law or forgo what is believed to be constitutionally protected activity. In this situation, the federal court may give declaratory relief and, at least, preliminary injunctive relief.

c. **Genuine threat of prosecution--Wooley v. Maynard,** 430 U.S. 705 (1977).

   1) **Facts.** New Hampshire required that noncommercial vehicles bear license plates embossed with the state motto "Live Free or Die." Another New Hampshire statute made it a misdemeanor to knowingly obscure the figure or letters on any number plate. The term "letters" had been interpreted to include the state motto. George Maynard (D) and his wife Maxine are followers of the Jehovah's Witnesses faith. They consider the New Hampshire state motto to be repugnant to their moral, religious, and political beliefs, and therefore began in 1974 to cover up the motto on their license plates. Subsequently, D was charged on three separate occasions with violating the state statutes. He appeared in court on his own behalf and was found guilty on all three occasions, serving one jail term of 15 days as a consequence. Thereafter, D brought this action pursuant to the federal civil rights statute, 42 U.S.C. section 1983, seeking both injunctive and declaratory relief against the enforcement of the state statute. On March 11, 1975, a temporary restraining order was issued, and the state (P) then filed this appeal, contending that the relief sought by D violated the principles of restraint enunciated in *Younger v. Harris.*

   2) **Issue.** When a genuine threat of prosecution exists, is a litigant entitled to resort to a federal forum to seek redress for an alleged violation of federal rights?

   3) **Held.** Yes. Judgment affirmed.

   a) In *Younger,* this Court stated that principles of judicial economy, as well as proper state-federal relations, preclude federal courts from exercising equitable jurisdiction to enjoin ongoing state prosecutions.

   b) However, when a genuine threat of prosecution exists, a litigant is entitled to resort to a federal forum to seek redress for an alleged deprivation of federal rights. Here, D finds himself placed between "the Scylla of intentionally flouting state law and the Charybdis of forgoing what he believes to be constitutionally protected activity in order to avoid becoming enmeshed in another criminal proceeding." Under these circumstances he cannot be denied consideration of a federal remedy.

   c) Here, the suit is in no way designed to annul the results of a state trial, because the relief sought is wholly prospective, to preclude a further prosecution under a statute alleged to violate D's constitutional rights.

   d) The threat of repeated prosecutions in the future against D and the effect of such a continuing threat on his ability to perform the ordinary tasks of daily life that require an automobile is sufficient to justify injunctive relief.

4) **Dissent** (White, Blackmun, Rehnquist, JJ.). The general rule is that equity will not interfere to prevent the enforcement of a criminal statute even though unconstitutional. Here, P's enforcement of its statute prior to the declaration of unconstitutionality by the federal court would appear to be no more than the performance of their duty by P's enforcement officers. If doing this much prior to the declaration of unconstitutionality amounts to unusual circumstances sufficient to warrant an injunction, the standard is obviously seriously eroded.

5) **Comment.** This case additionally involved serious First Amendment issues regarding freedom of speech. On the merits, the Court found that it was inconsistent with First Amendment protections to require persons to be coerced into advocating public adherence to a point of view that they found to be ideologically unacceptable.

Pennzoil Co. v. Texaco, Inc.

d. **No federal injunction against enforcement of state judgment--Pennzoil Co. v. Texaco, Inc.,** 481 U.S. 1 (1987).

1) **Facts.** Under Texas law, a judgment creditor can secure and execute a lien on a judgment debtor's property unless the debtor files a bond in at least the amount of the judgment, interest, and costs. Pennzoil (P) obtained a jury verdict of $10.53 billion in a Texas state court suit alleging that Texaco, Inc. (D) had tortiously induced Getty Oil to breach a contract to sell its shares to P. Because it was clear that D would not be able to post a bond in the necessary amount, D filed suit in federal district court before the trial court entered judgment on the verdict. The suit alleged that the Texas proceedings violated the rights of D under the Constitution. The district court concluded that D's constitutional claims had a clear probability of success and issued a preliminary injunction barring any action to enforce the state court's judgment, which had now been entered. The court of appeals affirmed, and the Supreme Court granted certiorari.

2) **Issue.** May a federal district court enjoin a plaintiff from executing a judgment in its favor in a state court when that judgment is pending appeal in a state appellate court?

3) **Held.** No. Judgment reversed.

a) While the action was pending appeal in the state court, the federal district court should have abstained from issuing the injunction against P's enforcement of its judgment. Abstention helps to avoid unwarranted determination of federal constitutional questions. Because D chose not to present its constitutional claims to the Texas courts, it is impossible to determine whether the governing Texas statutes and rules actually involved those claims.

b) The *Younger v. Harris* abstention is mandated if the state's interest in the proceedings is so important that exercise of the federal judicial power would disregard the comity extended between the states and the federal government. The states have important interests in administering certain aspects of their judicial systems. These include enforcing the orders and judgment of the states' courts.

c) The argument that the *Younger* abstention was inappropriate because no Texas court could have heard D's constitutional claims fails because D has not satisfied its burden of showing that state procedural law barred presentation of its claim. D made no effort to present its claim in state court; when a litigant has made no effort to present its claim in state court, a federal court should assume that state procedures will afford an adequate remedy, in the absence of unambiguous authority to the contrary.

4) **Concurrence** (Scalia, O'Connor, JJ.). There was no jurisdictional bar to the Supreme Court's decision in this case because the Court is not deciding any issue that was litigated in Texas courts or inextricably intertwined with the issues so litigated.

5) **Concurrence** (Brennan, Marshall, JJ.). The claim that the Texas bond and lien provisions violated the Due Process and Equal Protection Clauses was without merit because D could exercise its right to appeal even if it were forced to file for bankruptcy. The underlying issues in this case—arising out of a commercial contract dispute—did not involve fundamental constitutional rights.

6) **Concurrence** (Marshall, J.). The district court lacked jurisdiction because the constitutional claims presented to it were inextricably intertwined with the merits of the judgment rendered in the Texas state court.

7) **Concurrence** (Blackmun, J.). The district court ought to have abstained because unsettled questions of state law remained and the state court could interpret the challenged state provisions so as to eliminate, or at least alter, the constitutional question presented.

8) **Concurrence** (Stevens, Marshall, JJ.). Texas was not constitutionally required to suspend the execution of the money judgment pending appeal without posting a bond. The Court's duty to deal with both rich and poor did not admit of a special exemption for multibillion-dollar corporations or transactions.

G. HABEAS CORPUS

1. **Applicant Must Exhaust State Court Remedies.** Before a federal court will issue a writ of habeas corpus for one who is held under a state commitment, the applicant must have exhausted whatever remedies are then available in the state court. Under 28 U.S.C. section 2254, a writ of habeas corpus may not be granted unless the applicant has exhausted available state remedies, or there is either an absence of an available state corrective process or the existence of circumstances that make the corrective process ineffective to protect the rights of the applicant.

a. **Need to show cause and prejudice--Wainwright v. Sykes,** 433 U.S. 72 (1977).

1) **Facts.** Sykes (P) was convicted of third degree murder. P testified at trial that he told the police when they arrived that he had shot the deceased. P was immediately arrested and taken to the police station. Once there, P was read his *Miranda* rights, but declined to seek the aid of counsel and confessed to having shot the deceased. At no time during the trial was the admissibility of any of P's statements challenged by his counsel on the ground that P had not understood the *Miranda* warnings. P appealed his conviction, but did not challenge the admissibility of the inculpatory statements. P later filed in state court to vacate the conviction, challenging, for the first time, the statements made to the police on grounds of involuntariness. All these efforts were unsuccessful. P initiated the present federal habeas action, asserting the inadmissibility of his statements by reason of his lack of understanding of the *Miranda* warnings. The district court held that P was entitled to a hearing prior to the admission of the statements and that this right had not been waived. The court of appeals affirmed. The Supreme Court granted certiorari.

2) **Issue.** Is the requirement that federal habeas review be barred absent a showing of cause and prejudice applicable to a situation where a criminal defendant has waived objection to the admission of a confession at trial?

3) **Held.** Yes. Judgment reversed.

    a) Florida procedure did, consistent with the Constitution, require that P's confession be challenged at trial or not at all, and thus his failure to timely object to its admission amounted to an independent and adequate state procedural ground that would have prevented direct review here.

    b) Thus, barring federal habeas review absent a showing of cause and prejudice attendant to a state procedural waiver is applicable to a waived objection to the admission of a confession at trial. P has advanced no explanation whatever for his failure to object at trial. Furthermore, the other evidence of guilt was substantial enough to negate any possibility of actual prejudice.

4) **Concurrence** (Burger, C.J.). The "deliberate bypass" standard is inapplicable to errors alleged to have been committed during trial.

5) **Dissent** (Brennan, Marshall, JJ.). Today, the court erroneously decides that the deliberate bypass standard should no longer apply with respect to procedural defaults occurring during the trial of a criminal defendant. The mistakes of a trial attorney should be visited on the head of a habeas corpus applicant only when the court is convinced of the client's participation in the lawyer's decision.

6) **Comment.** The Supreme Court ruled that the decision in *Sykes* in no way changes its holding in *Brown v. Allen*, 344 U.S. 443 (1953). In that case, the Court held that a federal habeas petitioner who claims he is detained pursuant to a final judgment of a state court in violation of the United States Constitution is entitled to have the federal habeas court make its own independent determination of his federal claim, without being bound by the determination on the merits in state proceedings.

b. **Standard of review--Matteo v. Superintendent, SCI Albion,** 171 F.3d 877 (3d Cir. 1999) (en banc).

Matteo v. Superintendent, SCI Albion

1) **Facts.** Anthony Matteo seeks habeas relief from his state convictions for first-degree murder, robbery, theft, and marijuana possession, contending that the Commonwealth of Pennsylvania violated his Sixth Amendment right to counsel by using incriminatory statements he made in two telephone conversations from prison to an outside informant. The district court dismissed Matteo's petition.

2) **Issue.** Was the state court's decision contrary to, or an unreasonable application of, clearing established federal law as determined by the Supreme Court of the United States?

3) **Held.** No. Judgment affirmed.

a) We must determine what deference, if any, the Antiterrorism and Effective Death Penalty Act of 1996 ("AEDPA") requires a federal habeas court to accord to a state court's construction of federal constitutional issues and interpretation of Supreme Court precedent.

b) The amount of deference requires a two-pronged inquiry: (i) whether the state court decision was "contrary to" clearly established federal law; if not, (ii) whether the state court judgment rests upon an objectively unreasonable application of clearly established Supreme Court jurisprudence.

c) The "contrary to" provision of AEDPA requires something more than a recognition that the Supreme Court has articulated a general standard that covers the claim. The inquiry must be whether the Supreme Court has established a rule that determines the outcome of the litigation.

d) Absent such a showing, the federal habeas court must ask whether the state court decision represents an "unreasonable application" of Supreme Court precedent and would result in an outcome that cannot be reasonably justified.

e) The informant did not act as a government agent at the time of the calls nor did he deliberately elicit incriminating information from Matteo in either phone call.

H. EFFECT OF PRIOR STATE JUDGMENT

1. **State Court Judgments Generally Accorded Preclusive Effects.** Usually, a state court judgment is accorded preclusive effect in the federal court on any issues that were or should have been litigated in the state court proceeding. Thus, the doctrines of res judicata and collateral estoppel apply to state court judgments unless there is some clear indication by Congress limiting the application of these doctrines to federal causes of action.

Allen v.
McCurry

a. **Relitigating state claims in federal section 1983 action--Allen v. McCurry, 449 U.S. 90 (1980).**

1) **Facts.** At a hearing before his criminal trial in the state court, McCurry (P) invoked the Fourth and Fourteenth Amendments to suppress evidence that had been seized by police officers. The state court denied the motion in part, and P was subsequently convicted after a jury trial. The conviction was affirmed on appeal. Because P did not assert that the state courts had denied him a "full and fair opportunity" to litigate his search and seizure claim, he was barred from seeking a writ of habeas corpus in a federal district court. Instead, P filed a 42 U.S.C. section 1983 action in the federal court against the officers against whom P alleged a violation of his constitutional rights. The district court granted summary judgment against P on the ground that collateral estoppel precluded P from relitigating the search and seizure question already decided against him in the state courts. The court of appeals reversed the judgment and directed the trial court to allow P to proceed to trial. The Supreme Court granted certiorari.

2) **Issue.** Does the unavailability of federal habeas corpus relief prevent raising a state criminal court's partial rejection of the constitutional claim as a collateral estoppel defense to a section 1983 suit for damages?

3) **Held.** No. Judgment reversed.

a) The federal courts generally have accorded preclusive effect to issues decided by state courts. Thus, res judicata and collateral estoppel not only reduce unnecessary litigation but also promote comity between state and federal courts that has been recognized in *Younger v. Harris* as a bulwark of the federal system.

b) While section 1983 says nothing about the preclusive effect of state court judgments, the legislative history of the section does not in any clear way suggest that Congress intended to repeal or restrict the traditional doctrine of preclusion. Congress intended to afford an opportunity for legal and equitable relief in a federal court for certain types of injuries.

c) It is doubtful that the drafters of section 1983 considered it a substitute for a federal writ of habeas corpus, the purpose of which is not to redress civil injury, but to release the applicant from unlawful physical confinement.

4) **Dissent.** (Blackmun, Brennan, Marshall, JJ.). The Court's ruling ignores the clear import of the legislative history of the statutes and disregards the important federal policies that underlie its enforcement. Although Congress did not expressly state whether the then-existing common law doctrine of preclusion would survive enactment of section 1983, they plainly anticipated more than the creation of a federal statutory remedy to be administered indifferently by either a state or federal court. Congress deliberately opened the federal courts to individuals in response to the states' failure to provide justice in their own courts. It is inconsistent now to narrow our previous

understanding of the distribution of power between state and federal courts. The criminal defendant is an involuntary litigant in the state tribunal. To force him to choose between forgoing either a potential defense or a federal forum for hearing his constitutional civil claim is fundamentally unfair.

b. **Federal court must grant full faith and credit to state court judgment--Matsushita Electric Industrial Co. v. Epstein,** 516 U.S. 367 (1996).

1) **Facts.** Matsushita Electric Industrial Company (D) made a tender offer for the stock of MCA, Inc. A class action was filed in a Delaware state court by MCA's common stockholders against its directors for failing to maximize shareholder value and waste of corporate assets. D was later added as a defendant to the suit for conspiring with the MCA directors. While the state class action was pending, the instant suit was filed in a California federal district court against D claiming that D's tender offer violated the Securities and Exchange Commission rules. The district court declined to certify the class and entered summary judgment for D. After the federal plaintiffs filed their notice of appeal, but before the decision, the parties to the Delaware suit negotiated a settlement. In exchange for a release, D deposited $2 million in a settlement fund to be distributed to class members. The Delaware court certified the class for purposes of the settlement and approved a notice of the proposed settlement. Some plaintiffs of both the state and classes (Ps) neither opted out of the settlement class nor appeared at the hearing to contest the settlement on the representation of the class. On appeal in the circuit court, D invoked the Delaware judgment as a bar to further prosecution of that action under the Full Faith and Credit Act. The circuit court rejected D's argument. The Supreme Court granted certiorari.

2) **Issue.** May a federal court withhold full faith and credit from a state court judgment approving a class action settlement simply because the settlement releases claims within the exclusive jurisdiction of the federal courts?

3) **Held.** No. Judgment reversed and remanded.

   a) The fact that the judgment is the result of a class action is irrelevant to the applicability of full faith and credit.

   b) Even if a claim could not have been raised in the court that rendered the settlement judgment in a class action, a state court could still find that the judgment bars subsequent pursuit of the claim. The settlement judgment would be res judicata under Delaware law.

   c) The SEC Act was not intended to give plaintiffs more than one day in court. Although claims under the Act are within exclusive federal jurisdiction, it does not prohibit state courts from approving the release of Exchange Act claims in the settlement of suits over which they have properly exercised jurisdiction.

   d) Even when exclusively federal claims are at stake, there is no universal right to litigate a federal claim in a federal district court.

4) **Concurrence and dissent** (Stevens, J.). While the SEC Act does not create a partial repeal of the Full Faith and Credit Act, the question of Delaware law should be addressed by the court of appeals in the first instance and that

court should be free to consider whether Delaware courts fully and fairly litigated the adequacy of class representation.

5) **Concurrence and dissent** (Ginsberg, Stevens, Souter, JJ.). This case should be remanded because the court of appeals did not evaluate the preclusive effect of the Delaware judgment through the lens of that state's preclusion law.

IX. THE LAW APPLIED IN THE FEDERAL COURTS

A. THE *ERIE* DOCTRINE

1. **Rules of Decision Act.** Under 28 U.S.C. section 1652, except where federal law otherwise requires, the laws of several states shall be regarded as the rules of decisions in civil actions in the courts of the United States.

   a. **Federal law in relation to state law.** Determining that a federal court has jurisdiction to hear a case does not determine what law it should look to in deciding the case. Broadly speaking, it can be said that federal substantive law operates in relation to state law in certain principal ways.

      1) As to certain matters, federal law assumes the authority of the states and seeks simply to regulate the exercise of state authority (*e.g.*, by the Due Process Clause of the Fourteenth Amendment).

      2) In others, federal law preempts state law and federal law is deemed to be determinative of the substantive rights of the parties.

   b. **Initial interpretation of "laws."** Initially, the word "laws" in the Rules of Decision Act was interpreted narrowly to include only statutory laws and local customs. The word "laws" was not read to include state decisions or state common law.

2. **The Evolution of Federal General Common Law.** Under the interpretation of "laws" in *Swift v. Tyson,* 41 U.S. (16 Pet.) 1 (1842), there evolved a body of federal substantive law that the federal courts applied even though the litigation did not raise any issues that related to federal law and despite the fact that the state courts would have decided the same litigation as a matter of state law. Accordingly, parties were allowed to forum shop between the state and federal courts for the application of either state law or federal general common law depending on which body of law was more favorable.

3. **"There Is No Federal General Common Law"**—*Swift* **Overturned.** In the *Erie* case, below, the Court overruled the rule of *Swift* that federal courts were free to disregard state decisions and to decide cases as a matter of federal general common law. Federal courts must decide cases according to local state law, including both statutes and court decisions, so that the same substantive result will be reached irrespective of whether the suit is commenced in a state or federal court.

   a. **State case law applies--Erie Railroad Co. v. Tompkins,** 304 U.S. 64 (1938).

      1) **Facts.** Tompkins (P) was walking in a right of way parallel to some railroad tracks when an Erie Railroad (D) train came by. P was struck and injured by what he would claim to be an open door extending from one of the rail cars. Under Pennsylvania case law (the applicable law because the accident occurred there), state courts would have treated P as a trespasser in denying him

recovery for other than wanton or willful misconduct on D's part. Under "general" law, recognized in federal courts, P would have been regarded as a licensee and would only have been obligated to show ordinary negligence. Because D was a New York corporation, P brought suit in a federal district court in New York, where he won a judgment for $30,000. Upon appeal to a federal court of appeals, the decision was affirmed. The Supreme Court granted certiorari.

2) **Issue.** Was the trial court in error in refusing to recognize state case law as the proper rule of decision in deciding the substantive issue of liability?

3) **Held.** Yes. Judgment reversed.

   a) *Swift v. Tyson,* 41 U.S. (16 Pet.) 1 (1842), which held that federal courts exercising jurisdiction on the ground of diversity of citizenship need not, in matters of general jurisprudence, apply the unwritten law of the state as declared by its highest court, is overruled. Section 34 of the Federal Judiciary Act of 1789, c. 20, 28 U.S.C. section 725, requires that federal courts, in all matters except those where some federal law is controlling, apply as their rules of decision the law of the state, unwritten as well as written. Up to this time, federal courts had assumed the power to make "general law" decisions even though Congress was powerless to enact "general law" statutes.

   b) *Swift* had numerous political and social defects. The hoped-for uniformity among state courts had not occurred; there was no satisfactory way to distinguish between local and general law. On the other hand, *Swift* introduced grave discrimination by noncitizens against citizens. The privilege of selecting the court for resolving disputes rested with the noncitizen, who could pick the more favorable forum. The resulting far-reaching discrimination was due to the broad province accorded "general law" in which many matters of seemingly local concern were included. Furthermore, local citizens could move out of the state and bring suit in a federal court if they were disposed to do so; corporations, similarly, could simply reincorporate in another state. More than statutory relief is involved here; the unconstitutionality of *Swift* is clear.

   c) Except in matters governed by the federal Constitution or by acts of Congress, the law to be applied in any case is the law of the state. There is no federal general common law. The federal courts have no power derived from the Constitution or by Congress to declare substantive rules of common law applicable in a state, whether they be "local" or "general" in nature.

   d) The federal district court was bound to follow the Pennsylvania case law, which would have denied recovery to P.

4) **Concurrence** (Butler, J.). Congress gave the United States the power to be heard in every case involving the constitutionality of an act affecting the public interest. The question herein was never certified to the attorney general for an opinion. The question is one of major public significance. The attorney general should be permitted to issue an interpretation of section 34 to see if the constitutional question may be mooted by a narrowly drawn construction. While the Court does not make section 34 unconstitutional, its construction renders the section virtually without meaning. However, I concur with the ultimate result solely on the ground that the evidence required a finding that P's negligence contributed to his injuries.

5) **Concurrence** (Reed, J.). Federal courts are not necessarily bound by state decisions in the absence of federal legislation, and I would also find questionable a holding that prevents federal courts from passing on what rules of substantive law should govern. While I concur in the decision to overturn *Swift v. Tyson*, it seems preferable to overturn an established construction of an act of Congress, rather than to interpret the Constitution as herein.

6) **Comment.** *Erie* can fairly be characterized as one of the most significant and sweeping decisions on civil procedure ever handed down by the Supreme Court. As interpreted in subsequent decisions, *Erie* held that while federal courts may apply their own rules of procedure, issues of substantive law must be decided in accord with the applicable state law—usually the state in which the federal court sits. Note, however, how later Supreme Court decisions have made inroads into the broad doctrine enunciated here.

B. BINDING EFFECTS OF STATE LAW

1. **Lower State Court Decisions Are Afforded Weight.** State trial and intermediate appellate courts are an integral part of the state judicial machinery. Absent evidence to the contrary of what the state law is on a particular subject, the decisions of lower state courts are to be accorded some weight by federal courts deciding similar state law issues.

a. **Intermediate state appeals court is entitled to great deference--Fidelity Union Trust Co. v. Field,** 311 U.S. 169 (1940).

Fidelity Union Trust Co. v. Field

1) **Facts.** Peck informed her bank that her savings account was being held in trust for Field (P). Peck retained absolute control over the account. Upon Peck's death, P applied for the funds. Fidelity Union Trust Co. (D), Peck's executor, also claimed the funds. P brought suit in federal court for the funds. D prevailed on the basis of two state court of appeals decisions stating that such designations were ineffective and no trust or gift occurred. These decisions held that state law had not been changed by the enactment of section 1 of chapter 40 of the state's statutes, which appeared to grant superior title to the beneficiary as opposed to the executor of the will. The court held that this section did not alter the prior common law. The federal court of appeals reversed on the ground that the state statute was clear, unambiguous, and constitutional. It held that the state court interpretations were clearly erroneous and could be ignored since the decisions were not by the highest court of the state. The Supreme Court granted certiorari.

2) **Issue.** May a federal court ignore decisions of lower state courts interpreting state statutes?

3) **Held.** No. Decree of the court of appeals reversed and that of the district court affirmed.

a) The highest court in a state has the final say in interpreting state statutes, except where federal questions exist. The fact that this court has not interpreted the issue does not mean that federal courts may ignore all other decisions by lower courts. An intermediate state court in declaring and applying state law is acting as an organ of the state.

b) In the absence of more convincing evidence of what state law is, its decisions are entitled to great deference. Federal courts are not entitled to interpret state law as they think it should be. Their only function is to apply it as state courts would if the question were before them. Intermediate decisions can only be ignored for important reasons.

c) Federal court plaintiffs should not receive a different result from state court plaintiffs. Since the decisions of the intermediate court have not been reversed, they stand as the definitive statement of state law unless contraindications, not present here, indicate that the highest state court would reverse.

4) **Comment.** In *King v. Order of United Commercial Travelers,* 333 U.S. 153 (1948), the Court held that an unreported decision of a state trial court was not controlling in the federal court. If conflicts exist within the lower state courts, the federal courts are free to decide how the state supreme court would decide the issue.

C. SUBSTANCE AND PROCEDURE IN THE FEDERAL COURTS

1. **Procedure—Law and Equity Merged.** Prior to 1938 and the adoption of the Federal Rules of Civil Procedure, procedure in the federal court was divided into law and equity. Suits in equity were controlled by federal equity rules. On the other hand, suits at law were governed by the Conformity Act, which required the federal district courts to follow as nearly as possible the procedure of the state in which the federal court was located. The purpose of the adoption of the Federal Rules of Civil Procedure was to provide a set of uniform rules of procedure for all federal district courts. The Federal Rules no longer made a distinction between law and equity and provided for only one form of action known as the civil action. [*See* Fed. R. Civ. P. 2] The major limitations on the Federal Rules are that they shall not abridge, enlarge, or modify any substantive right and shall preserve the Seventh Amendment right to jury trial. [*See* 28 U.S.C. §2072]

2. **Substance—Purpose Is to Ensure Uniformity.** The substantive law in the federal courts is governed by the Rules of Decision Act [28 U.S.C. §1652], which requires that the federal district courts apply the law of the state in which the federal court sits. The objective of the Rules of Decision Act is to ensure uniformity in the substantive result in litigation irrespective of whether the suit is brought in the state or federal court.

   a. **Suits based on state-created rights.** If the suit in the federal court is based on a state-law-created right, the federal court must deny recovery if no recovery could be had under the applicable state law.

1) **Outcome determinative state statutes--Guaranty Trust Co. of New York v. York,** 326 U.S. 99 (1945).

a) **Facts.** Van Sweringen Corporation in 1930 issued notes and named Guaranty Trust Company of New York (D) as trustee with power and obligations to enforce the rights of the noteholders in the assets of the corporation and of the Van Sweringens. In 1931, when it was apparent that the corporation could not meet its obligations, D cooperated in a plan for the purchase of the outstanding notes for 50% of their face value and an exchange of 20 shares of the corporation's stock for each $1,000 note. In 1934, York (P) received some cash, her donor not having accepted the rate of exchange. In 1940, three accepting noteholders sued D, charging fraud and misrepresentation, in state court. P was not allowed to intervene. Summary judgment in favor of D was affirmed. In 1942, P brought a class action suit in federal court based on diversity of citizenship and charged D with failing to protect the interest of the noteholders and for breach of trust. D moved for and was granted summary judgment on the basis of the earlier state decision. The court of appeals reversed on the basis that the earlier state decision did not foreclose this federal court action, and held that, even though the state statute of limitations had run, the fact that the action was brought in equity releases the federal court from following the state rule. The Supreme Court granted certiorari.

b) **Issue.** Does a state statute of limitations, which would bar a suit in state court, also act as a bar to the same action if the suit is brought in equity in federal court and jurisdiction is based on diversity of citizenship?

c) **Held.** Yes. Judgment reversed and remanded.

(1) *Erie Railroad Co. v. Tompkins* overruled a particular way of looking at law. Federal courts have traditionally given state-created rights in equity greater respect than rights in law because the former are more frequently defined by legislative enactment. Even though federal equity must be thought of as a separate legal system, the substantive right is created by the state, and federal courts must respect state law governing that right.

(2) While state law cannot define the remedies that a federal court must give simply because a federal court in diversity jurisdiction is available as an alternative, a federal court may afford an equitable remedy for a substantive right recognized by a state even though a state court cannot give it.

(3) Federal courts enforce state-created substantive rights if the mode of proceeding and the remedy are consonant with the traditional body of equitable remedies, practice, and procedure. Matters of "substance" and of "procedure" turn on different considerations.

(4) Here, because the federal court is adjudicating a state-created right solely because of diversity of citizenship of the parties and is, in effect,

only another court of the state, it cannot afford recovery if the right to recovery is made unavailable by the state.

(5) The question is not whether a statute of limitations is "procedural," but whether the statute so affects the result of litigation as to be controlling in state law. It is, therefore, immaterial to make a "substantive/procedure" dichotomy— *Erie Railroad Co. v. Tompkins* was not an endeavor to formulate scientific legal terminology, but rather was an expression of a policy that touches the distribution of judicial power between state and federal courts. *Erie* insures that insofar as legal rules determine the outcome of litigation, the result should not be any different in a federal court extending jurisdiction solely on the basis of diversity of citizenship.

(6) Through diversity jurisdiction, Congress meant to afford out-of-state litigants another tribunal, and not another body of law.

d) **Dissent** (Rutledge, J.). Applicable statutes of limitations in state tribunals are not always the ones that would apply if suit was instituted in the courts of the state that created the substantive rights for which enforcement is sought. The forum state is free to apply its own period of limitations, regardless of whether the state originating the right has barred suit. Whether the action will be held to be barred depends, therefore, not upon the law of the state that creates the substantive right, but upon the law of the state where suit may be brought. It is not clear whether today's decision puts it into the power of corporate trustees by confining their jurisdictional presence to states that allow their courts to give equitable remedies only within short periods of time, to defeat the purpose and intent of the law of the state creating the substantive right. The Constitution does not require this nor does the Judiciary Act permit it.

e) **Comment.** *Guaranty Trust,* which clarified *Erie,* may itself be in the process of being slowly eroded by modern courts. *Hanna v. Plumer, infra,* held that where state law conflicts with the Federal Rules of Civil Procedure, the latter prevail regardless of the effect on outcome of the litigation. In *Byrd v. Blue Ridge Electric Cooperative, Inc. infra,* the Court suggested that some constitutional doctrines (there, the right of a jury trial in federal court) are so important as to be controlling over state law—once again, the outcome notwithstanding.

3. **Balancing State and Federal Interests.** The federal courts should not blindly follow the outcome determinative test in determining whether to use state or federal law. In some cases, for example the right to jury trial on issues of fact, it is not possible to determine whether the outcome of litigation will be affected by use of federal over state law. In such instances, the federal court should weigh the interests of using the federal rule against the interests involved in applying state law to determine whether *Erie* requires the application of state law.

a.   **Jury or judge decides--Byrd v. Blue Ridge Electric Cooperative, Inc.,** 356
     U.S. 525 (1958).

1)   **Facts.** Byrd (P), a lineman, was working on a project for Blue Ridge
     Electric Cooperative (D). P was injured on the job and brought suit for
     personal injuries in federal court based on diversity. D alleged P was
     deemed an employee under state law and was entitled only to workers'
     compensation benefits. The jury found for P, but was reversed by the court
     of appeals. P appealed on the ground that the issue of whether he was
     entitled only to workers' compensation had not been adequately tried in the
     lower court and that the jury under federal law had to decide the issue even
     though, under state law, the judge was to decide the fact. The Supreme
     Court granted certiorari.

2)   **Issue.** Does state procedural law control in federal court if it would alter the
     essential character or function of the court?

3)   **Held.** No. Judgment reversed and remanded.

     a)   A state may distribute its judicial function as it sees fit. Such proce-
          dural rules will normally be binding on federal courts. However, the
          federal system is independently administered. An essential characteris-
          tic of the system is that juries are to decide all factually disputed
          matters. This procedure may be mandated by the Seventh Amendment.
          However, it is not necessary to decide that question.

     b)   State law cannot alter the essential character or function of a federal
          court. In some cases, depending on the issue, an exception might be
          made where it is highly likely that the issue involved may be outcome
          determinative. A conflict would then exist because federal courts are
          to reach the same result as a state court.

     c)   While the matter of who decides the issue in state court might be
          crucial, it is less relevant in federal proceedings. The power of the
          federal judge to comment on evidence and the credibility of witnesses
          and the discretion to grant a new trial lessen the chance of differing
          results.

     d)   The case is remanded for a decision on the issue of whether P is a
          statutory employee. State law provides that the judge renders this
          decision, and the majority concedes that it may be outcome determina-
          tive. The judge should therefore rule on the question.

4)   **Concurrence and Dissent** (Whittaker, J.). In this diversity case the
     jurisdictional issue must be determined by the judge—not by the jury.

5)   **Dissent** (Frankfurter, Harlan, JJ.). The evidence of record establishes as a
     matter of law that D was P's "statutory employer" and hence is entitled to
     judgment n.o.v.

6)   **Comment.** See also *Herron v. Southern Pacific Co.,* 283 U.S. 91 (1930),
     which holds that state laws that conflict with the federal system are not a
     local matter, and state statutes that would interfere with the appropriate

performance of that function are not binding upon the federal courts under either the Conformity Act or the Rules of Decision Act.

4. **Federal Rules of Civil Procedure Control Except When They Interfere with Substantive Rights.** The Federal Rules of Civil Procedure were adopted to provide uniform rules of procedure in the federal courts. The Federal Rules should not yield to state law unless the rules abridge, enlarge, or modify a substantive right. When a Federal Rule covers a specific situation, there is a presumption that the Rules do not violate the Enabling Act or other constitutional restrictions.

Hanna v.
Plumer

a. **Service of process--Hanna v. Plumer,** 380 U.S. 460 (1965).

1) **Facts.** Hanna (P), a citizen of Ohio, filed a tort action in federal court in Massachusetts against Plumer (D), the executor of the estate of Louise Plumer Osgood, a Massachusetts citizen. It was alleged that Mrs. Osgood caused injuries to P in an auto accident in South Carolina. Service on D was accomplished pursuant to Federal Rule 4(d)(1) by leaving copies of the summons with D's wife. At trial, a motion for summary judgment by D was granted on the grounds that service should have been accomplished pursuant to Massachusetts law (under the *Erie* doctrine), which requires service by hand to the party personally. On appeal, P contended that *Erie* should not affect the application of the Federal Rules of Civil Procedure to this case. D, however, contended that: (i) a substantive law question under *Erie* is any question in which permitting application of federal law would alter the outcome of the case (the so-called outcome determination test); (ii) the application of federal law here will necessarily affect the outcome of the case (a necessary dismissal to litigation); and (iii) *Erie* thus requires that the state substantive law requirement of service by hand be upheld along with the trial court's summary judgment. The court of appeals affirmed, and the Supreme Court granted certiorari.

2) **Issue.** Does the *Erie* doctrine classification of "substantive law questions" extend to embrace questions involving both substantive and procedural considerations merely because such questions might have an effect on the determination of the substantive outcome of the case?

3) **Held.** No. Judgment reversed.

a) The *Erie* doctrine mandates that federal courts are to apply state substantive law and federal procedural law, and where matters fall roughly between the two and are rationally capable of classification as either, the Constitution grants the federal court system the power to regulate their practice and procedure.

b) It is well settled that the Enabling Act for the Federal Rules of Civil Procedure requires that a procedural effect of any rule on the outcome of a case be shown to actually "abridge, enlarge, or modify" the substantive law in a case for the *Erie* doctrine to come into play.

c) Where, as here, the question only goes to procedural requirements—*i.e.*, service of summons—a dismissal for improper service would not alter the substantive right of P to serve D personally and refile, or affect the substantive law of negligence in the case.

d) Article III and the Necessary and Proper Clause provide that Congress has a right to provide rules for the federal court system such as Rule 4(d)(1). Outcome determination analysis was never intended to serve as a talisman for the *Erie* doctrine.

4) **Concurrence** (Harlan, J.). I agree with the result of the Court and its rejection of the outcome determination test. However, the Court was wrong in stating that anything arguably procedural is constitutionally placed within the province of the federal government to regulate. My test for "substantive" would be whether "the choice of rule would substantially affect those primary decisions respecting human conduct which our constitutional system leaves to state regulation."

5) **Comment.** This case points up a return to the basic rationales of *Erie Railroad Co. v. Tompkins*. First, the Court asserts that one important consideration in determining how a particular question should be classified is the avoidance of forum shopping. Second, the court seeks to avoid inequitable administration of the laws that would result from allowing jurisdictional considerations to determine substantive rights. Justice Warren, in rejecting the "outcome determination" test, asserts that any Federal Rule of Civil Procedure must be measured ultimately against the Federal Rules Enabling Act and the Constitution.

D. FINDING THE STATE LAW

1. **In General.** In a diversity case, a federal district court sits as another court of the state. The judge must decide the case the way the judge believes the highest court in the state would decide the case.

2. **No Pronouncement by Highest State Court.** If there has been no pronouncement by the highest state court, the federal judge should look to whatever sources a state court judge would examine to resolve the litigation.

   a. **Effect of lower and intermediate level courts.** The decisions of lower state courts are not binding absent a decision by a state's highest court. An intermediate appellate state court decision is data for ascertaining state law. Thus, the decisions of the intermediate courts are not to be disregarded unless the federal court is convinced by other persuasive data that the highest court of the state would decide otherwise.

   b. **State court decision with federal consequences--Commissioner of Internal Revenue v. Estate of Bosch,** 387 U.S. 456 (1967).

      1) **Facts.** Two cases came before the federal district courts as a result of holdings in a state trial court allowing a reduction and a prorating of the federal estate tax. The lower federal courts were unable to determine whether a federal court or agency in a federal

Commissioner of Internal Revenue v. Estate of Bosch

estate tax controversy is conclusively bound by a state trial court adjudication of property rights or characterization of property interests. One federal court held that a state court ruling was binding and the other held that it was not.

2) **Issue.** If there is no decision by the highest court of a state, must a federal court apply the rulings of lower state courts?

3) **Held.** No. The federal court finding that the state probate court ruling was not binding is affirmed, while the contrary holding is reversed and remanded.

a) If Congress had intended state trial court determinations to be conclusive and binding in the area of federal estate tax issues in federal courts, it would have so indicated.

b) The highest court of the state decides the law of the state, and if there is no decision by that court on the issue, then federal authority must apply what it finds to be the state law after giving proper regard to relevant rulings of the other courts of the state.

c) Thus, a federal court or agency in a federal estate tax controversy such as the case at bar is not conclusively bound by a state trial court application of property rights or characterization of property interests since the highest state court has not made a determination on the issues involved.

4) **Dissent** (Douglas, J.). In a long line of cases this court has held that federal courts must look to state court decisions for the state law that is to be applied and it was never suggested that the federal court may ignore a relevant state court decision because it was not entered by the highest state court.

5) **Dissent** (Harlan, Fortas, JJ.). Although not every state judgment has to be accepted by federal courts as conclusive and binding, in cases in which state-adjudicated property rights are contended to have federal tax consequences, federal courts must attribute conclusiveness to any judgment of a state court.

3. **State Choice of Law Rules.** State conflict of law rules must be applied by the federal courts. The rationale is that to allow otherwise would constantly disturb the equal administration of justice in coordinate state and federal courts. Federal courts may not decline to follow state law merely because they would decide differently or have a better method or procedure.

Day and Zimmermann, Inc. v. Challoner

a. **Federal court may not arbitrarily ignore state choice of law rules--Day and Zimmermann, Inc. v. Challoner,** 423 U.S. 3 (1975).

1) **Facts.** The parents (Ps) of Nelms, who was killed, and Challoner (P), who was injured, brought an action in federal court in Texas against Day and Zimmermann, Inc. (D), the manufacturer of a howitzer shell that exploded prematurely in Cambodia. Jurisdiction was based on diversity. The district court applied Texas's law of strict liability, and

the jury found for Ps. The court of appeals affirmed, holding that while Texas's choice of law rules would have applied Cambodian law, it felt that Texas's law should be applied in this case.

2) **Issue.** May a federal court refuse to apply a state's choice of law rules?

3) **Held.** No. Judgment reversed and remanded.

a) Federal courts are to apply state law so that the same result would occur in either state or federal court. A federal court cannot arbitrarily decline to follow the state's choice of law rules. The court must identify the appropriate state conflict of law rule and apply it as it would be applied in state court.

b) In no other way may comparable state and federal results be reached.

4) **Concurrence** (Blackmun, J.). As I read the Court's opinion, the court of appeals on remand is not flatly required to apply Cambodian law, but instead may conclude that a Texas state court would apply Texas strict liability law.

E. FEDERAL PRACTICE AND FEDERAL RULE OF CIVIL PROCEDURE DISTINGUISHED

When the scope of the Federal Rule of Civil Procedure is broad enough so as to directly conflict with the state law, the proper test for determining whether to use the Federal Rule of Civil Procedure is whether it abridges, enlarges, or modifies a substantive right. On the other hand, when the conflict is between the state law and some aspect of federal practice not covered by the Federal Rules, the proper test is whether the outcome of the litigation will be affected and whether the use of the federal practice will promote forum shopping or interfere with the equitable administration of state laws.

1. **No Rule 3 Tolling Effect--Walker v. Armco Steel Corp.,** 446 U.S. 740 (1980).

Walker v. Armco Steel Corp.

a. **Facts.** Walker (P), a carpenter, claimed a defect in a nail manufactured by Armco (D) caused a portion of the nail head to shatter and strike him in the right eye, causing injury. He brought a diversity-based action in federal court to recover damages. Although P filed his complaint within Oklahoma's two-year limit, service of process was not made on D within the two-year period or within the 60-day extension period granted under Oklahoma law. However, P claimed that Federal Rule of Civil Procedure 3 governed the tolling of the Oklahoma statute of limitations and that it tolled the statute on the date the complaint was filed. Rule 3 simply provides that an action is commenced by the filing of the complaint. The district court dismissed the complaint, finding that the statute of limitations had not been tolled under applicable Oklahoma law. The court of appeals affirmed. The Supreme Court granted certiorari.

b.   **Issue.** Should state law be used in a diversity action in federal court to determine when an action is commenced for the purpose of tolling the state statute of limitations?

c.   **Held.** Yes. Judgment affirmed.

   1)   There is no indication that Federal Rule 3 was intended to toll a state statute of limitations or displace state tolling rules for purposes of state statutes of limitations. Thus, there is not the "direct collision" between Federal Rule and state law that must be present before a *Hanna*-type analysis is required to determine if the Federal Rule should prevail.

   2)   *Hanna* applies when a "direct collision" occurs and requires that the Federal Rule be followed if it is within the scope of the Rules Enabling Act and within the constitutional power of Congress.

   3)   Here, the Federal Rule simply does not cover the tolling issue. There is no "collision" requiring a *Hanna*-type analysis, and state law is left alone to govern.

d.   **Comment.** In its note, the Advisory Committee on the Federal Rules of Civil Procedure acknowledged that Rule 3 might have the effect of a tolling provision for statute of limitations purposes. However, the important point in terms of the analysis in this case is that the Committee never indicated that Rule 3 was intended to serve as a tolling provision for such purposes.

Burlington Northern Railroad Co. v. Woods
2.   **Application of *Erie* to Mandatory Affirmance Penalties--Burlington Northern Railroad Co. v. Woods,** 480 U.S. 1 (1987).

a.   **Facts.** Alan and Cara Woods (Ps) sued Burlington Northern Railroad Co. (D) in Alabama state court for damages resulting from a motorcycle accident. D removed the case to federal district court on the basis of diversity jurisdiction. Ps won the suit with Alan receiving $300,000 and Cara receiving $5,000 in damages. D posted a bond, which stayed the judgment, and appealed the case. The Court of Appeals affirmed. Ps then sued for an additional 10% of the judgment under a statute that authorized this amount to be paid to one whose judgment is stayed pending appeal and subsequently affirmed. D alleged that the penalty violated the equal protection and due process guarantees of the United States Constitution. Moreover, D alleged the rule was a procedural rule that federal courts did not have to apply. The Court of Appeals affirmed the application of the penalty. The Supreme Court granted certiorari.

b.   **Issue.** In a diversity action, must a federal court apply a state statute that imposes a fixed penalty on all appellants who obtain stays of judgment pending unsuccessful appeals?

c.   **Held.** No. Judgment reversed.

   1)   When a potential conflict exists between a state law and a federal rule, a two-step approach is used to resolve the conflict. First, the court must determine if application of the federal rule puts it in direct conflict with a state law. Second, a court must determine the reasonableness of the federal rule. If reasonable, a rule is constitutional. Rules of proce-

dure are presumed reasonable and therefore constitutional. Rules are also reasonable if they do not abridge, modify, or enlarge a substantive right.

2) Applying the above approach, a conflict exists and the Alabama state law must be held inapplicable by federal courts in diversity suits. Federal Rule of Appellate Procedure 38 conflicts with the Alabama law in two ways. First, the federal rule's application is discretionary as to when it is used in a case and how much of a penalty is assessed. In contrast, the Alabama law applies in every unsuccessful appeal with a court of appeals affirmance and will always be a 10% penalty.

3) The second conflict can be seen in the scope of the federal rule. If one of these rules and only one governed in every situation, no conflict in scope would occur. However, the purposes of the federal rule are sufficiently similar to the state law's purposes so that the federal rule would apply in all federal diversity cases to the total exclusion of the Alabama statute.

4) Federal Appellate Rule 38 is procedural in nature. It "affects only the process of enforcing litigants' rights and not the rights themselves." As the rule is procedural, it is reasonable and shall be upheld as constitutional. Therefore the Alabama mandatory affirmance penalty does not apply in federal diversity cases.

F. DEFERRAL TO STATE DECISIONMAKING PROCESS

1. **Standard of Review Used by Federal Courts of Appeals--Salve Regina College v. Russell,** 499 U.S. 225 (1991).

Salve Regina College v. Russell

a. **Facts.** Russell (P), after her first year of attending school at Salve Regina College (D), applied for the nursing program there. P was accepted. At the time of her admission, P weighed over 300 pounds. Before beginning her second year in the program, P was required to sign a document entitled a contract that specified that she lose two pounds a week or she would be expelled from the program. P did not fully comply and was forced to withdraw from D's nursing program. P went to another college where she completed a nursing program although it took an extra year because of transfer problems P had between the two programs. P sued D on three bases. She alleged intentional infliction of emotional distress, invasion of privacy, and nonperformance by D to educate P. The trial court granted D's motion for directed verdict on the first two bases, but denied a directed verdict on the nonperformance basis. A jury awarded P $30,000 in damages on the nonperformance claim. Both P and D appealed. The court of appeals affirmed. D sought a writ of certiorari from the Supreme Court, challenging the standard of review that the court of appeals applied. The Supreme Court granted certiorari.

b. **Issue.** Was the standard of deference used by the court of appeals the correct standard for appellate review of the district court decision?

c. **Held.** No. Judgment reversed and case remanded.

1) Courts of appeals should review de novo a district court's determination of state law. Appellate courts have the capacity to more thoroughly and intensely evaluate the legal issues in a case as they are not faced with the need to preside over an entire trial from hearing witnesses to final verdict. An appellate court need only examine legal issues. With the focus on questions of law only, an appellate court can give a more reflective and careful analysis of these questions than a district court can give. This consideration should not be limited by a standard of deference to the district's analysis.

2) At the same time, an appellate court should defer in some areas to the district court especially in the area of fact finding. Indeed, deference refers to an accommodation between the district court's expertise and the appellate court's capacity for closer scrutiny of issues. However, accommodation does not change the need for independent review of the district court, especially in light of *Erie*.

3) Independent de novo review serves the goals set out in *Erie*. Independent review discourages forum shopping. Deferential review permits differing development of state law between district courts even in a single state. If an appellate court must defer to a district court that holds one opinion on a legal issue, and another appellate court must defer to a district court with a different opinion, plaintiffs will look for the jurisdiction best suited in their favor. *Erie* sought to prevent this, and independent review will prevent forum shopping.

4) P, in support of the deferential standard, suggests that appellate courts now independently review cases even though the courts use deferential language. P cites cases where the courts used deferential language, but either reversed the district court decision or carefully scrutinized the district court's legal conclusions. Neither reversal nor close scrutiny implies an independent standard of review used by an appellate court.

5) P also argues that there is little difference between independent review and the deferential review standard currently applied in appellate courts. However, in cases dealing with unresolved issues of state law where an appellate and district court differ, an independent standard has a great impact. For these instances alone, an independent standard is necessary.

6) Finally, P argues that district judges can better determine an unsettled state law issue because they have knowledge and experience as to how a particular state would resolve such an issue since the judges practiced in the state. This argument fails because a decision on a new issue must have some basis that is articulable to many people. Such bases should be communicable to both district and appellate judges. One judge's experience or prior practice should not influence a decision at all. A judge's decision should have a basis that is rational and understandable to people with or without experience in a state's court system. For these reasons, an independent de novo review of the district court's determination of state law should be done at the appellate level.

d. **Dissent** (Rehnquist, C.J., White, Stevens, JJ.). The federal courts' task in a case such as this is to predict how the highest state court would decide the question at issue. In making this prediction, the judge must consider not only an analysis of the law but also judicial behavior in the state. District court judges are better positioned than appellate judges to evaluate the behavior of state court judges, and their perspective on local law should thus be given special weight. By according weight to the conclusions of a particular district judge, the appellate court does not suspend its own thought processes. The court of appeals did no more than that here, and should not be reversed.

G. FEDERAL COMMON LAW AND IMPLIED RIGHTS OF ACTION

1. **In General.** Although *Erie* held that there is no federal general common law, there is nevertheless federal common law that may apply in those cases where the litigation raises the implementation of the Constitution or federal statutes or the litigation concerns areas that have been preempted by the federal law.

2. **Uniformity May Require Federal Common Law.** Where there is a need for uniformity with respect to a federal function, the federal courts may apply federal common law.

   a. **Federal government's commercial paper--Clearfield Trust Co. v. United States,** 318 U.S. 363 (1943).

   Clearfield Trust Co. v. United States

      1) **Facts.** A check drawn on the Treasurer of the United States and made payable to Clair Barner was cashed by an unknown party who indorsed the check in the name of Barner and transferred it to J. C. Penney Co. J. C. Penney Co. indorsed the check over to Clearfield Trust Co. (D). D collected on the check from the United States (P), expressly guaranteeing prior indorsements. Barner then informed his employer that he had not received the check. Over a year later, D received notice that P was seeking reimbursement. Suit was instituted over another year later by P in the federal district court based on the express guarantee of prior indorsements made by D. The district court dismissed the complaint on the ground that the rights of the parties were to be determined by the law of Pennsylvania, the place of the transaction, and that, since P unreasonably delayed in giving notice of the forgery to D, it was barred from recovery. The court of appeals reversed. The Supreme Court granted certiorari.

      2) **Issue.** Are the rights and duties of the United States on commercial paper that it issues governed by federal rather than local law?

      3) **Held.** Yes. The decision of the court of appeals is affirmed.

         a) When the United States disburses its funds or pays its debts, it is exercising a constitutional function.

         b) This check was issued for services performed under the Federal Emergency Relief Act of 1935. The authority to issue the check had its origin in the Constitution and the statutes of the United States and was in no way dependent on the laws of Pennsylvania or any other state.

c)   In the absence of an applicable act of Congress, it is for the federal courts to fashion the governing rule of law according to their own standards. Although in our choice of the applicable federal rule we have occasionally selected state law, the reasons that make state law at times the appropriate federal rule are inappropriate in the instant case.

d)   The issuance of commercial paper by the United States is on a vast scale, commonly occurring in several states. Therefore, the application of state law would subject the rights and duties of the United States to exceptional uncertainty.

e)   The desirability of a uniform rule is plain. As to the issue of prompt notice, this Court holds that lack of such notice will be a defense. If it is shown that the drawee, on learning of the forgery, did not give prompt notice of it and that damage resulted, recovery by the drawee is barred.

f)   But the damages must be established and not left to conjecture as was done in the case at bar. No such damage has been shown by D, who can still recover from J. C. Penney Co.

4)   **Comment.** Justice Jackson, concurring in the case of *D'Oench, Duhme & Co. v. F.D.I.C.*, 315 U.S. 447 (1942), stated that "a federal court sitting in a nondiversity case does not sit as a local tribunal. In some cases it may see fit for special reasons to give the law of a particular state highly persuasive or even controlling effect, but in the last analysis its decision turns upon the law of the United States. Federal law is no judicial chameleon changing complexion to match that of each state wherein lawsuits happen to be commenced because of the accidents of service of process and of the application of the venue statutes."

3.   **If No Federal Interest Involved, Then State Law Controls.** When the suit is between private parties and the federal interest is either not involved or tangential, state law rather than federal common law controls.

DeSylva v.
Ballentine

a.   **Disposition of copyright--DeSylva v. Ballentine,** 351 U.S. 570 (1956).

1)   **Facts.** DeSylva died possessed of copyrights secured by federal law. Federal law provided that "the widow, widower, or children" had the rights to copyright payments and the rights to renew the copyright. Ballentine (P), the illegitimate child of DeSylva, brought suit to obtain an interest in the copyright and renewal rights. DeSylva's widow (D) contended that she had the sole right of the payments under federal law because the statute did not create a class interest in the widow and the child. It was also contended that an illegitimate child did not fall within the statutory definition of "children." P contended he was a "child" under California descent rules.

2)   **Issue.** Are state rules of descent used to determine whether the proper familial relationship existed to qualify under a federal statute?

3)   **Held.** Yes. Judgment affirmed.

a) Familial relationships are more properly a state concern. There is no federal common law in such areas. We hold that the copyright statute grants rights to a class including the widow and a child.

b) To determine if P qualifies as a "child," we look to state law. Because the interest involves the disposition of property by a decedent, the proper state statutes to consider for definitional purposes are the rules of descent.

c) Because P would qualify as an intestate heir under California law, he is deemed to be a child under the copyright statute.

4) **Concurrence** (Douglas, Black, JJ.). While we concur in the result, it is felt that this is a federal question that can be decided based on the rights of illegitimate children to other benefits. Uniformity is the desired end in federal statutes. This is not served by obtaining diverse results based on state law.

5) **Comment.** If a state were to define "children" in an unusual or impermissible manner, federal courts could reject the construction. [Seaboard Air Line Railway v. Kenney, 240 U.S. 489 (1915)] The concurrence in *DeSylva*, however, appears to more correctly reflect congressional policy. "Children" were to be given an interest in copyrights. There is no purpose served by applying a law conferring a federal benefit differently across the country.

4. **Damages for Violation of Constitutionally Protected Rights.** Federal courts have the power to determine whether a violation of constitutionally protected rights gives rise to remedial relief as a matter of federal common law. If the plaintiff states a cause of action under the Constitution, the federal court may award money damages as an available remedy.

a. **Recovery in federal court for constitutional violations by federal officers--Carlson v. Green,** 446 U.S. 14 (1980).

Carlson
v. Green

1) **Facts.** Green (P) brought suit in the United States District Court for the Southern District of Indiana on behalf of the estate of her deceased son, alleging that he suffered personal injuries from which he died because Carlson and other federal prison officials (Ds) had violated his due process, equal protection, and Eighth Amendment rights. The district court held that the allegations pleaded a violation of the Eighth Amendment's proscription against infliction of cruel and unusual punishment, giving rise to a cause of action for damages, but dismissed the complaint because, in its view, the damages remedy as a matter of federal law was limited to that provided by Indiana's survivorship and wrongful death laws, and the damages available under those laws failed to meet the jurisdictional amount requirement. The court of appeals reversed, reasoning that the Indiana law, if applied, would subvert the policy of allowing complete vindication of constitutional rights by making it more advantageous for a tortfeasor to kill rather than to injure. Ds then brought this appeal, contending that the Federal Tort Claims Act ("FTCA") was the exclusive remedy for unconstitutional tortious acts.

2) **Issue.** Do the victims of a constitutional violation by a federal agent have a right to recover damages against the official in federal court if Congress has not explicitly provided an alternative remedy?

3) **Held.** Yes. Judgment affirmed.

    a) The defendants may show that Congress has provided an alternative remedy that it explicitly declared to be a substitute for recovery directly under the Constitution and viewed as equally effective.

    b) That situation is not present here. There has been no explicit congressional declaration that persons injured by federal officers' violations of the Eighth Amendment may not recover money damages from the agents but must be remitted to another remedy, equally effective in the view of Congress.

    c) The FTCA contemplates that victims of the kind of intentional wrongdoing alleged in this complaint shall have an action under the FTCA against the United States, as well as a direct action against the individual officers alleged to have infringed on their constitutional rights.

4) **Concurrence** (Powell, Stewart, JJ.). The Court's willingness to infer federal causes of action that cannot be found in the Constitution or in a statute denigrates the doctrine of separation of powers and hardly comports with a rational system of justice.

5) **Dissent** (Burger, C.J.). Under the test enunciated by the Court, the adequacy of the FTCA remedy is irrelevant. The sole inquiry called for by the Court's new test is whether Congress has provided an alternative remedy that it explicitly declared to be a substitute for recovery directly under the Constitution.

6) **Dissent** (Rehnquist, J.). Absent a clear indication from Congress, federal courts lack the authority to grant damage relief for constitutional violations. Because Congress has never provided for a direct action for damages in this situation, the appropriate course is for federal courts to dismiss such actions for failure to state a claim upon which relief can be granted.

7) **Comment.** Although in his dissent Chief Justice Burger was concerned that a preemptive remedy could not be established absent some explicit "magical words," the majority indicates that specific intent is the main focus of inquiry. In footnote 68, Justice Brennan states that "our inquiry at this step in the analysis is whether Congress has indicated that it intends the statutory remedy to replace, rather than to complement, the *Bivens* remedy."

5. **Congressional Intent to Create a Private Right of Action.** In those areas where there is a federal intent, federal courts will apply federal common law even though there is no statutory mandate to do so. In such situations, the court will examine the intent of Congress and whether the right is created by Congress.

a. **No implied cause of action for conflicting state custody decisions--Thompson v. Thompson,** 484 U.S. 174 (1988).

1) **Facts.** In July 1978, Matthew Thompson's mother (D) filed for divorce in a California state court. The court awarded the parents joint custody of Matthew, but when D decided to move from California to Louisiana, the court entered an order giving D sole custody pending a more studied custody determination. D moved with Matthew to Louisiana in December 1980, and three months later, she filed a petition in Louisiana state court for enforcement of the California custody determination. The court granted the petition and awarded D sole custody. Two months later, the California state court awarded full custody to the father (P). In August 1983, P brought an action in federal court in California in which he requested that the Louisiana decree be invalidated and the California decree be recognized. P's claim was based on the Parental Kidnapping Prevention Act ("PKPA"), which requires all states to accord full faith and credit to a child custody determination entered by a court of a sister state. P had not attempted to enforce the California decree in a Louisiana state court before he filed suit in federal court. The district court dismissed the complaint for lack of subject matter and personal jurisdiction. The court of appeals affirmed. The United States Supreme Court granted certiorari.

2) **Issue.** Does a federal act give a party an implied cause of action to determine two conflicting state custody decisions?

3) **Held.** No. Judgment affirmed.

   a) A federal act does not furnish an implied cause of action in federal court to determine which of two conflicting state custody determinations is valid.

   b) The PKPA was created by Congress to extend the requirements of full faith and credit to custody determinations in sister states and not to create an entirely new cause of action. The context, purpose, heading, structure, and history of the Act indicate that Congress intended the Act only to furnish a rule of decision for courts to use in adjudicating custody disputes, and not to create a new cause of action.

4) **Concurrence** (Scalia, J.). It is misleading to state that in determining the existence of a private right of action the Court has relied on the four factors set out in *Cort v. Ash.* That case was effectively overruled by *Transamerica Mortgage Advisors, Inc. v. Lewis,* which converted one of the four factors (congressional intent) into the determinative one. Also, the Court's dicta today moves in the wrong direction. The Court should move away from the congressional intent test to the categorical position that federal private rights of action will not be implied.

X. PROCEDURE IN THE DISTRICT COURT

A. SERVICE OF PROCESS

1. **In General.** The issue of service of process can be divided into two categories: manner of service and amenability to service. Manner of service deals
with the methods by which a defendant may be properly served with process
in a particular litigation. Amenability to service deals with whether a court
has power to order a defendant to appear in a suit if the defendant is properly
served with process.

   a. **Manner and method of service of process.** The manner of service of
   process is governed by Federal Rule of Civil Procedure 4. Rule 4
   provides for various methods of serving process. These methods of
   service are interpreted as a matter of state law rather than federal law.

Henderson v.
United States

   1) **Rule 4 supersedes other federal act--Henderson v. United
       States,** 517 U.S. 654 (1996).

      a) **Facts.** Lloyd Henderson (P), a merchant mariner, brought
      suit against the United States (D) for injuries he sustained
      aboard a United States vessel. As required by the Suits in
      Admiralty Act, P served the United States Attorney General
      and the United States Attorney. The Attorney General was
      served 47 days after P filed suit, but service on the United
      States Attorney was 148 days after the complaint was filed.
      D moved to dismiss the action. The district court dismissed
      P's complaint for lack of subject matter jurisdiction, and the
      court of appeals affirmed. The Supreme Court granted
      certiorari.

      b) **Issue.** Does Federal Rule of Civil Procedure 4, which
      authorizes an extendable 120-day period for service of
      process, supersede the Suits in Admiralty Act provision that
      service on the United States be made "forthwith?"

      c) **Held.** Yes. Judgment reversed and remanded.

         (1) Rule 4 conflicts irreconcilably with the Suits in Admi-
         ralty Act's service "forthwith" provision.

         (2) Upon commencement of an action under the Suits in
         Admiralty Act, the plaintiff must immediately resort to
         Rule 4 for instructions on service of process.

         (3) The core function of service is to supply notice of a
         legal action in a manner and at a time that affords the
         defendant a fair opportunity to answer the complaint
         and present defenses and objections. In this light,
         Federal Rule 4 has displaced the "forthwith" provision
         of the Suits in Admiralty Act.

      d) **Concurrence** (Scalia, Kennedy, JJ.). It is not my view, and do not believe that the Court now holds, that no procedural provision can be jurisdictional.

e) **Dissent** (Thomas, J., Rehnquist, C.J., O'Connor, J.). The majority's conclusion is irreconcilable with our sovereign immunity jurisprudence. The government's waiver of its immunity through the Suits in Admiralty Act requires strict compliance with the Act's time restriction on service.

2) **Rule 4 can be waived by defendant--McCurdy v. American Board of Plastic Surgery**, 157 F.3d 191 (3d Cir. 1998).

McCurdy v. American Board of Plastic Surgery

a) **Facts.** McCurdy (P), a plastic surgeon, filed a complaint in the United States District Court for the District of Hawaii against several defendants including the American Board of Plastic Surgery (D) alleging unfair competition, unlawful restraint of trade, and various antitrust violations under the Clayton Act, the Sherman Act, and Hawaii law. D was served 20 days after the expiration of the original 120-day period provided for under Rule 4. D moved to dismiss the complaint, asserting that Hawaii lacked personal jurisdiction over it and that venue was improper. D did not allege a defect in service of process at that time. After the Hawaii district court granted a similar motion made by another defendant in the case, P attempted to reserve D under the Clayton Act. This service was also untimely, and P's motion to extend the time was denied. D moved to quash this service, but the record contains no indication of any ruling on that motion. In ruling on D's first motion, the Hawaii district court found that it lacked personal jurisdiction over D and that venue was improper, but transferred the suit to the Eastern District of Pennsylvania "in the interest of justice." P did not re-serve D. D then filed a motion to dismiss arguing that the original service was untimely. P argued that D had waived this objection by failing to raise it in the original motion to dismiss. The Pennsylvania district court granted D's motion finding that Rule 4's 120-day service requirement is mandatory and not subject to waiver. P appeals.

b) **Issue.** Is compliance with Rule 4 subject to waiver by the defendant?

c) **Held.** Yes, but order affirmed on other grounds.

(1) Under Rule 12, if a motion to dismiss is made and the defendant omits an objection to the timeliness or effectiveness, that objection is waived. Rule 12 has universal application; Rule 4 does not override its waiver provisions.

(2) However, P's attempts at service on D were ineffective. The original service made pursuant to the Hawaii long arm provision was ineffective because the district court in Hawaii lacked personal jurisdiction. As to P's second attempt, the court did not abuse its discretion in refusing to grant P an extension to file the Clayton Act complaint because P did not request an extension before the time allotted had lapsed.

b. **Amenability to service of process determined by state law.** Earlier court decisions held that whether a defendant was amenable to suit was to be decided based on federal. Later decisions make it clear that a defendant's amenability to suit must be determined as a matter of state law.

B. JOINDER OF PARTIES AND CLAIMS

1. **Compulsory Joinder.** In certain instances, a court must determine whether a person who has not been included in the litigation must be joined in the suit as a party. If the court determines that the absentee is indispensable, then the absentee must be joined as a party. In many cases, joining the absentee will have the result of destroying diversity jurisdiction.

    a. **Requirements for determining whether an absentee is indispensable.** Although Federal Rule of Civil Procedure 19 does not speak in terms of indispensable, necessary, or nominal parties, the rule does address the question of persons to be joined if feasible and, in addition, the rule sets out four guidelines for determining when it is equitable to proceed in the absence of such a party. The factors are: (i) to what extent a judgment rendered in the party's absence might be prejudicial to him or to those already parties; (ii) the extent to which, by protective provisions in the judgment, by the shaping of relief, or by other measures, the prejudice can be lessened or avoided; (iii) whether a judgment rendered in the indispensable party's absence will be adequate; and (iv) whether the plaintiff will have an adequate remedy if the action is dismissed for nonjoinder.

Temple v.
Synthes
Corporation

    b. **Indispensable parties under Rule 19--Temple v. Synthes Corporation,** 498 U.S. 5 (1990)

        1) **Facts.** Temple (P) sued Synthes, Ltd. (D1) in federal court in Louisiana, alleging defective design and manufacture of a "plate and screw device" that was implanted in P's lower spine during surgery. At the same time, P sued Dr. S. Henry LaRocca (D2), who performed the surgery, and St. Charles General Hospital (D3), where the surgery was performed, in Louisiana state court following a state administrative proceeding P had brought against D2 and D3 for malpractice and negligence. The federal trial court ordered P to join D2 and D3 in the federal action, on the grounds that D2 and D3 were indispensable parties under Rule 19(b), and hence joinder would be in the interest of judicial economy. When P failed to join D2 and D3, the federal court dismissed the lawsuit with prejudice. The court of appeals affirmed, and the United States Supreme Court granted certiorari.

        2) **Issue.** Was it error to label potential joint tortfeasors (D2 and D3) as indispensable parties under Rule 19(b)?

        3) **Held.** Yes. Judgment reversed; case remanded.

            a) Rule 19(a) has been interpreted to mean that "a tortfeasor with the usual 'joint and several' liability is merely a permissive party to an action against another with like liability." Thus, it is not necessary for all joint tortfeasors to be joined as defendants in a single lawsuit.

b)   Given the fact that the threshold requirements of Rule 19(a) have not been satisfied, no inquiry under Rule 19(b) is necessary.

4)   **Comment.** Compulsory joinder under Rule 19 requires a twofold finding: that the nonparty is necessary (or one who should be joined if feasible) [Rule 19(a)] and indispensable [Rule 19(b)] to the pending lawsuit. Following the prior interpretation of Rule 19(a), the Court simply finds that there is not enough to reach the second prong of the analysis—the indispensability question. Note that D1 could have impleaded D2 and D3 under Rule 14(a) only on the basis of derivative liability, such as a claim that the device failed because D2 and D3 failed to follow the manufacturer's instructions, and on that basis D2 and D3 are liable if D1 is liable. The mere claim that D2 and D3 are liable and not D1 is insufficient for impleader; there must be a claim over from D1 to D2 and D3.

c.   **Necessary and indispensable parties—Cases before the same judge--Western Maryland Railway Co. v. Harbor Insurance Co.,** 910 F.2d 960 (D.C. Cir. 1990).

Western Maryland Railway Co. v. Harbor Insurance Co.

1)   **Facts.** Following a multitude of asbestosis claims by employees, Western Maryland Railway Co. (P) sued nine insurers seeking damages and a declaration of its rights under 40 insurance polices. The same day the Chesapeake and Ohio Railway filed suit against 40 insurance companies on 600 policies seeking the same relief. P is a wholly-owned subsidiary of the Chesapeake, and 36 of the policies in question in P's case were issued to the Chesapeake Railway. The insurance companies (Ds) in each case sought to join the other railway as a necessary and indispensable party to the respective lawsuits. Ds further sought dismissal from federal court if the railways were joined because joinder would destroy diversity, the basis of the court's jurisdiction. The district court held that the railways were not necessary parties under FRCP 19(a)(1) or 19(a)(2)(i), but that they were under 19(a)(2)(ii); *i.e.*, that Ds would risk incurring multiple or inconsistent liability. Consequently, the court dismissed both suits. The railways appeal.

2)   **Issue.** Were the railways necessary and indispensable parties to each other's suits such that the present parties in each suit would incur substantial risk of inconsistent obligations without the railways?

3)   **Held.** No. Judgment reversed.

a)   Ds seek to join the other railway in both suits to prevent a situation where in one case a judge requires Ds to pay one of the plaintiffs under the policies without considering a reduction of payments made to the other plaintiff based on payments made to the first plaintiff. If the employees' asbestosis claims are occupational diseases and subject to "aggregate limits" in the policies, then both plaintiffs are claimants to a common, limited fund. If one plaintiff is paid out first, there may not be enough left to cover successful employee claims against the second plaintiff. The railways sought to avoid this problem by filing separate suits.

b)   Ds claim that allowing the railways to proceed in separate suits subjects Ds to a substantial risk of double payout as one suit settles before the other. In this situation, the risk to Ds is minimized. The cases are before the same judge who has treated the cases consistently by "delimiting the scope of the occupational disease clauses the same in both suits." If the aggregate limits apply, the judge will limit the insurer's liability to those limits and these limits should be no more than the total amount of the policies. The railways concede that this will be the case if the aggregate limits apply. Thus, Ds do not face a substantial risk of inconsistent obligations, and joinder may be denied.

2.   **Interpleader.** Interpleader is a form of joinder available to a party uncertain as to which of several claimants he is liable, if he is liable at all. It allows him to join the claimants in a single action and to require them to litigate among themselves to decide which, if any, has a valid claim. There are two kinds of federal interpleader: 28 U.S.C. section 1335 authorizes interpleader with liberal provisions as to venue, jurisdiction, and service of process. Nonstatutory interpleader is available under Federal Rule 22, but the jurisdictional and procedural requirements there are identical to an ordinary civil action.

State Farm
Fire &
Casualty Co.
v. Tashire

a.   **Interpleader by insurer--State Farm Fire & Casualty Co. v. Tashire,** 386 U.S. 523 (1967).

1)   **Facts.** State Farm Fire & Casualty Company (P), insurer for a defendant in a multiple tort suit arising out of a bus crash, sought to consolidate all claims against its insured and limit its obligations under the policy. Under 28 U.S.C. section 1335, the federal interpleader statute, P persuaded the district court to enjoin the filing and prosecution of any action arising out of the incident with its insured, except in the interpleader proceeding. The Ninth Circuit reversed, holding that in states like Oregon that do not permit "direct action" suits against insurance companies until judgments are obtained against the insured, the insurance companies may not invoke federal interpleader until the claims against the insured have been reduced to judgment. Until that is done, said the court, claimants with unliquidated tort claims are not "claimants" within the meaning of section 1335 nor are they "persons having claims against the plaintiff" within Federal Rule 22. The Supreme Court granted certiorari.

2)   **Issue.** In the absence of a state law or contractual provision for "direct action" suits against an insurance company, must the company wait until persons asserting claims against its insured have reduced those claims to judgment before seeking to invoke the benefits of federal interpleader?

3)   **Held.** No. Judgment reversed and case remanded.

a)   Were an insurance company required to await reduction of claims to judgment, the first claimant to obtain such a judgment or to negotiate a settlement might appropriate all, or a disproportionate slice of, the fund before his fellow claimants were able to establish their claims. The difficulties such a "race to judgment" pose for the insurer and the unfairness that might result to some claimants were among the principal evils the interpleader device was intended to remedy.

b) The fact that P had properly invoked the interpleader jurisdiction of section 1335 did not, however, entitle it to an order both enjoining prosecution of suits against it outside the confines of the interpleader proceeding and also extending such protection to its insured, the alleged tortfeasor. Here, the scope of the litigation was vastly more extensive than the confines of the "fund," the deposited proceeds of the insurance policy.

c) In these circumstances the mere existence of such a fund cannot by use of interpleader be employed to accomplish purposes that exceed the needs of orderly contest with respect to the fund.

4) **Dissent** (Douglas, J.). While I agree with the Court's view as to "minimal diversity" and that the injunction, if granted, should run only against prosecution of suits against the insurer, I feel that the use that we today allow to be made of the federal interpleader statute is, with all deference, unwarranted. How these litigants are "claimants" to this fund in the statutory sense is indeed a mystery. If they are not "claimants" of the fund, neither are they in the category of those who "are claiming" or who "may claim" to be entitled to it.

3. Counterclaims and Cross-claims.

a. **Counterclaims.** As with other joinder rules, the modern theory as to counterclaims in federal courts is to allow unlimited joinder at the pleading stage, with power in the court to order the separate trial of particular issues if more convenient or desirable.

1) **Classes of counterclaims.** The modern rules of federal civil procedure recognize two distinct classes of counterclaims.

a) **Compulsory counterclaim.** If the defendant's claim arises out of the same transaction or occurrence as the main claim, then the defendant's claim is termed a "compulsory counterclaim" under Rule 13(a) and must be asserted as such or be forever barred.

b) **Permissive counterclaim.** Other claims the defendant has against the plaintiff that do not fit the definition of 13(a) are "permissive counterclaims" under 13(b), which permits a defendant to assert such a claim, but does not require her to do so. It has been said that the test is whether the issues of fact and law embraced in the counterclaim are largely the same.

2) **Jurisdictional basis.** Compulsory counterclaims are supported by ancillary jurisdiction, now codified at 28 U.S.C. section 1367 under the name supplemental jurisdiction, and therefore no independent jurisdictional basis need be asserted. Permissive counterclaims need an independent jurisdictional basis.

3) **Meaning of "arising out of the transaction"--Moore v. New York Cotton Exchange,** 270 U.S. 593 (1926).

a) **Facts.** Moore (P) sued the New York Cotton Exchange (D) under the antitrust laws, challenging the validity of a contract

Moore v.
New York
Cotton
Exchange

between D and Western Union that provided for cotton exchange quotations to be distributed only to selected persons. P sought a decree canceling the contract and adjudging D to be a monopoly, and an injunction requiring Western Union to install a ticker in the Odd-Lot Cotton Exchange. D counterclaimed, alleging that Odd-Lot had been refused permission to use the quotations but had been purloining them and distributing them to its members, and seeking an injunction halting this practice. The district court denied the injunction sought by P and granted the one sought by D. The court of appeals affirmed. P appeals, claiming that D's counterclaim did not arise out of any transaction that was the subject matter of the suit.

b) **Issue.** Under Equity Rule 30, are there two classes of counterclaims?

c) **Held.** Yes. Decree affirmed.

(1) Under Equity Rule 30, there are two classes of counterclaims: (i) one "arising out of the transaction" that is the subject matter of the suit, which must be pleaded, and (ii) another "which might be the subject of an independent suit in equity" and which may be brought forward at the option of the defendant. The counterclaim here is of the first type, so no independent basis of jurisdiction is required.

(2) "Transaction" is a word of flexible meaning. It may comprehend a series of many occurrences, depending not so much upon immediateness of their connection as upon their logical relationship.

(3) Here, the refusal to furnish the quotations is one of the links in the chain that constitutes the transaction upon which D bases its cause of action. It is an important part of the transaction constituting the subject matter of the counterclaim. It is the circumstance without which neither party would have found it necessary to seek relief.

(4) That the counterclaim embraces additional allegations does not matter.

b. **Cross-claims.** Courts have not always clearly distinguished between counterclaims and cross-claims and frequently used one name when the other was appropriate. This confusion occurs, perhaps, because in several states and in the old equity practice the term cross-complaint or cross-bill was used for what the modern rules regard as a counterclaim. According to Federal Rule 13, a counterclaim is a claim against an opposing party, while a cross-claim is against a co-party. Unlike counterclaims, there is only one type of cross-claim. All cross-claims must arise out of the same transaction or occurrence as the main claim. Cross-claims are supported by ancillary (supplemental) jurisdiction.

Scott v. Fancher

1) **Jurisdiction--Scott v. Fancher,** 369 F.2d 842 (5th Cir. 1966).

a) **Facts.** A three-truck collision occurred between Fancher (P), Scott (D), and Short, in which Short was killed. P filed suit in district court alleging negligence on the part of both D and Short. Short's estate counterclaimed against P and cross-claimed against D, the other named defendant. Jurisdiction was based on diversity of citizenship, P being a Texan and D and Short being Oklahomans. The jury absolved P and Short of liability and returned a verdict against D. D appeals, claiming the court was without jurisdiction as to both the original action and the cross-claim by Short because the required diversity of citizenship was lacking and because the cross-claim was not ancillary to the original suit.

b) **Issues.**

    (1) Is realignment of the parties to be accomplished on the basis of the facts available at the commencement of the action?

    (2) Do cross-claims arising out of the same transaction and involving the same parties require independent jurisdictional grounds?

c) **Held.** (1) Yes. (2) No. Judgment affirmed.

    (1) Realignment of the parties is to be accomplished on the basis of the facts available at the commencement of the action. Here, D asserts that a proper alignment of the parties would cast D and Short as opposing parties because under no theory of facts could Short have been at fault. Thus, he concludes the district court was without jurisdiction because Short and D are both Oklahomans. However, P had charged both D and Short with negligence and at the time it could not be said that the allegation was baseless. Accordingly, no realignment was required.

    (2) Cross-claims by definition must be closely related to the existing action. Therefore, they are always treated as within the ancillary jurisdiction of the court and independent jurisdictional grounds are not required, nor can there be any venue objection. Here, Short's cross-claim arose out of the same transaction and involved the same parties as did the original action. In such cases, jurisdiction rests with the primary suit.

d) **Comment.** As previously stated, courts have not always clearly distinguished between counterclaims and cross-claims and have frequently used one name when the other was appropriate. As Rule 13 makes clear, a counterclaim is a claim against an opposing party, while a cross-claim is against a co-party.

4. Intervention.

a. **Intervention as of right protects parties' interests.** Rule 24, permitting persons not named as parties to a lawsuit to intervene therein, was added as a viable procedure by which parties not included originally can protect themselves from being excluded from an action that might be detrimental to them, or from an action where they might be able to litigate their claims inexpensively.

1) Rule 24(a) defines situations in which intervention is "of right." Anyone may intervene as of right when: (i) a United States statute confers the unconditional right to intervene [*see, e.g.,* 28 U.S.C. §2403]; or (ii) when the applicant claims an interest relating to the property or transaction that is the subject of the action and the applicant is so situated that the disposition of the action may impair or impede his ability to protect his interest, unless the applicant's interest is adequately represented by existing parties. The right to intervene in federal actions is governed by Rule 24, rather than state law.

2) If an applicant qualifies under Rule 24(a), he should be allowed to intervene rather than being obliged to test the validity of the judgment as applied to his interest by a later collateral attack.

b. **Permissive intervention is discretionary.** Permissive intervention is governed by Rule 24(b) and is in the court's discretion. The court should consider whether the intervention will unduly delay the original action. Anyone may be permitted to intervene under Rule 24(b) when: (i) a United States statute confers a conditional right to intervene; or (ii) an applicant's claim or defense and the main action have a common question of law or fact.

Johnson v. San Francisco Unified School District

1) **Interest in the outcome--Johnson v. San Francisco Unified School District,** 500 F.2d 349 (9th Cir. 1974).

a) **Facts.** Litigation seeking desegregation was initiated by parents of black children attending public elementary schools in the San Francisco Unified School District. Before court hearings commenced, Chinese-American parents sought leave to intervene under Federal Rule 24(a)(2), which was denied, and the hearings were held without their participation. The parents opposed the compulsory reassignment of their children, which they claimed made it impossible for them to attend community schools offering education in Chinese culture. The Chinese-American parents appeal on constitutional and equitable grounds, asserting that they were not properly bound by the district court desegregation decree and plan, or that, if they were so bound, they were entitled to participate in the fashioning of that decree.

b) **Issue.** Must a party claim sufficient interest in the outcome of an action to intervene in federal court under Rule 24(a)(2)?

c) **Held.** Yes. Decree vacated and case remanded.

(1) Rule 24(a)(2) permits timely intervention when the applicant shows: (i) an interest relating to the property or transaction that is the subject of the action; (ii) that the disposition of the action may, as a practical matter, impair or impede his ability to protect that interest; and (iii) that the interest is not adequately represented by existing parties.

(2) Other courts have recognized that for purposes of Rule 24(a)(2), all students and parents, whatever their race, have an interest in a sound educational system and in the operation of that system in accordance with the law. That interest is surely no less significant where, as here, it is entangled with the constitutional claims of a racially defined class.

c. **Jurisdictional basis—permissive intervention and intervention as of right distinguished.** If the claim of an intervenor is so clearly related to the main action that the applicant is allowed to intervene as of right, the intervention is supported by ancillary (supplemental) jurisdiction and no independent grounds of jurisdiction need exist. Generally, independent jurisdictional grounds have been required under a Rule 24(b) permissive intervention.

d. **Third party's interest in outcome--Wodecki v. Nationwide Insurance Co.,** 107 F.R.D. 118 (W.D. Pa. 1985).

Wodecki v. Nationwide Insurance Co.

1) **Facts.** In an action to recover health insurance benefits from Nationwide Insurance (D), Wodecki (P) received a jury verdict of $8,200. Following the judgment, the court permitted Hamot Medical Center, the hospital where P stayed, to file a claim for intervention. P now moves to dismiss Hamot's claim of intervention on the grounds that Hamot's claim does not have independent jurisdictional basis since the parties are not diverse and that the court lacks subject matter jurisdiction because the underlying action against D has been terminated by judgment. Hamot contends that since the disposition of the judgment monies currently in the court would negate its ability to protect its interest in these monies, and since its interest is not represented by either of the parties, it has a right to intervene pursuant to Federal Rule 24(a)(2).

2) **Issue.** Does a third party not privy to a contract between two parties in a lawsuit but who has an interest in the judgment have a right to intervene to protect this interest?

3) **Held.** No. P's motion to dismiss Hamot's intervention claim is granted.

   a) When a third party can otherwise assert its right through a state court claim, the court may not grant intervention of right.

   b) The disposition of P's case depended on the terms of her contract with D. Hamot's claim for hospital cost and expenses arose after P assigned health benefits to it. Hamot's claim does not provide a sufficient nexus to establish intervention of right. Hamot may more expeditiously complete the litigation of its claims in the pending state action.

5. **Class Actions.**

a. **In general.** The class action under Rule 23 is a device whereby representatives of a defined group may either sue or be sued and the entire group will benefit or be bound by the judgment.

b. **Prerequisites for a class action.** There are four prerequisites under Rule 23(a) for maintaining a class action:

1) The class is so numerous that joinder of all individual members is impracticable;

2) There are questions of law and fact common to all class members;

3) The claims or defenses of the representative members are typical; and

4) The representatives will adequately protect the class interest.

c. **Situations where class action is appropriate.** If the requirements of Rule 23(a) are met, there are three situations where a class action is appropriate under Rule 23(b):

1) Where the prosecution of separate actions by or against individual members of the class would create a risk of inconsistent judgments that might create incompatible standards of conduct for the party opposing the class, or where the judgments would affect the ability of nonparty class members to protect their interest [Rule 23(b)(1)];

2) Where injunctive or declaratory relief is sought against a person who has acted on or refused to act on grounds that are generally applicable to the class [Rule 23(b)(2)]; and

3) Where the questions of law or fact common to class members predominate over the questions affecting only individual members and the class action is the superior device for settling the dispute [Rule 23(b)(3)].

Amchem Products, Inc. v. Windsor

d. **Class action requirements not met--Amchem Products, Inc. v. Windsor**, 521 U.S. 591 (1997).

1) **Facts.** During the 1940s and 1950s millions of Americans were exposed to asbestos. This exposure resulted in numerous diseases and lawsuits. Facing an asbestos-litigation crisis, in 1991, the Judicial Panel on Multidistrict Litigation transferred all asbestos cases then filed, but not yet on trial, to a single court. After negotiations between the Center for Claims Resolution ("CCR"), a consortium of 20 former asbestos manufacturers, and those representing the plaintiffs, the parties agreed to a settlement. The present case was launched to resolve the claims of potential asbestos-litigation plaintiffs who had not yet filed suit. A class action was instituted for the purpose of settlement only. The class proposed for certification was all persons who had not yet filed a lawsuit against a member of the CCR and who had been exposed to asbestos or whose family member had been so exposed. The proposed settlement specified a range of damages for qualified claimants based on type of disease suffered and would preclude nearly all class members from litigating against CCR companies in the future. The district court certified the class, finding that the class was fair and that representation and notice had been adequate. Objecting class members appealed. The court of appeals vacated the certification, holding that the class certification failed to satisfy Rule 23. The Supreme Court granted certiorari.

2) **Issues.**

a) Should settlement be considered in determining the propriety of class certification?

b) Does the proposed class in this case meet the requirements of Rule 23?

3) **Held.** a) Yes. b) No. Judgment of court of appeals affirmed.

   a) Settlement is relevant to a class certification. However, federal courts lack authority to substitute for Rule 23's certification criteria a standard that if a settlement is fair, then certification is proper.

   b) Class actions must satisfy all of the relevant requirements of Rule 23, such as predominance of common question of law or fact over any questions affecting only individual members and adequacy of representation.

   c) The district court concluded that predominance was satisfied because the class members shared asbestos exposure and a common interest in compensation for their claims, but given the great number of questions particular to the different categories of class members, the predominance standard of Rule 23(b)(3) is not met.

   d) Furthermore, due to the disparity between those currently injured and those only exposed to asbestos, and the diversity within each category, the interests of those within the class are not aligned. For example, for those currently injured the goal is immediate payment, for those exposure-only plaintiffs it is ensuring an ample fund for the future.

   e) Because this class cannot meet the above requirements, we need not rule on the issue of notice.

4) **Concurrence and Dissent** (Breyer, Stevens, JJ.). The need for settlement in this case is greater than the Court suggests. I would give more weight to settlement-related issues for purposes of determining whether common questions predominate. The Court should not second-guess the adequacy of representation without having the court of appeals consider it. I am uncertain about the tenor of the Court's opinion that suggests that the settlement is unfair. I cannot accept the majority's suggestion that notice is inadequate.

6. **Impleader.**

a. **In general.** Federal Rule of Civil Procedure 14 permits a party to join anyone who is or may be liable to the party for all or part of a claim against the party. The party seeking the joinder is a third-party plaintiff and the party joined is a third-party defendant.

b. **Claims by a plaintiff against third-party defendant are impermissible without independent jurisdiction.** A plaintiff may not assert a claim against a third-party defendant unless there is an independent basis for subject matter jurisdiction. The theory behind this rule is to prevent a plaintiff from doing indirectly something that the plaintiff could not have done directly. Since the plaintiff could not sue the third-party defendant directly without an independent jurisdictional basis, the plaintiff cannot sue the third party merely because he has been joined in the suit by the defendant.

1) **Plaintiff's claim against third party destroys diversity--Owen
Equipment & Erection Co. v. Kroger,** 437 U.S. 365 (1978).

a) **Facts.** James Kroger was electrocuted when the boom of a
steel crane next to which he was walking came too close to
a high-tension wire. Kroger (P), the decedent's widow,
filed a wrongful death action in federal district court against
the Omaha Public Power District (D1). Federal jurisdiction
was based on diversity because P was a citizen of Iowa. D1
then filed a third-party complaint against Owen Equipment
and Erection Company (D2), alleging that the crane was
owned and operated by D2. P amended her complaint
naming D2 as an additional defendant. D2 was incorporated in Nebraska and, due to a mistake of geography, was
initially believed to have its principal place of business
there. It was, however, actually located in Iowa. The district court granted D1's motion for summary judgment and
the case went to trial between P and D2 alone. D2 moved
to dismiss the action for lack of diversity jurisdiction. The
court denied the motion and the jury held for P. D2 appealed and the court of appeals affirmed. The Supreme
Court granted certiorari.

b) **Issue.** In an action in which federal jurisdiction is based on
diversity, may a plaintiff assert a claim against a third-party
defendant when this would destroy diversity and there is no
independent basis for federal jurisdiction?

c) **Held.** No. Judgment reversed.

(1) Section 1332 requires complete diversity between a
plaintiff and a defendant. It is clear that P could not
have originally brought suit in federal court naming
D2 and D1 as co-defendants, since citizens of Iowa
would have been on both sides of the litigation. Yet
the identical lawsuit resulted when she amended her
complaint.

(2) Complete diversity was destroyed just as surely as if
she had sued D2 initially.

d) **Dissent** (White, Brennan, JJ.). Once a claim has been
stated that is of sufficient substance to confer subject matter
jurisdiction on the federal district court, the court has judicial power to consider a nonfederal claim if it and the federal claim are derived, as in the present case, from a common nucleus of operative fact.

C. TRIAL

1. **In General.** The right to a jury trial in the federal court is preserved by the
Seventh Amendment to the United States Constitution. The Seventh
Amendment grants the right to jury trial in suits at common law (as it existed
in 1791) when the value in controversy exceeds $20. There is no right to

jury trial in equity suits because equity proceedings were not "suits at common law" at the time that the Seventh Amendment was adopted in 1791.

2. **Jury Trial in Suits Raising Both Legal and Equitable Claims.** When there are issues common to both the legal and equitable claims in the same action, the legal claim must first be tried by a jury. Even if the legal issue is raised in the context of a predominantly equitable proceeding, the legal issue must still be tried by a jury.

   a. **Legal relief incidental to equitable claim--Dairy Queen, Inc. v. Wood,** 369 U.S. 469 (1962).

   Dairy Queen, Inc. v. Wood

   1) **Facts.** The owners of the name "Dairy Queen" (Ps) sued a franchisee (D), in federal district court seeking temporary and permanent injunctions to restrain D from future use of Ps' trademark, an accounting to determine the exact amount of money owing by D and a judgment for that amount, and an injunction pending accounting to prevent D from collecting any money from Dairy Queen stores in the territory. D requested a jury trial, which the district court judge (Wood) denied. The court of appeals denied D's application for mandamus to compel the district court to grant D a jury trial. D contended that since Ps sought a money judgment, Ps' action was at law and D must be given its requested jury trial. Ps contended that their claim was purely "equitable," since it was framed in terms of an "accounting" rather than as an action for "debt" or "damages," and that any included legal claim was merely "incidental" to the equitable issues.

   2) **Issues.**

      a) Does a party lose its Seventh Amendment right to trial by jury in federal court when the legal issues are incidental to equitable issues?

      b) Does the framing of an issue in equitable terms make it equitable in nature?

   3) **Held.** a) No. b) No. Judgment reversed and remanded.

      a) *Beacon Theatres, Inc. v. Westover*, 359 U.S. 500 (1959), established the rule that when both legal and equitable claims coexist in a single case, "only under the most imperative circumstances" can a party's right to jury trial be lost through prior determination of equitable claims. A claim for a money judgment is a claim wholly legal in its nature, however the complaint is construed.

      b) The Federal Rules of Civil Procedure did not change the Supreme Court's holding in *Scott v. Neely*, 140 U.S. 106 (1891), that a party's right to trial by jury must be preserved; rather, Rule 38(a) expressly reaffirms the principle. If a legal issue exists in the instant case, the court must afford D a jury trial, even if such issue is merely incidental to existing equitable issues. Although Ps have framed their complaint in equitable terms of an "accounting," the part of the claim demanding money judgment is legal in nature and entitles D to a jury trial.

4) **Concurrence** (Harlan, Douglas, JJ.). The fact that an "accounting" is sought is not in itself dispositive of the jury trial issue. To render this aspect of the complaint truly "equitable" it must appear that the substantial claim is one cognizable only in equity or that the "accounts between the parties" are of such a "complicated nature" that they can be satisfactorily unraveled only by a court of equity.

5) **Comment.** In *Ross v. Bernhard, infra,* a shareholders' derivative suit, the Supreme Court, observing that legal claims are not transformed into equitable claims merely by being filed in a court of equity, declared that when parties join equitable and legal claims in the same action, they have a right to trial by jury on the legal claims that the court must not infringe either by trying the legal issues as incidental to the equitable ones or by court trial of a common issue shared by the claims. The Court has reemphasized this principle in many cases. The Court has also declared that the Seventh Amendment right to trial by jury depends on the true nature of the type of relief sought (*i.e.*, equitable or legal) and not on the form of the action. Finally, even though the Court in *Dairy Queen* specifically disapproved the practice of circumventing jury trials by first litigating equitable issues, it has given its approval to the use of bifurcated trials (*i.e.*, one trial for the legal issues and one for the equitable issues) in cases where this best serves the interests of the parties.

3. **Legal Claims Raised by an Equitable Procedure Tried by Jury.** Certain procedures such as declaratory judgment actions, interpleader, and shareholder derivative suits, could only be maintained in equity. If a legal claim is raised in such a historically equitable proceeding, the legal issue must still be tried by a jury.

Ross v.
Bernhard

a. **Shareholder derivative suits--Ross v. Bernhard,** 396 U.S. 531 (1970).

1) **Facts.** Shareholders (Ps) brought a shareholder derivative suit in federal court against the directors of their closed-end investment company. They contended that the company's brokers, Lehman Brothers, controlled the corporation through an illegally large representation on the corporation's board of directors, and that they used this control to extract excessive brokerage fees from the corporation. Ps demanded a jury trial on these claims. Considering this issue, the court of appeals held that in no event does the right to a jury trial under the Seventh Amendment extend to derivative actions brought by shareholders of a corporation. From this holding, Ps appeal.

2) **Issue.** Does the Seventh Amendment guarantee the right to a jury trial in shareholder derivative actions?

3) **Held.** Yes. Judgment reversed.

a) We hold that the right to jury trial attaches to those issues in derivative actions as to which the corporation, if it had been suing in its own right, would have been entitled to a jury.

b) In the instant case we have no doubt that the corporation's claim is, at least in part, a legal one. The corporation, had it sued on its own behalf, would have been entitled to a jury's determination of its damages against its broker under the brokerage contract and of its rights against its own directors because of their negligence.

4) **Dissent** (Stewart, J., Burger, C.J., Harlan, J.). In holding as it does that the plaintiff in a shareholder derivative suit is constitutionally entitled to a jury trial, the Court today seems to rely upon some sort of ill-defined combination of the Seventh Amendment and the Federal Rules of Civil Procedure. Somehow the Amendment and the Rules magically interact to do what each separately was intended expressly not to do, namely, to enlarge the right to a jury trial in civil actions brought in United States courts.

5) **Comment.** *Ross* was an important innovation in the right to jury trial problem, confronted previously in *Beacon Theatres* and *Dairy Queen*. *Ross* extended the right to jury trial to certain shareholder derivative actions, which historically could have only been brought in equity. Thus, *Ross* seems a necessary result from the doctrines espoused in *Beacon Theatres* and *Dairy Queen*, and it seems a result that should be reached in all situations in which a party is seeking relief that would by itself pose legal issues, but is doing so by a procedural device historically available solely in equity. The Court seems to indicate this in *Ross*, where it states "[N]othing turns now upon . . . the procedural devices by which the parties happen to come before the court."

4. **Collateral Estoppel Based on Finding in Equity Suit.** A litigant who has lost because of adverse factual findings in an equity action is equally deprived of a jury trial whether he is collaterally estopped from relitigating the factual issues against the same party or a new party. In either case, there is no further fact-finding function for the jury to perform, because the common factual issues have been resolved in the previous action.

a. **Offensive collateral estoppel--Parklane Hosiery Co. v. Shore,** 439 U.S. 322 (1979).

Parklane
Hosiery Co.
v. Shore

1) **Facts.** Shore and others (Ps) brought this shareholders' class action, alleging that Parklane (D) had issued a materially false and misleading proxy statement in connection with a merger in violation of the Securities Exchange Act. Before this action came to trial, the Securities and Exchange Commission ("SEC") filed suit against D, alleging essentially the same facts as Ps. The district court in the SEC action found that the proxy statement was materially false and misleading and entered a declaratory judgment to that effect. Ps, in the present case, then moved for partial summary judgment, asserting that D was collaterally estopped from relitigating the issues that had been resolved against it in the SEC action. The court denied the motion on the ground that such an application of collateral estoppel would deny D its Seventh Amendment right to a jury trial. The court of appeals reversed. D appeals.

2) **Issue.** Is a party who has had issues of fact adjudicated adversely to it in an equitable action collaterally estopped from relitigating the same issues before a jury in a subsequent legal action brought against it by a new party?

3) **Held.** Yes. Judgment of court of appeals affirmed.

    a)   This is known as offensive collateral estoppel. Under certain circumstances, offensive collateral estoppel is not allowed. However, these circumstances do not exist in the present case. Here the application of offensive collateral estoppel will not reward a private plaintiff who could have joined in the previous action, since Ps probably could not have joined in the SEC action. Also, there is no unfairness to D in applying collateral estoppel.

    b)   Therefore, since D received a full and fair opportunity to litigate its claim in the SEC action, it is collaterally estopped from relitigating the question of whether the proxy statements were materially false and misleading.

4) **Dissent** (Rehnquist, J.). The Court has reduced the right of trial by jury in civil cases to a mere neutral factor and in the name of procedural reform denies the right of jury trial to defendants in a vast number of cases in which defendants heretofore have enjoyed jury trials.

5. Evidence in Jury Trial.

    a. **Admissibility of evidence.** The admissibility of evidence is usually characterized as procedural. Therefore, *Erie Railroad v. Tompkins, supra,* does not require a federal court to follow state rules of evidence.

<table>
<tr><td>Conway v.
Chemical
Leaman Tank
Lines, Inc.</td><td>

1) **Federal Rules of Evidence govern--Conway v. Chemical Leaman Tank Lines, Inc.,** 540 F.2d 837 (5th Cir. 1976).

    a)   **Facts.** Conway (P), widow of the decedent, brought a wrongful death action in federal court against Chemical Leaman Tank Lines, Inc. (D) based on diversity of citizenship. In its appeal from a judgment for P, D claimed that the trial court erred by improperly refusing to permit reference to P's remarriage after her husband's death. At the time of trial, Federal Rule of Civil Procedure 43(a) provided that any evidence admissible in a Texas state court was admissible in this federal court. The relevant Texas statute provides that evidence of the actual ceremonial remarriage of the surviving spouse is admissible as evidence.

    b)   **Issue.** Is admissibility of evidence in federal court governed by the Federal Rules of Evidence rather than by state law?

    c)   **Held.** Yes. Judgment reversed and remanded.

        (1)   The policy of the new Rules of Evidence is one of broad admissibility, and the generous definition of "relevant evidence" in Rule 401 was specifically intended to provide that background evidence is admissible.

        (2)   Although the Rules do not deal specifically with proof of a surviving spouses's remarriage, their treatment of comparable issues suggests that the evidence is, as here, admissible for background and perhaps other limited purposes.

</td></tr>
</table>

b. **Sufficiency of evidence.** There is still confusion as to whether, in a diversity case, the sufficiency of the evidence to go to the jury is measured by a federal or state standard. The courts have, in addition, failed to agree on the appropriate standard to be used if in fact the federal measure of sufficiency of evidence is to be used.

1) **Federal or state standard--Wratchford v. S.J. Groves & Sons Co.,** 405 F.2d 1061 (4th Cir. 1969).

a) **Facts.** Wratchford, the plaintiff's (P's) conservatee, was found at the bottom of an open highway drainage hole, suffering from retrograde amnesia and a fractured skull. Extensive construction work had been underway on the road by S.J. Groves & Sons (D), and P claimed D was negligent in leaving an open, unprotected hole. Under Maryland law, if the evidence showed that an injury could have occurred with equal probability in each of two ways, only one of which was laid to the defendant's responsibility, it was the duty of the court to direct a verdict for the defendant. D contended that the circumstances gave rise to an inference of equal probability that Wratchford was crossing the road, slipped on the ice and snow, and either slid or crawled into the open hole. Because the district judge was of the opinion that the injury could have been sustained either way, he directed a verdict for D under his understanding of the Maryland rule. From his order, P appeals.

b) **Issue.** In the diversity jurisdiction of federal district court, are state standards to be applied by the court in determining the sufficiency of the evidence to go to the jury?

c) **Held.** No. Judgment reversed and remanded.

(1) A grave disruption of the federal system would result from the application of state law rules as to the sufficiency of evidence to go to the jury. Faith in the ability of a jury, selected from a cross-section of the community, to choose wisely among competing rational inferences in the resolution of factual questions lies at the heart of the federal judicial system.

(2) That faith requires consistency within the system and does not permit the accommodation of more restrictive state laws.

(3) The relevant question here, therefore, is not whether the judge is of the opinion that the evidence did not make it more probable that Wratchford stepped into the hole before his skull was fractured, but whether a jury might reasonably conclude from the evidence that he was injured after stepping into the hole D had negligently left uncovered.

(4) We conclude that the case should have been submitted to a jury under appropriate instructions as to D's negligence and its proximate relation to the injury.

XI. APPELLATE JURISDICTION AND PROCEDURE

A. THE COURT OF APPEALS

1. **Final Decision Rule.** Under 28 U.S.C. section 1291, the courts of appeals have jurisdiction over appeals from final decisions of the district courts.

   a. **Rationale behind the rule.** The primary rationale behind the final decision rule is to avoid appeals of issues that may become moot when viewed in the context of the entire litigation and to avoid delay and interference with the efficiency of trial process by allowing piecemeal review of trial court rulings.

   b. **Finality difficult to determine.** A judgment is deemed to be final when all that remains is the execution on the judgment. However, what constitutes a final decision is often difficult to determine. In addition, because a rigid application of the rule sometimes causes hardship, the Supreme Court and the Congress have created exceptions to the finality rule.

   Gulfstream Aerospace Corp. v. Mayacamas Corp.

   1) **Appealability of decision not to stay or dismiss federal court suit while state court suit is pending--Gulfstream Aerospace Corp. v. Mayacamas Corp., 485 U.S. 271 (1988).**

      a) **Facts.** Gulfstream Aerospace Corp. (P) agreed to manufacture a plane for sale to Mayacamas Corp. (D). When the plane was ready, D refused to pay P, alleging unfair trade practices. P filed suit for breach of contract in Georgia state court. D filed an answer and a counterclaim, as well as filing its own suit in federal court against P. P moved for a stay or dismissal of the federal court action because of the pending state court suit. The district court denied P's motion. P appealed the decision on three bases: (i) the decision was final; (ii) the order was an interlocutory one pertaining to an injunction; or (iii) the notice of appeal should be treated as an application for a writ of mandamus. The appellate court found no jurisdiction under the first two bases and declined to accept the notice of appeal as a writ of mandamus. P appeals.

      b) **Issue.** May a party immediately appeal a district court decision that denies a motion to stay or dismiss an action because there is a similar suit pending in state court?

      c) **Held.** No. Judgment affirmed.

         (1) P first argues that the court's order denying the motion to stay or dismiss is a collateral order. Collateral orders are permissible exceptions to the final judgment

rule and thus appealable under 28 U.S.C. section 1291. Collateral orders do not end the litigation, but are appealable. A collateral order exists if a three-prong test is met. The order must conclusively determine the disputed question. Second, the order must resolve an important issue completely separate from the merits of the action. Third, the order must effectively not be reviewable on appeal.

(2)   The order denying P's motion is not appealable because it does not meet the first prong of the collateral order test. Denial of an order that would stay or dismiss an action in federal court because of a pending state court proceeding does not conclusively resolve the disputed question. In denying the motion, the court might simply be reserving the question for some future date when the litigation has progressed further and the court has more information.

(3)   P next argues that the order is appealable under 28 U.S.C. section 1292(a)(1) as an appeal of an interlocutory order granting or denying an injunction. Under the *Enelow-Ettelson* doctrine, certain orders that stay or do not stay litigation are considered injunctions and are appealable. P argues that the order in this case fits within the *Enelow-Ettelson* doctrine.

(4)   This Court now believes that it is time to overturn the *Enelow-Ettelson* doctrine. The doctrine was formulated at a time when law and equity were two separate systems. With the merger of law and equity, the need for the rule no longer exists. As a consequence, P's reliance on this doctrine fails and the order is not appealable as an interlocutory order under section 1292(a)(1).

(5)   P's final argument is that the court of appeals should issue a writ of mandamus requiring the district court to vacate the order and grant its motion. P asserts that D's decision to file a separate suit in federal court rather than removing the state court case to federal court is sufficient reason for issuing a writ. This court disagrees with P's reasoning. A writ is an extraordinary remedy, which will be issued only if there is a usurpation of power by one court over another. The party seeking the writ must show that "issuance of the writ is clear and indisputable."

(6)   P has failed to meet the standard for issuance of a writ. P has not shown that the district court usurped its authority in not issuing a stay of the federal court proceedings. Deciding to file a federal suit rather than remove a state suit to federal court does not establish grounds for issuance. In light of the above, P's appeal is denied and the court of appeals is affirmed.

d)   **Concurrence** (Scalia, J.). With respect to P's argument that its motion is appealable as a collateral order, it is an oversimplification to give as a reason for denial that the order is inherently tentative. Other types of orders that have been considered final for purposes of immediate review are in fact subject to reconsideration at a later date. For cases like this where the basis for the requested stay is the pendency of state proceedings, the more general conclusion should be that denial of a stay is not immediately appealable. The collateral order exception should be subject to limiting principles so that, as the exception originally envisioned, review is available only for a small class of decisions too important to be denied review.

2. Final Decisions Involving Multiple Claims and/or Multiple Parties.
Federal Rule of Civil Procedure 54(b) provides for appeals in certain situations in suits involving either multiple claims and/or multiple parties.

a. Rule 54 gives district courts discretion to grant appeals of claims.
Rule 54(b) does not expand the definition of finality as required under 28 U.S.C. section 1291 because under 54(b) only otherwise "final" decisions can be appealed. Rule 54(b) recognizes that in some suits where there are multiple claims and/or parties, it may be a hardship to require parties, whose claims have been finally adjudicated before disposition of the entire proceeding, to wait until the entire proceeding is finally adjudicated. Rule 54(b) gives the district court the discretion to act as a dispatcher to the court of appeals for claims that have been finally decided when there is no just reason for delay of an appeal of these claims.

b. Requirements for certification.
In order to satisfy the requirement of Rule 54(b), the district court must determine that: (i) the decision is final; (ii) the certification for appeal will not result in unnecessary appellate review; (iii) the claims certified are sufficiently separate and distinct from the remaining claims; and (iv) it would cause undue hardship to delay immediate appeal of these otherwise final decisions.

B. EXCEPTIONS TO THE FINAL DECISION RULE

1. Statutory Exceptions.

a. Interlocutory decisions of the district courts.
Title 28 U.S.C. section 1292(a) authorizes appeals from: (i) orders granting, modifying or dissolving injunctions; (ii) interlocutory orders appointing receivers or refusing orders to wind up receiverships; and (iii) interlocutory decrees determining the rights and liabilities of parties to admiralty cases in which appeals from final decrees are allowed.

b. Certification on nonfinal orders.
In addition to 28 U.S.C. section 1292(a), the court of appeals, under 28 U.S.C. section 1292(b), has the discretion to review any interlocutory order if the district court states in writing that the order involves a controlling question of law as to which there is a substantial ground for difference of opinion, and that an immediate appeal may materially advance the ultimate termination of the litigation. The opinion of the district court judge that a controlling question is involved is not binding on the court of appeals under the section 1292(b) certification procedure. If the court of appeals determines that an interlocutory appeal will delay rather than shorten the litigation, the court of appeals will deny the certification.

Katz v. Carte Blanche Corp.

1) Certification of question arising from discretionary determination--Katz v. Carte Blanche Corp., 496 F.2d 747 (3d Cir. 1974).

a) **Facts.** Katz (P) brought a class action against Carte Blanche Corp. (D) for alleged violations of the Truth in Lending Act ("TILA"). The district court granted class action status over objection, but certified the question for appeal under 28 U.S.C. section 1292(b) since it involved (i) a controlling question of law, (ii) substantial grounds for difference of opinion, and (iii) if appealed immediately, it would materially advance termination of the litigation.

b) **Issue.** Can the certification of a question for appeal under 28 U.S.C. section 1292(b) as to class action status be prevented merely because the district court made the determination based on its discretion?

c) **Held.** No. Order reversed and case remanded.

(1) P contends that the question of appealability of a class action status determination under section 1292(b) is not available when the district court relied on its discretion in making the determination. However, this is not the law. The determination of what orders are properly reviewable cannot be made by a mechanical application of labels.

(2) The policies underlying the rule must be examined to prevent piecemeal litigation and wasted trial time. The certification of a class action requires an analysis of alternative methods of adjudication, fairness to all those involved, and the comparative efficiency of a class or individual action. And since these criteria involve questions of fact and law, discretion alone is not determinative.

(3) However, the district court erred in granting the class action because it would be more appropriate to allow P to first proceed individually to establish whether there was any violation of the TILA.

d) **Dissent** (Seitz, C.J.). The majority is correct in deciding that discretionary determinations are equally appealable, but there is a further question of whether the TILA implicitly prohibits maintenance of class actions to enforce its provisions. This is clearly a question of law that is appealable. However, because the district court applied the three criteria noted in section 1292(b) as to controlling question, difference of opinion, and advancement of termination of the litigation, its decision should not be reversed for abuse of discretion.

e) **Dissent** (Aldisert, J.). If factual determinations become issues of appealability, the appellate courts will be swamped with second-guessing class determinations rather than determining the "controlling question of law."

f) **Comment.** As an alternative to seeking certification to appeal a controlling question of law in an interlocutory order by the district court, the losing party may seek an "Appeal by Permission" under Rule 5 of the Federal Rules of Appellate Procedure. This section provides for the filing of a petition within 10 days after the entry of the district court's order. The petition must contain all the essential elements of 28 U.S.C. section 1292(b), and it must include copies of the underlying order with its findings and conclusions of law.

2. **Judicial Exceptions.**

   a. **An order is appealable if it affects important rights.** Some court decisions have demonstrated a willingness to give the finality requirement a practical construction. If the order affects important rights and, on balance, the need to hear the appeal immediately outweighs the reasons for delaying appellate review, the court of appeals will deem the order appealable under 28 U.S.C. section 1291.

Gillespie v.
United States
Steel Corp.

   1) **"Final decision" need not be last order possible--Gillespie v. United States Steel Corp.,** 379 U.S. 148 (1964).

      a) **Facts.** Mrs. Gillespie (P1) is the mother and administrator of the estate of Daniel Gillespie, who was killed in an accident while working aboard a ship belonging to United States Steel Corporation (D). P1 brought an action in the federal district court for herself and Daniel's brother (P2) and sisters (P3) under the Jones Act, a statute that subjects employers to liability for a seaman's death. However, on the motion of D, the district court judge held that the Jones Act supplied the exclusive remedy for P1, but that P2 and P3 must be stricken from the complaint since they were entitled to no recovery while P1 was living. Further, since the Jones Act was the exclusive remedy, the district court judge struck from the complaint all reference to an Ohio statute. P1 appealed. However, D moved to dismiss the appeal on the ground that the district court's ruling was not a "final decision" as required by 28 U.S.C. section 1291. Thereupon P1, now joined by P2 and P3, filed in the court of appeals a petition for mandamus commanding the district court judge to either vacate his original order and enter a new one denying the motion to strike, or grant the motion to strike but take the necessary steps under section 1292(b) to render the order appealable. However, the court of appeals did neither, but instead decided the controversy on the merits as the merits had been submitted on appeal. The court of appeals reasoned that it was free to take such action because its resolution of the merits did no prejudice to D. The United States Supreme Court granted P1's petition for writ of certiorari.

      b) **Issue.** In order to be a "final decision" within the meaning of 28 U.S.C. section 1291, must a decision be the last order possible to be made in the case?

      c) **Held.** No. Judgment affirmed on the merits.

         (1) A final decision does not necessarily mean the last order possible to be made in the case but rather is a practical, rather than technical, decision arrived at by balancing the competing interests. In fact, it is often impossible, in close cases, to devise a formula to resolve all marginal cases that fall within the "twilight zone" of finality.

         (2) Therefore we should balance the inconvenience and costs of piecemeal review on one hand, against the danger of denying justice by delay on the other.

(3) In the instant case it seems clear that, if we now decide the final issue: (i) the cost to all parties will be less; and (ii) P2 and P3 will be saved the burden of otherwise having to wait a number of years to have their rights in this matter decided.

d) **Dissent in part** (Goldberg, J.). I agree that this case is properly here, but disagree with the Court on the merits of the basic question presented for decision.

e) **Dissent** (Harlan, J.). This decision is a striking example of piecemeal litigation of the issues in a lawsuit—the very vice that section 1291 was intended to avoid. The decision of the district court, affirmed by the majority, surely lacked the essential quality of finality since the issues here decided had not even been tried.

b. **Collateral orders may be appealable.** Some cases involve procedural matters that are not directly related to the substantive issues presented in the litigation. An order on a collateral issue may constitute a final decision on that issue and, if so, the order is generally appealable if appellate review does not require the appellate court to determine the other pending issues of the litigation.

C. THE SUPREME COURT

1. **Congress May Limit the Appellate Jurisdiction of the Supreme Court.** The Constitution is both a grant and a limitation on federal jurisdiction. No federal court, including the Supreme Court, can exercise jurisdiction that is beyond the limits set out in Article III, Section 2, of the United States Constitution.

a. **The repeal of an act giving the Supreme Court jurisdiction divests the court of that jurisdiction--*Ex Parte* McCardle,** 7 Wall. (74 U.S.) 506 (1868). *Ex Parte* McCardle

1) **Facts.** McCardle (D) was a civilian newspaper editor who was taken into military custody for alleged libelous news articles. D was brought before a military commission pursuant to Civil War Reconstruction Statutes. Upon a hearing, D was remanded to military custody and allowed to appeal to the Supreme Court under the Act of 1867. This Act granted to the federal courts power to issue writs of habeas corpus in all cases where a person may be restrained of his liberty in violation of the Constitution or any treaty or law of the United States from which appeal could be taken to the Supreme Court. The Supreme Court granted jurisdiction for an appeal on the merits. However, while the appeal was pending, Congress passed another Act in 1868 that repealed the 1867 Act. Consequently, the Supreme Court dismissed the appeal for lack of jurisdiction.

2) **Issue.** Does the Constitution grant to Congress the power to affect the appellate jurisdiction of the Supreme Court and thus deprive the Court of jurisdiction?

3) **Held.** Yes. The appeal is dismissed.

    a) Although the appellate jurisdiction of the Supreme Court is not derived from acts of Congress, but is conferred by the Constitution, it is conferred with such exceptions and under such regulations as Congress shall make. Thus the effect of the repealing act on the case at bar is to deny to the Supreme Court jurisdiction in habeas corpus cases.

    b) When an act of the legislature is repealed, it must be considered, except as to transactions past and closed, as if it never existed.

    c) The effect of repealing acts upon suits under acts repealed is that no judgment can be rendered. Therefore, it is clear that this Court cannot proceed to pronounce judgment, for it no longer has jurisdiction of the appeal.

4) **Comment.** In the case at bar the Supreme Court considered it immaterial that the repealing act was passed after the Court had already taken jurisdiction. Although the *McCardle* case is usually interpreted as granting to Congress full power over the appellate jurisdiction of the Supreme Court, there has been some suggestion that this might be too broad an interpretation. That is to say, it is argued that this broad power of Congress does not extend to such exceptions as might destroy the primary functions of the Supreme Court in the constitutional scheme. Reinforcing this suggestion is the fact that shortly after the *McCardle* case, it was held in *Ex Parte Yerger* that review of cases such as *McCardle* might be accomplished under the Supreme Court's power to issue original writs of habeas corpus and certiorari.

2. Appellate Jurisdiction of the Supreme Court.

    a. **Scope.** The appellate jurisdiction of the Supreme Court was significantly changed in 1988 by amendments to title 28 U.S.C. The effect of these amendments was to make review in the Supreme Court discretionary in virtually all cases. Before the amendments, title 28 provided, in general, for direct appeals to the Supreme Court of: (i) Any federal court decision invalidating an act of Congress in an action in which the United States is a party [§1252]; (ii) Any federal court of appeals decision holding unconstitutional a state statute on which a party has relied [§1254(2)]; and (iii) Any state supreme court decision finding, when its validity was questioned, a federal law unconstitutional or a state law constitutional [§§1257(1), (2)]. The 1988 amendments repealed all of the above sections. Thus, most Supreme Court review is now by writ of certiorari. An exception exists for decisions granting or denying injunctions in actions required to be heard by a three-judge federal district court. Also, provision is made for the courts of appeals to certify questions of law to the Supreme Court.

    b. **Finality in the Supreme Court.** The Supreme Court has appellate jurisdiction over final judgments or decrees of the highest court of the state in which a decision could be had. However, there are times when it is not feasible to wait for a final decision. For example, there are cases in which an important right may be destroyed if a party is not able to secure immediate review. In other cases, the issue that needs review is capable of being separated from the rest of the case and prompt review will prevent the entire trial court proceeding from being held in abeyance. For these reasons, as well as others, the decisions of the Supreme Court concerning the finality issue are not altogether harmonious. Indeed the Court has stated that there is not even a sure test as to what constitutes a final decision that can be applied universally to all cases.

1) **Jurisdiction when state supreme court rules, but returns case to lower court--** Cox Broad-
Cox Broadcasting Corp. v. Cohn, 420 U.S. 469 (1975). casting Corp.
v. Cohn

    a) **Facts.** Cox Broadcasting Corporation (D), reporting on the court proceedings in a prosecution for rape, gave the name of the rape victim, which it had learned from public records. Cohn (P), the rape victim's father, sued D for damages for invasion of privacy under a Georgia statute that made it a misdemeanor to publish or broadcast the name of a rape victim. D claimed that its use of the name was privileged under the First and Fourteenth Amendments. The trial court gave summary judgment for P. D appealed, and the Georgia Supreme Court held that the Georgia statute was inapplicable since it created no civil cause of action. Consequently it need not consider the issue of the constitutionality of the statute. Instead, it reversed the summary judgment, holding that P had a common law tort claim for invasion of privacy and that the trier of fact must determine whether the public disclosure of the daughter's name actually invaded the father's privacy. On rehearing, the Georgia trial court relied on the misdemeanor statute as an authoritative declaration of state policy and held that the name of a rape victim is not a matter of public concern. It then held that the Georgia statute was a legitimate limitation on the First Amendment right of freedom of expression. D appealed to the Supreme Court, invoking jurisdiction under 28 U.S.C. section 1257, which stated that the Court's appellate jurisdiction with respect to state litigation can be granted only after the highest state court in which judgment could be had has rendered a final judgment or decree.

    b) **Issues.**

        (1) When the highest state court has ruled on a constitutional issue in an action and returned the case to a lower state court for further proceedings, has a "final judgment or decree" been issued that will satisfy the requirements for United States Supreme Court jurisdiction?

        (2) Does the Constitution bar a civil action against the press for publishing true information disclosed in public documents open to public inspection?

    c) **Held.** (1) Yes. (2) Yes. Judgment reversed.

        (1) Although the ultimate issue was one of the constitutionality of civil actions against the press, this Court must resolve two questions of jurisdiction arising under 28 U.S.C. section 1257. First, was the constitutional validity of the Georgia statute drawn into issue and upheld by the Georgia Supreme Court? Second, was the decision from which this appeal has been taken a final judgment or decree?

(2) Historically, this Court has appellate jurisdiction with respect to state litigation only after the highest state court in which judgment could be had has rendered a final judgment or decree. However, there are cases in which the highest state court has finally determined the federal issue present, but in which there are further proceedings in lower state courts. In these cases the Supreme Court has taken jurisdiction, and such is the case at bar.

(3) Consequently, we conclude that this Court has jurisdiction to review the judgment of the Georgia Supreme Court rejecting the challenge under the First and Fourteenth Amendments to the state law authorizing damage suits against the press for publishing the name of a rape victim whose identity is revealed in the course of a public prosecution.

(4) The Georgia Supreme Court's judgment is plainly final on the federal issue and is not subject to further review in the state courts. Although the trial court's decision as to which party might prevail is still unsettled, if the Georgia Supreme Court erroneously upheld the statute, there should be no trial at all.

(5) Moreover, delaying final decision of the First Amendment claim after trial will leave unanswered an important question of freedom of the press that could only further harm the operation of a free press. Given these factors, that the litigation could be terminated by a decision on the merits now and that a failure to decide the issue will leave the operation of the press in Georgia hampered by civil and criminal sanctions, this Court finds it necessary to reach the merits.

(6) On the merits this Court holds that the Constitution bars a civil action against the press for publishing true information disclosed in public court documents open to public inspection.

d) Dissent (Rehnquist, J.). The decision that is the subject of this appeal is not a final judgment as that term is used in 28 U.S.C. section 1257. The appeal should be dismissed for want of jurisdiction. The finality requirement should not be disturbed, except in very few situations, where intermediate rulings may carry serious public consequences. The Court here, far from eschewing a constitutional holding in advance of the necessity for one, construes section 1257 so that it may virtually rush out and meet the prospective constitutional litigant as he approaches our doors.

Jefferson v. City of Tarrant, Alabama

2) No jurisdiction when state supreme court rules on interlocutory appeal-- Jefferson v. City of Tarrant, Alabama, 522 U.S. 75 (1997).

a) Facts. Alberta Jefferson, an African-American woman, died in a fire in her home. The survivors of Alberta Jefferson (Ps) sued the city of Tarrant, Alabama (D) under state law for wrongful death and the common law tort of outrage. Ps also sued D under 42 U.S.C. section1983, alleging that the death resulted from racial discrimination in the selective denial of fire protection to minorities. D moved for judgment on the pleadings on the section 1983 claims and for summary judgment on all claims. The state court denied the summary judgment motion in its entirety and it denied in part the motion for judgment on the pleadings. As to the latter motion, the court ruled that notwithstanding the punitive damages only limitation in the state Wrongful Death

Act, Ps could recover compensatory damages upon proof that D violated Alberta Jefferson's constitutional rights. On interlocutory appeal, the Alabama Supreme Court reversed and remanded the case. The United States Supreme Court granted certiorari.

b) **Issue.** Can the Supreme Court review an interlocutory order of a state court?

c) **Held.** No. Writ of certiorari dismissed.

   (1) The Alabama Supreme Court decision affected only two of the four counts in the complaint.

   (2) Resolution of the state law claims could effectively moot the federal law question. If D prevails on the facts, then the federal law claim necessarily fails.

   (3) If the Alabama Supreme Court's decision on the federal claim ultimately makes a difference to Ps, they will be free to seek review once the state court litigation comes to an end.

   (4) A state court decision is not final until it has effectively determined the entire litigation.

d) **Dissent** (Stevens, J.). In *Pennsylvania v. Ritchie*, 480 U.S. 39 (1987), this court held that a judgment of the Pennsylvania Supreme Court resolving a federal question was final even though the federal question could have been relitigated in the state court if the appeals had been dismissed, and even though it could have been raised in a second appeal to this Court after conclusion of further proceedings in the state courts. Although I would prefer to overrule *Ritchie*, since *Ritchie* is still the law, it requires us to take jurisdiction and reach the merits.

c. **Timeliness in raising the federal question.** The question of the timeliness in raising a federal issue is left primarily to regulation by a state's own rules of procedure. A party's failure to raise such questions as required by state law can preclude review, unless the state rules disallow a fair opportunity to be heard or deliberately evade consideration of the federal question. It is thus wise procedure to bring to the fore the federal question at each and every stage of the proceedings. This avenue of caution prevents such mistakes as raising a federal question in the trial court but not preserving it as an issue on appeal. However, it must always be kept in mind that should the highest state court consider a federal question, it is reviewable by the Supreme Court no matter at what stage of the proceedings it is first initiated.

1) **Timeliness of issue raised in petition for rehearing--Herndon v. Georgia,** 295 U.S. 441 (1935).

Herndon v. Georgia

   a) **Facts.** Herndon (D) was convicted under section 56 of the Georgia Penal Code of an attempt to incite insurrection and sentenced to a term of imprisonment. D was convicted after a charge by the trial court that to incur a verdict of guilty he must have advocated violence with the intent that his advocacy would be acted upon immediately and with reasonable grounds for the expectation that the intent would be fulfilled. Upon appeal from the judgment of conviction, the Georgia Supreme Court repudiated the trial court's construction of section 56 and substituted another interpretation. D then moved for a rehearing on the ground that the substituted meaning made the statute unconstitutional and, in connection with that motion, invoked the protection of the Fourteenth Amendment. A rehearing was denied and the Georgia Supreme Court again construed the statute and again rejected the trial court's interpretation. D appeals to the United States Supreme Court, renewing his contention that the substituted meaning makes the statute unconstitutional.

b) **Issue.** Was the federal question invoking the Fourteenth Amendment upon petition for rehearing made in a timely fashion, enabling the Supreme Court to exercise jurisdiction?

c) **Held.** No. Appeal dismissed for want of jurisdiction.

   (1) The long-established general rule is that the attempt to raise a federal question after judgment, upon a petition for rehearing, comes too late unless the court actually entertains the question and decides it.

   (2) D, however, contends that the present case falls within an exception to the rule, namely, that the question respecting the validity of the statute as applied by the lower court first arose from its unanticipated act in giving the statute a new construction that threatened rights under the Constitution. There is no doubt that the federal claim was timely, if the ruling of the state court could not have been anticipated and a petition for rehearing presented the first opportunity for raising it.

   (3) However, prior to the action of the trial court on the motion for a new trial, the Georgia Supreme Court had decided *Carr v. State* in which the statute in question was construed in like manner to the case at bar. Consequently, Herndon was bound to anticipate the probability of a similar ruling in his own case.

   (4) It therefore follows that Herndon's contention that he raised the federal question at the first opportunity is without substance.

d) **Dissent** (Cardozo, Brandeis, Stone, JJ.). The settled doctrine is that when a constitutional privilege or immunity has been denied for the first time by a ruling made on appeal, a litigant thus surprised may challenge the unexpected ruling by a motion for rehearing and the challenge will be timely made. In this case, the protection of the Constitution was seasonably invoked and the Court should proceed to adjudicate the merits of the case. Herndon came into the highest court of Georgia without notice that the statute defining his offense was to be given a new meaning. He was under no duty to put before the state court the possibility of a definition less favorable to himself, especially since the trial court had predicated its decision on a prior opinion of the Georgia Supreme Court. Therefore, Herndon could wait until the law of this case had been rejected by the reviewing court before asserting his constitutional rights on a petition for rehearing.

d. **Federal and nonfederal grounds.**

1) **Uncertainty as to basis for decision.** If the Supreme Court cannot determine the grounds for the state court decision, the Supreme Court can either issue a writ of certiorari or remand the case for clarification.

3. **Adequate State Grounds Bar Review by Supreme Court.** An adequate and independent state ground is a bar to Supreme Court review.

a. **Supreme Court may review if basis not clear--Michigan v. Long,** 463 U.S. 1032 (1983).

Michigan v. Long

1) **Facts.** Long (D) was convicted of possession of marijuana by a Michigan Circuit Court after the court denied D's motion to suppress marijuana seized from his car. Two officers had stopped to investigate after D swerved into a ditch. The officers observed a knife on the floorboard and, after shining a light into the interior of the vehicle to search for other weapons, found a pouch of marijuana under the armrest. D was then arrested and the officers found more marijuana in the trunk. The Michigan Court of Appeals affirmed D's conviction but the Michigan Supreme Court reversed, holding the search invalid. The United States Supreme Court granted certiorari.

2) **Issue.** May the United States Supreme Court review a state court's decision if it is not clear from the face of the opinion that the decision was based on an independent state law ground?

3) **Held.** Yes. Decision reversed and remanded.

a) When the adequacy and independence of any possible state law ground is not clear from the face of the state court's decision, the United States Supreme Court will accept as the most reasonable explanation that the state court decided the case the way it did because it believed that federal law required it to do so.

b) In this case, apart from two citations to the state constitution, the Michigan Supreme Court relied exclusively on its understanding of *Terry v. Ohio,* 392 U.S. 1 (1968), and other federal cases. Even if it is accepted that the Michigan Constitution has been interpreted to provide independent protection for certain rights also secured under the Fourth Amendment, it fairly appears that the Michigan court rested its decision primarily on federal law, and therefore the United States Supreme Court may review its decision.

4) **Dissent** (Stevens, J.).

a) The state law ground is clearly adequate to support the judgment, because the Michigan Supreme Court expressly stated that the judgment was based on both the United States and the Michigan Constitutions. The more difficult question is whether it is independent. In pursuit of efficient use of resources, two approaches are available to this Court: it may presume that the state grounds either (i) are or (ii) are not independent unless it clearly appears otherwise. The presumption chosen by the Court—that the state grounds are not independent—goes against the historical presumption against taking jurisdiction in cases based on both state and federal grounds.

b) In this case, Michigan has arrested one of its citizens and the Michigan Supreme Court has decided to turn him loose. The primary role of this Court is to make sure that persons who seek to vindicate federal rights have been heard. There is no claim that D has been mistreated; the final outcome of state processes offends no federal interest whatever. Until recently, this Court had virtually no interest in this type of case. The only reason the majority offers for asserting authority over these cases—"an important need for uniformity in federal law"—is no less present when an adequate and independent state ground exists, and we have never claimed jurisdiction to correct such errors.

Florida v.
Meyers

b. Remand by intermediate state court--Florida v. Meyers, 466 U.S. 380 (1984).

1) **Facts.** At his trial in a Florida state court on sexual battery charges, the accused (D) moved to suppress evidence seized in a second search of his automobile eight hours after it had been impounded in a locked, secure area. The motion was denied and D was convicted. The Florida District Court of Appeal reversed, holding that even though the accused conceded that the initial search of his automobile was valid, the second search violated the Fourth Amendment, and it remanded for a new trial. The Florida Supreme Court denied the State's (P's) petition for discretionary review. The United States Supreme Court granted certiorari.

2) **Issue.** Does a state intermediate appellate court's decision remanding a case for a new trial on the ground that the defendant's constitutional rights were violated constitute a final judgment reviewable by the United States Supreme Court?

3) **Held.** Yes. Judgment reversed.

a) A state court's decision constitutes a final judgment reviewable by the United States Supreme Court even though the state court remands the case for a new trial after holding that a warrantless search violated the Fourth Amendment, when if the state loses, governing state law prohibits it from presenting the federal claim for review, and if the state wins, the issue will be moot.

b) A second warrantless search of an impounded vehicle, locked in a secure area about eight hours after D's arrest and after a concededly valid search of the vehicle that resulted in the seizure of evidence, does not violate the Fourth Amendment merely because the car had been impounded and immobilized.

4) **Dissent** (Stevens, Brennan, Marshall, JJ.). Certiorari should be denied. First, the law is settled in this area. Second, the majority seems to extend *Michigan v. Long* unnecessarily. *Long* creates a presumption of jurisdiction when the state decision rests primarily on or is interwoven with federal law. But here the second error found by the Florida court, involving the scope of

cross-examination, does not involve federal law, and jurisdiction should be denied. The majority, however, implies that state courts must expressly state that there are no federal grounds, even when it is clearly a state law decision. Third, granting certiorari shows a lack of confidence in the ability of state judges to rule on Fourth Amendment issues. Fourth, this will increase the number of certiorari petitions, leaving us with less time for our primary responsibilities. Fifth, the trend shows a disregard for the basic role of the Court; to protect the individual against oppression by the federal or state governments.

4. **If State Grounds Are Inadequate, Supreme Court May Review.** When the state ground is considered to be inadequate, Supreme Court review is not barred.

a. **Procedural grounds inadequate--National Association for the Advancement of Colored People v. Alabama *ex rel*. Flowers,** 377 U.S. 288 (1964).

1) **Facts.** The Attorney General of Alabama (P) filed suit against the National Association for the Advancement of Colored People (D) to oust it from the state, alleging that D failed to comply with Alabama statutes for doing business in the state. P obtained an ex parte restraining order barring D from conducting any business within Alabama and from taking any steps to qualify to do business under state law. Then the court issued a contempt order against D for failure to produce records and membership lists. The Alabama Supreme Court refused to review the contempt order. On appeal to the United States Supreme Court, D obtained a reversal of the contempt order, which the Alabama Supreme Court, on remand, proceeded to affirm again. Unable to obtain a hearing on the merits in the Alabama courts, D attempted to gain a hearing about the initial restraining order in a federal district court. The district court dismissed the action on the ground that the case should initially be litigated in the state courts. The court of appeals agreed, but vacated the judgment and remanded the case to the district court to deal with those issues pertaining to D's constitutional claims, leaving the other issues to be decided by the appropriate state courts. On appeal, the Supreme Court vacated the judgment and remanded the case to the court of appeals with the instructions to have the district court proceed to trial on the issues. After five years had elapsed, D was given a hearing in the Montgomery County Circuit Court, which permanently enjoined D from doing any further business in Alabama. D appealed to the Alabama Supreme Court, which affirmed the judgment without considering the merits, relying wholly on procedural grounds related to formal defects in D's brief. The United States Supreme Court granted certiorari.

2) **Issue.** May constitutional rights be thwarted by simply reciting that there has not been observance of a procedural rule that is novel in its application?

3) **Held.** No. Judgment reversed.

a) We consider first the nonfederal basis of the decision of the Alabama Supreme Court, which is asserted by the State as a barrier to consideration of the constitutionality of D's ouster from Alabama. The Alabama Supreme Court based its decision entirely on the asserted failure of D's brief to conform to rules of the court that unrelated assignments of error not be argued together. Indeed, the sole basis mentioned in the state court's opinion was that these errors were grouped together simply because of the numbering of subdivisions. The numbering was a mere stylistic device that cannot be regarded as detracting from the brief's full conformity with the rule in question.

b)   Furthermore, the Alabama courts have not heretofore applied their rules respecting the preparation of briefs with the pointless severity shown here. Novelty in procedural requirements cannot be permitted to thwart review in this Court applied for by those who, in justified reliance upon prior decisions, seek vindication in state courts of their federal constitutional rights.

c)   The State has urged that if the nonfederal procedural ground relied on be found inadequate, the case be remanded to the Alabama Supreme Court for decision on the merits.

d)   While this is the usual procedure, in view of what has gone before, we reject that contention and proceed to the merits.

e)   It is held that the suppression of the activities of D accomplished by the order below was a serious abridgement of the right to freedom of association of the members and that there was no legitimate governmental objective requiring such a restraint.

4)   **Comment.** The problem of the state courts attempting to evade the mandates of the Supreme Court was particularly apparent in the case at bar. Normally the Supreme Court does not specifically mandate the action a state should follow. Instead, the Court will remand a case to the state court for proceedings not inconsistent with the Supreme Court's opinion. However, if a litigant does not agree that the subsequent state court decision is consistent with the Supreme Court opinion, the Court can review the state court decision and for a second time reverse it and remand. The Court can also issue a writ of mandamus requiring that the state court conform its decision to the Supreme Court's previous opinion.

XII. ORIGINAL JURISDICTION OF THE SUPREME COURT

A. SUITS BY THE UNITED STATES AGAINST A STATE

The Supreme Court has original, but not exclusive, jurisdiction in suits by the United States against a state.

1. **Action to Determine State's Claim of Territory--United States v. Texas,** 143 U.S. 621 (1892).

   United States
   v. Texas

   a. **Facts.** An Act of Congress establishing a temporary government for the territory of Oklahoma provided that the Act would not apply to an area known as Greer County until title to that land was adjudicated to be in the United States and not in Texas. The Act directed the attorney general of the United States to prosecute a suit in equity in the United States Supreme Court to determine title. The state of Texas filed a demurrer to this action, arguing that the question presented is political in character and not susceptible to jurisdiction in the Supreme Court or any federal court, and that an action to recover real property is in fact legal, not equitable, in nature, and thus the Act directing a suit in equity to be brought is unconstitutional and void.

   b. **Issue.** Does the United States Supreme Court have original jurisdiction over a suit brought by the United States against a state for the purposes of determining title to property claimed by both parties?

   c. **Held.** Yes. Demurrer overruled.

      1) It cannot be claimed that a question involving a boundary dispute between the United States and a state is of a political nature and not capable of judicial determination.

      2) The important question, therefore, is whether the Court can, under the Constitution, take original jurisdiction of this case. Texas claims none exists and that disputes must be resolved by agreement of the parties. This is unwarranted under the Constitution since it cannot be doubted that the national courts have jurisdiction over cases in which the United States is a party, for, without this right, the sovereignty would be at the mercy of the states.

      3) The Constitution gives to the judiciary of the United States all cases, in law and equity, in which the United States is a party. Further, the Supreme Court is given original jurisdiction in all cases in which a state is a party. In all other cases in which the United States has judicial power, the Supreme Court shall have appellate jurisdiction.

      4) It is clear that one class of cases over which the Court has power depends on the character of the cause, whoever the parties, and in other instances on the character of the parties, whatever the cause. This case comes within both, as a case in law or equity and also as one in which the United States is a party. Thus, it is one to which the judicial power extends.

5) By the Revised Statutes, the Supreme Court is given exclusive jurisdiction of all cases where a state is a party, except criminal cases, cases between a state and a citizen or between a state and a citizen of another state in which case it has original, but not exclusive, jurisdiction.

6) Thus, in cases involving a suit between the United States against a state, the circuit court does not have jurisdiction. This exclusive jurisdiction was given to afford the dignity of a state to the sovereignty in cases in which it is a party. The original jurisdiction given the Supreme Court in cases in which a state is a party does not depend on whether the state is a plaintiff or a defendant. It is said, however, that this refers only to suits in which a state is a party and the other party is also a state or a foreign state. This cannot be correct for it is conceded that a state can bring an original suit in this Court against a citizen or another state.

7) We cannot assume that the Framers of the Constitution, in extending the judicial power of the United States to cases between two states, intended to exempt cases between the United States and a state. It would be difficult to suggest a reason why this Court should be able to determine a boundary dispute between two states and not have jurisdiction to decide the same case between a state and the United States. Texas is called to the bar of this Court by another sovereign, but both are subject to the supreme law of the land, which does no violence to the nature of the sovereignty. When Texas was admitted to the Union it consented to the provision of the Constitution extending the judicial power to all cases in law and equity in which the United States is a party. Thus, the demurrer is overruled.

d. **Dissent** (Fuller, C.J., Lamar, J.). The Court has original jurisdiction over two classes of cases only: (i) those affecting ambassadors, other public ministers, and consuls, and (ii) those in which a state is a party. The judicial power extends to cases between two states, between a state and the citizens of another state, and between a state and a foreign state. Controversies in which the United States is a party are not included in the grant of original jurisdiction.

e. **Comment.** To have held other than it did would have meant that the Supreme Court possibly could be denied jurisdiction altogether in those cases involving the United States and a state and involving only state law questions. The primary rationale behind the Court's decision rests on a fundamental concept of federalism, namely that each state, while supreme unto itself, yields to the sovereignty of the United States and its judicial system.

B. SUITS BY A STATE AGAINST ANOTHER STATE

When the sovereign rights of a state are damaged by another state, it may invoke the original jurisdiction of the Supreme Court.

1. **In General.** The original jurisdiction of the Supreme Court does not cover every case to which a state is a party, but only those controversies within the judicial power as defined in Article III, Section 2. Thus, when a state brings suit against one of its own citizens, the case does not involve the original jurisdiction of the Supreme Court. The Supreme Court has also held that its original jurisdiction is restricted to civil cases.

2. **Supreme Court as the Only Appropriate Forum.** In certain suits by one state against another state, the Supreme Court, because of its superiority over all other courts, may be the only appropriate forum to hear such cases.

3. **Original Jurisdiction When the Parties Are Two States--Wyoming v. Oklahoma,** 502 U.S. 437 (1992).

   Wyoming v. Oklahoma

   a. **Facts.** Oklahoma (D) passed a law that required that plants producing electricity to be sold in Oklahoma and that used coal to generate the electricity must use coal that contained at least 10% of Oklahoma coal. Wyoming (P) brought suit in the United States Supreme Court requesting a permanent injunction against the law's enforcement because the law was per se a Commerce Clause violation. D filed a motion to dismiss based on P's lack of standing. A special master reported that P had standing and that a Commerce Clause violation existed.

   b. **Issue.** Does P have standing to come within the original jurisdiction of the United States Supreme Court?

   c. **Held.** Yes. Findings of the special master accepted.

      1) D first argues that a state is denied standing when actions taken by government agencies injure the state's economy and cause an overall decline in revenues. However, this argument fails here because P has suffered a direct injury. P, as a result of this law, faces a loss of severance taxes on coal that Oklahoma utilities would have purchased except for the Act.

      2) D further argues that P lacks standing because it does not participate in the sale of coal as a vendor or purchaser and therefore suffers no direct injury. However, the law could result in less severance taxes charged to Wyoming vendors of coal and therefore a decrease in state revenues. This decrease is a sufficient financial nexus to establish direct injury to P, and therefore standing exists.

      3) Additionally, D argues that P's loss is de minimis and therefore its injury slight because the loss of revenues from the severance tax has been less than 1% of the total taxes collected. However, P's loss is more than de minimis because the law interferes with P's ability to collect severance taxes. The ability to collect severance or any other kind of tax is a function of the state in its sovereign capacity and cannot be limited by the act of another sovereign state. As the Act limits P's ability to collect taxes, it is invalid.

      4) D also argues that other parties, besides P, could bring suit against enforcement of the Act. However, Wyoming mining companies have chosen not to sue under the Commerce Clause; thus there is no pending

action to which this court could defer adjudication. Further, such a suit may not adequately represent P's interests. Therefore P has standing to sue D.

    d.   **Dissent** (Scalia, J., Rehnquist, C.J., Thomas, J.). There has never been a shortage of suits brought by private parties in "negative Commerce Clause" actions. It is a major step to recognize a state's standing to bring such an action on the basis of its consequential loss of tax revenue and I think it is wrong.

    e.   **Dissent** (Thomas, J., Rehnquist, C.J., Scalia, J.). Even if I believed that P had standing, which I do not, I would decline to exercise the Court's original jurisdiction. Original jurisdiction should be invoked sparingly. The primary dispute here is not between the states but between Wyoming mining companies and D. An economic burden imposed by one state on another state's taxpayers frequently affects the other state. Under today's opinion a state that can show any loss in tax revenue, even a de minimis loss, that can be traced to the action of another state can proceed directly to this Court. The implications are both sweeping and troubling.

TABLE OF CASES

(Page Numbers of Briefed Cases in Bold)

NOTES

Publications Catalog

Publishers of America's Most Popular Legal Study Aids!

All Titles Available At Your Law School Bookstore.

Gilbert Law Summaries are the best selling outlines in the country, and have set the standard for excellence since they were first introduced more than twenty-five years ago. It's Gilbert's unique combination of features that makes it the one study aid you'll turn to for all your study needs!

Accounting and Finance for Lawyers
Professor Thomas L. Evans, University of Texas

Basic Accounting Principles; Definitions of Accounting Terms; Balance Sheet; Income Statement; Statement of Changes in Financial Position; Consolidated Financial Statements; Accumulation of Financial Data; Financial Statement Analysis.
ISBN: 0-15-900382-2   Pages: 232 $19.95

Administrative Law
By Professor Michael R. Asimow, U.C.L.A.

Separation of Powers and Controls Over Agencies; (including Delegation of Power) Constitutional Right to Hearing (including Liberty and Property Interests Protected by Due Process, and Rulemaking- Adjudication Distinction); Adjudication Under Administrative Procedure Act (APA); Formal Adjudication (including Notice, Discovery, Burden of Proof, Finders of Facts and Reasons); Adjudicatory Decision Makers (including Administrative Law Judges (ALJs), Bias, Improper Influences, Ex Parte Communications, Familiarity with Record, Res Judicata); Rulemaking Procedures (including Notice, Public Participation, Publication, Impartiality of Rulemakers, Rulemaking Record); Obtaining Information (including Subpoena Power, Privilege Against Self-incrimination, Freedom of Information Act, Government in Sunshine Act, Attorneys' Fees); Scope of Judicial Review; Reviewability of Agency Decisions (including Mandamus, Injunction, Sovereign Immunity, Federal Tort Claims Act); Standing to Seek Judicial Review and Timing.
ISBN: 0-15-900000-9   Pages: 306 $20.95

Agency and Partnership
By Professor Richard J. Conviser, Chicago Kent

Agency: Rights and Liabilities Between Principal and Agent (including Agent's Fiduciary Duty, Right to Indemnification); Contractual Rights Between Principal (or Agent) and Third Persons (including Creation of Agency Relationship, Authority of Agent, Scope of Authority, Termination of Authority, Ratification, Liability on Agents, Contracts); Tort Liability (including Respondeat Superior, Master-Servant Relationship, Scope of Employment). Partnership: Property Rights of Partner; Formation of Partnership; Relations Between Partners (including Fiduciary Duty); Authority of Partner to Bind Partnership; Dissolution and Winding up of Partnership; Limited Partnerships.
ISBN: 0-15-900327-X   Pages: 172 $17.95

Antitrust
By Professor Thomas M. Jorde, U.C. Berkeley, Mark A. Lemley, University of Texas, and Professor Robert H. Mnookin, Harvard University

Common Law Restraints of Trade; Federal Antitrust Laws (including Sherman Act, Clayton Act, Federal Trade Commission Act, Interstate Commerce Requirement, Antitrust Remedies); Monopolization (including Relevant Market, Purposeful Act Requirement, Attempts and Conspiracy to Monopolize); Collaboration Among Competitors (including Horizontal Restraints, Rule of Reason vs. Per Se Violations, Price Fixing, Division of Markets, Group Boycotts); Vertical Restraints (including Tying Arrangements); Mergers and Acquisitions (including Horizontal Mergers, Brown Shoe Analysis, Vertical Mergers, Conglomerate Mergers); Price Discrimination—Robinson-Patman Act; Unfair Methods of Competition; Patent Laws and Their Antitrust Implications; Exemptions From Antitrust Laws (including Motor, Rail, and Interstate Water Carriers, Bank Mergers, Labor Unions, Professional Baseball).
ISBN: 0-15-900328-8   Pages: 236 $18.95

Bankruptcy
By Professor Ned W. Waxman, College of William and Mary

Participants in the Bankruptcy Case; Jurisdiction and Procedure; Commencement and Administration of the Case (including Eligibility, Voluntary Case, Involuntary Case, Meeting of Creditors, Debtor's Duties); Officers of the Estate (including Trustee, Examiner, United States Trustee); Bankruptcy Estate; Creditor's Right of Setoff; Trustee's Avoiding Powers; Claims of Creditors (including Priority Claims and Tax Claims); Debtor's Exemptions; Nondischargeable Debts; Effects of Discharge; Reaffirmation Agreements; Administrative Powers (including Automatic Stay, Use, Sale, or Lease of Property); Chapter 7-Liquidation; Chapter 11-Reorganization; Chapter 13-Individual With Regular Income; Chapter 12-Family Farmer With Regular Annual Income.
ISBN: 0-15-900442-X   Pages: 368 $21.95

Business Law
By Professor Robert D. Upp, Los Angeles City College

Torts and Crimes in Business; Law of Contracts (including Contract Formation, Consideration, Statute of Frauds, Contract Remedies, Third Parties); Sales (including Transfer of Title and Risk of Loss, Performance and Remedies, Products Liability, Personal Property Security Interest); Property (including Personal Property, Bailments, Real Property, Landlord and Tenant); Agency; Business Organizations (including Partnerships, Corporations); Commercial Paper; Government Regulation of Business (including Taxation, Antitrust, Environmental Protection, and Bankruptcy).
ISBN: 0-15-900005-X   Pages: 289 $17.95

California Bar Performance Test Skills
By Professor Peter J. Honigsberg, University of San Francisco

Hints to Improve Writing; How to Approach the Performance Test; Legal Analysis Documents (including Writing a Memorandum of Law, Writing a Client Letter, Writing Briefs); Fact Gathering and Fact Analysis Documents; Tactical and Ethical Considerations; Sample Interrogatories, Performance Tests, and Memoranda.
ISBN: 0-15-900152-8   Pages: 229 $18.95

Civil Procedure
By Professor Thomas D. Rowe, Jr., Duke University, and Professor Richard L. Marcus, U.C. Hastings

Territorial (Personal) Jurisdiction, including Venue and Forum Non Conveniens; Subject Matter Jurisdiction, covering Diversity Jurisdiction, Federal Question Jurisdiction; Erie Doctrine and Federal Common Law; Pleadings including Counterclaims, Cross-Claims, Supplemental Pleadings; Parties, including Joinder and Class Actions; Discovery, including Devices, Scope, Sanctions, and Discovery Conference; Summary Judgment; Pretrial Conference and Settlements; Trial, including Right to Jury Trial, Motions, Jury Instruction and Arguments, and Post-Verdict Motions; Appeals; Claim Preclusion (Res Judicata) and Issue Preclusion (Collateral Estoppel).
ISBN: 0-15-900447-0   Pages: 460 $22.95

Commercial Paper and Payment Law
By Professor Douglas J. Whaley, Ohio State University

Types of Commercial Paper; Negotiability; Negotiation; Holders in Due Course; Claims and Defenses on Negotiable Instruments (including Real Defenses and Personal Defenses); Liability of the Parties (including Merger Rule, Suits on the Instrument, Warranty Suits, Conversion); Bank Deposits and Collections; Forgery or Alteration of Negotiable Instruments; Electronic Banking.
ISBN: 0-15-900367-9   Pages: 194 $19.95

Community Property
By Professor William A. Reppy, Jr., Duke University

Classifying Property as Community or Separate; Management and Control of Property; Liability for Debts; Division of Property at Divorce; Devolution of Property at Death; Relationships Short of Valid Marriage; Conflict of Laws Problems; Constitutional Law Issues (including Equal Protection Standards, Due Process Issues).
ISBN: 0-15-900422-5   Pages: 188 $18.95

Conflict of Laws
By Dean Herma Hill Kay, U.C. Berkeley

Domicile; Jurisdiction (including Notice and Opportunity to be Heard, Minimum Contacts, Types of Jurisdiction); Choice of Law (including Vested Rights Approach, Most Significant Relationship Approach, Governmental Interest Analysis); Choice of Law in Specific Substantive Areas; Traditional Defenses Against Application of Foreign Law; Constitutional Limitations and Overriding Federal Law (including Due Process Clause, Full Faith and Credit Clause, Conflict Between State and Federal Law); Recognition and Enforcement of Foreign Judgments.
ISBN: 0-15-900424-1   Pages: 273 $20.95

Constitutional Law
By Professor Jesse H. Choper, U.C. Berkeley

Powers of Federal Government (including Judicial Power, Powers of Congress, Presidential Power, Foreign Affairs Power); Intergovernmental Immunities, Separation of Powers; Regulation of Foreign Commerce; Regulation of Interstate Commerce; Taxation of Interstate and Foreign Commerce; Due Process, Equal Protection; "State Action" Requirements; Freedoms of Speech, Press, and Association; Freedom of Religion.
ISBN: 0-15-900375-X   Pages: 355 $21.95

Contracts
By Professor Melvin A. Eisenberg, U.C. Berkeley

Consideration (including Promissory Estoppel, Moral or Past Consideration); Mutual Assent; Defenses (including Mistake, Fraud, Duress, Unconscionability, Statute of Frauds, Illegality); Third-Party Beneficiaries; Assignment of Rights and Delegation of Duties; Conditions; Substantial Performance; Material vs. Minor Breach; Anticipatory Breach; Impossibility; Discharge; Remedies (including Damages, Specific Performance, Liquidated Damages).
ISBN: 0-15-900014-9   Pages: 326 $21.95

Corporations
By Professor Jesse H. Choper, U.C. Berkeley, and Professor Melvin A. Eisenberg, U.C. Berkeley

Formalities; "De Jure" vs. "De Facto"; Promoters; Corporate Powers; Ultra Vires Transactions; Powers, Duties, and Liabilities of Officers and Directors; Allocation of Power Between Directors and Shareholders; Conflicts of Interest in Corporate Transactions; Close Corporations; Insider Trading; Rule 10b-5 and Section 16(b); Shareholders' Voting Rights; Shareholders' Right to Inspect Records; Shareholders' Suits; Capitalization (including Classes of Shares, Preemptive Rights, Consideration for Shares); Dividends; Redemption of Shares; Fundamental Changes in Corporate Structure; Applicable Conflict of Laws Principles.
ISBN: 0-15-900342-3   Pages: 319 $21.95

Criminal Law
By Professor George E. Dix, University of Texas

Elements of Crimes (including Actus Reus, Mens Rea, Causation); Vicarious Liability; Complicity in Crime; Criminal Liability of Corporations; Defenses (including Insanity, Diminished Capacity, Intoxication, Ignorance, Self-Defense); Inchoate Crimes; Homicide; Other Crimes Against the Person; Crimes Against Habitation (including Burglary, Arson); Crimes Against Property; Offenses Against Government; Offenses Against Administration of Justice.
ISBN: 0-15-900217-6   Pages: 317 $20.95

Criminal Procedure
By Professor Paul Marcus, College of William and Mary, and Professor Charles H. Whitebread, U.S.C.

Exclusionary Rule; Arrests and Other Detentions; Search and Seizure; Privilege Against Self-Incrimination; Confessions; Preliminary Hearing; Bail; Indictment; Speedy Trial; Competency to Stand Trial; Government's Obligation to Disclose Information; Right to Jury Trial; Right to Counsel; Right to Confront Witnesses; Burden of Proof; Insanity; Entrapment; Guilty Pleas; Sentencing; Death Penalty; Ex Post Facto Issues; Appeal; Habeas Corpus; Juvenile Offenders; Prisoners' Rights; Double Jeopardy.
ISBN: 0-15-900449-7   Pages: 271 $20.95

Estate and Gift Tax
By Professor John H. McCord, University of Illinois

Gross Estate; Allowable Deductions Under Estate Tax (including Expenses, Indebtedness, and Taxes, Deductions for Losses, Charitable Deduction, Marital Deduction); Taxable Gifts; Deductions; Valuation; Computation of Tax; Returns and Payment of Tax; Tax on Generation-Skipping Transfers.
ISBN: 0-15-900425-X   Pages: 327 $20.95

Evidence
By Professor Jon R. Waltz, Northwestern University, and Roger C. Park, University of Minnesota

Direct Evidence; Circumstantial Evidence; Rulings on Admissibility; Relevancy; Materiality; Character Evidence; Hearsay and the Hearsay Exceptions; Privileges; Competency to Testify; Opinion Evidence and Expert Witnesses; Direct Examination; Cross-Examination; Impeachment; Real, Demonstrative, and Scientific Evidence; Judicial Notice; Burdens of Proof; Parol Evidence Rule.
ISBN: 0-15-900385-7   Pages: 387 $22.95

Federal Courts
By Professor William A. Fletcher, U.C. Berkeley

Article III Courts; "Case or Controversy" Requirement; Justiciability; Advisory Opinions; Political Questions; Ripeness; Mootness; Standing; Congressional Power Over Federal Court Jurisdiction; Supreme Court Jurisdiction; District Court Subject Matter Jurisdiction (including Federal Question Jurisdiction, Diversity Jurisdiction); Pendent and Ancillary Jurisdiction; Removal Jurisdiction; Venue; Forum Non Conveniens; Law Applied in the Federal Courts (including Erie Doctrine); Federal Law in the State Courts; Abstention; Habeas Corpus for State Prisoners; Federal Injunctions Against State Court Proceedings; Eleventh Amendment.
ISBN: 0-15-900232-X   Pages: 313 $21.95

Future Interests & Perpetuities
By Professor Jesse Dukeminier, U.C.L.A.

Reversions; Possibilities of Reverter; Rights of Entry; Remainders; Executory Interest; Rules Restricting Remainders and Executory Interest; Rights of Owners of Future Interests; Construction of Instruments; Powers of Appointment; Rule Against Perpetuities (including Reforms of the Rule).
ISBN: 0-15-900218-4   Pages: 185 $19.95

Income Tax I - Individual
By Professor Michael R. Asimow, U.C.L.A.

Gross Income; Exclusions; Income Splitting by Gifts, Personal Service Income, Income Earned by Children, Income of Husbands and Wives, Below-Market Interest on Loans, Taxation of Trusts; Business and Investment Deductions; Personal Deductions; Tax Rates; Credits; Computation of Basis, Gain, or Loss; Realization; Nonrecognition of Gain or Loss; Capital Gains and Losses; Alternative Minimum Tax; Tax Accounting Problems.
ISBN: 0-15-900421-7   Pages: 312 $21.95

Income Tax II - Partnerships, Corporations, Trusts
By Professor Michael R. Asimow, U.C.L.A.

Taxation of Partnerships (including Current Partnership Income, Contributions of Property to Partnership, Sale of Partnership Interest, Distributions, Liquidations); Corporate Taxation (including Corporate Distributions, Sales of Stock and Assets, Reorganizations); S Corporations; Federal Income Taxation of Trusts.
ISBN: 0-15-900384-9   Pages: 238 $19.95

Labor Law
By Professor James C. Oldham, Georgetown University, and Robert J. Gelhaus

Statutory Foundations of Present Labor Law (including National Labor Relations Act, Taft-Hartley, Norris-LaGuardia Act, Landrum-Griffin Act); Organizing Campaigns, Selection of the Bargaining Representative; Collective Bargaining (including Negotiating the Agreement, Lockouts, Administering the Agreement, Arbitration); Strikes, Boycotts, and Picketing; Concerted Activity Protected Under the NLRA; Civil Rights Legislation; Grievance; Federal Regulation of Compulsory Union Membership Arrangements; State Regulation of Compulsory Membership Agreements; "Right to Work" Laws; Discipline of Union Members; Election of Union Officers; Corruption.
ISBN: 0-15-900340-7   Pages: 260 $19.95

Legal Ethics
By Professor Thomas D. Morgan, George Washington University

Regulating Admission to Practice Law; Preventing Unauthorized Practice of Law; Contract Between Client and Lawyer (including Lawyer's Duties Regarding Accepting Employment, Spheres of Authority of Lawyer and Client, Obligation of Client to Lawyer, Terminating the Lawyer-Client Relationship); Attorney-Client Privilege; Professional Duty of Confidentiality; Conflicts of Interest; Obligations to Third Persons and the Legal System (including Counseling Illegal or Fraudulent Conduct, Threats of Criminal Prosecution); Special Obligations in Litigation (including Limitations on Advancing Money to Client, Duty to Reject Certain Actions, Lawyer as Witness); Solicitation and Advertising; Specialization; Disciplinary Process; Malpractice; Special Responsibilities of Judges.
ISBN: 0-15-900026-2   Pages: 258 $20.95

Legal Research, Writing and Analysis
By Professor Peter J. Honigsberg, University of San Francisco

Court Systems; Precedent; Case Reporting System (including Regional and State Reporters, Headnotes and the West Key Number System, Citations and Case Finding); Statutes, Constitutions, and Legislative History; Secondary Sources (including Treatises, Law Reviews, Digests, Restatements); Administrative Agencies (including Regulations, Looseleaf Services); Shepard's Citations; Computers in Legal Research; Reading and Understanding a Case (including Briefing a Case); Using Legal Sourcebooks; Basic Guidelines for Legal Writing; Organizing Your Research; Writing a Memorandum of Law; Writing a Brief; Writing an Opinion or Client Letter.
ISBN: 0-15-900436-5   Pages: 187 $17.95

Multistate Bar Examination
By Professor Richard J. Conviser, Chicago Kent

Structure of the Exam; Governing Law; Effective Use of Time; Scoring of the Exam; Jurisdictions Using the Exam; Subject Matter Outlines; Practice Tests, Answers, and Subject Matter Keys; Glossary of Legal Terms and Definitions; State Bar Examination Directory; Listing of Reference Materials for Multistate Subjects.
ISBN: 0-15-900246-X   Pages: 776 $24.95

Personal Property
Gilbert Staff

Acquisitions; Ownership Through Possession (including Wild Animals, Abandoned Chattels); Finders of Lost Property; Bailments; Possessory Liens; Pledges; Trover; Gift; Accession; Confusion (Commingling); Fixtures; Crops (Emblements); Adverse Possession; Prescriptive Rights (Acquiring Ownership of Easements or Profits by Adverse Use).
ISBN: 0-15-900360-1   Pages: 140 $14.95

Professional Responsibility
(see Legal Ethics)

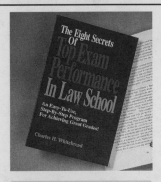

Criminal Procedure
By Professor Charles H. Whitebread
USC School of Law

TOPICS COVERED: Incorporation Of The Bill Of Rights; Exclusionary Rule; Fruit Of The Poisonous Tree; Arrest; Search & Seizure; Exceptions To Warrant Requirement; Wire Tapping & Eavesdropping; Confessions (Miranda); Pretrial Identification; Bail; Preliminary Hearings; Grand Juries; Speedy Trial; Fair Trial; Jury Trials; Right To Counsel; Guilty Pleas; Sentencing; Death Penalty; Habeas Corpus; Double Jeopardy; Privilege Against Compelled Testimony.
3 Audio Cassettes
ISBN: 0-15-900281-8 $39.95

Evidence
By Professor Faust F. Rossi
Cornell Law School

TOPICS COVERED: Relevance; Insurance; Remedial Measures; Settlement Offers; Causation; State Of Mind; Rebuttal; Habit; Character Evidence; "MIMIC" Rule; Documentary Evidence; Authentication; Best Evidence Rule; Parol Evidence; Competency; Dead Man Statutes; Examination Of Witnesses; Present Recollection Revived; Past Recollection Recorded; Opinion Testimony; Lay And Expert Witness; Learned Treatises; Impeachment; Collateral Matters; Bias, Interest Or Motive; Rehabilitation; Privileges; Hearsay And Exceptions.
5 Audio Cassettes
ISBN: 0-15-900282-6 $45.95

Family Law
Professor Roger E. Schechter
George Washington University Law School

TOPICS COVERED: Marital Relationship; Formalities And Solemnization; Common Law Marriage; Impediments; Conflict Of Laws; Non-Marital Relationship; Void And Voidable Marriages; Annulment; Divorce; Separation; Full Faith And Credit; Temporary Orders; Property Division; Community Property Principles; Equitable Distribution And Reimbursement; Marital And Separate Property; Alimony; Child Support; Enforcement Of Orders; Antenuptial And Postnuptial Agreements; Separation And Settlement Agreements; Custody; Visitation Rights; Termination Of Parental Rights; Adoption; Illegitimacy; Paternity Actions.
3 Audio Cassettes
ISBN: 0-15-900283-4 $39.95

Federal Courts
Professor John C. Jeffries
University of Virginia School of Law

TOPICS COVERED: History Of The Federal Court System; "Court Or Controversy" And Justiciability; Congressional Power Over Federal Court Jurisdiction; Supreme Court Jurisdiction; District Court Subject Matter Jurisdiction—Federal Question Jurisdiction, Diversity Jurisdiction And Admiralty Jurisdiction; Pendent And Ancillary Jurisdiction; Removal Jurisdiction; Venue; Forum Non Conveniens; Law Applied In The Federal Courts; Federal Law In The State Courts; Collateral Relations Between Federal And State Courts; The Eleventh Amendment And State Sovereign Immunity.
3 Audio Cassettes
ISBN: 0-15-900372-5 $39.95

Federal Income Tax
By Professor Cheryl D. Block
George Washington University Law School

TOPICS COVERED: Administrative Reviews; Tax Formula; Gross Income; Exclusions For Gifts; Inheritances; Personal Injuries; Tax Basis Rules; Divorce Tax Rules; Assignment Of Income; Business Deductions; Investment Deductions;

Passive Loss And Interest Limitation Rules; Capital Gains & Losses; Section 1031, 1034, and 121 Deferred/Non Taxable Transactions.
4 Audio Cassettes
ISBN: 0-15-900284-2 $45.95

Future Interests
By Dean Catherine L. Carpenter
Southwestern University Law School

TOPICS COVERED: Rule Against Perpetuities; Class Gifts; Estates In Land; Rule In Shelley's Case; Future Interests In Transferor and Transferee; Life Estates; Defeasible Fees; Doctrine Of Worthier Title; Doctrine Of Merger; Fee Simple Estates; Restraints On Alienation; Power Of Appointment; Rules Of Construction.
2 Audio Cassettes
ISBN: 0-15-900285-0 $24.95

Law School Exam Writing
By Professor Charles H. Whitebread
USC School of Law

TOPICS COVERED: With "Law School Exam Writing," you'll learn the secrets of law school test taking. Professor Whitebread leads you step-by-step through his innovative system, so that you know exactly how to tackle your essay exams without making point draining mistakes. You'll learn how to read questions so you don't miss important issues; how to organize your answer; how to use limited exam time to your maximum advantage; and even how to study for exams.
1 Audio Cassette
ISBN: 0-15-900287-7 $19.95

Professional Responsibility
By Professor Erwin Chemerinsky
USC School of Law

TOPICS COVERED: Regulation of Attorneys; Bar Admission; Unauthorized Practice; Competency; Discipline; Judgment; Lawyer-Client Relationship; Representation; Withdrawal; Conflicts; Disqualification; Clients; Client Interests; Successive And Effective Representation; Integrity; Candor; Confidences; Secrets; Past And Future Crimes; Perjury; Communications; Witnesses; Jurors; The Court; The Press; Trial Tactics; Prosecutors; Market; Solicitation; Advertising; Law Firms; Fees; Client Property; Conduct; Political Activity.
3 Audio Cassettes
ISBN: 0-15-900371-7 $39.95

Real Property
By Professor Paula A. Franzese
Seton Hall Law School

TOPICS COVERED: Estates—Fee Simple, Fee Tail, Life Estate; Co-Tenancy—Joint Tenancy, Tenancy In Common, Tenancy By The Entirety; Landlord-Tenant Relationship; Liability For Condition Of Premises; Assignment & Sublease; Easements; Restrictive Covenants; Adverse Possession; Recording Acts; Conveyancing; Personal Property.
4 Audio Cassettes
ISBN: 0-15-900289-3 $45.95

Remedies
By Professor William A. Fletcher
University of California at Berkeley, Boalt Hall School of Law

TOPICS COVERED: Damages; Restitution; Equitable Remedies; Tracing; Rescission and Reformation; Injury and Destruction of Personal Property; Conversion; Injury to Real Property; Trespass; Ouster; Nuisance; Defamation; Trade Libel; Inducing Breach of Contract; Contracts to Purchase Personal Property; Contracts to Purchase Real Property (including Equitable Conversion); Construction Contracts; and Personal Service Contracts.
4 Audio Cassettes
ISBN: 0-15-900353-9 $45.95

Sales & Lease of Goods
By Professor Michael I. Spak
Chicago Kent College of Law

TOPICS COVERED: Goods; Contract Formation; Firm Offers; Statute Of Frauds; Modification; Parol Evidence; Code Methodology; Tender; Payment; Identification; Risk Of Loss; Warranties; Merchantability; Fitness; Disclaimers; Consumer Protection; Remedies; Anticipatory Repudiation; Third Party Rights.
3 Audio Cassettes
ISBN: 0-15-900291-5 $39.95

Secured Transactions
By Professor Michael I. Spak
Chicago Kent College of Law

TOPICS COVERED: Collateral; Inventory; Intangibles; Proceeds; Security Agreements; Attachment; After-Acquired Property; Perfection; Filing; Priorities; Purchase Money Security Interests; Fixtures; Rights Upon Default; Self-Help; Sale; Constitutional Issues.
3 Audio Cassettes
ISBN: 0-15-900292-3 $39.95

Securities Regulation
By Professor Therese H. Maynard
Loyola Marymount School of Law

TOPICS COVERED: Securities Markets; IPOs; Brokers-Dealers; Securities Acts (1933, 1934); Self-Regulatory Organizations; Insider Trading; the SEC; Securities—Howey Test; Publicly Held Corporation; Underwriting; Who is Subject to Section 5 of 1933 Securities Act; Offers; Prospectuses; Registration Statements; Liability for Material Misstatements; Exemptions from Section 5 Registration; Foreign Issuers and Offshore Offerings; Regulations A and D; Rules 504, 505, 506, 701; Liability Provisions of 1933 Act; Due Diligence Defense; Damages; Liability Under Sections 12 (a)(1) and (2).
5 Audio Cassettes
ISBN: 0-15-900359-8 $45.95

Torts
By Professor Richard J. Conviser
Chicago Kent College of Law

TOPICS COVERED: Essay Exam Techniques; Intentional Torts—Assault, Battery, False Imprisonment, Intentional Infliction Of Emotional Distress, Trespass To Land, Trespass To Chattels, Conversion; Defenses. Defamation—Libel, Slander; Defenses; First Amendment Concerns; Invasion Of Right Of Privacy; Misrepresentation; Negligence—Duty, Breach, Actual And Proximate Causation, Damages; Defenses; Strict Liability, Products Liability; Nuisance; General Tort Considerations.
4 Audio Cassettes
ISBN: 0-15-900293-1 $45.95

Wills & Trusts
By Professor Stanley M. Johanson
University of Texas School of Law

TOPICS COVERED: Attested Wills; Holographic Wills; Negligence; Revocation; Changes On Face Of Will; Lapsed Gifts; Negative Bequest Rule; Nonprobate Assets; Intestate Succession; Advancements; Elective Share; Will Contests; Capacity; Undue Influence; Creditors' Rights; Creation Of Trust; Revocable Trusts; Pourover Gifts; Charitable Trusts; Resulting Trusts; Constructive Trusts; Spendthrift Trusts; Self-Dealing; Prudent Investments; Trust Accounting; Termination; Powers Of Appointment.
4 Audio Cassettes
ISBN: 0-15-900294-X $45.95

Call To Order: 1-800-787-8717 or Order On-Line at http://www.gilbertlaw.com

NO
QUESTIONS

ASKED.

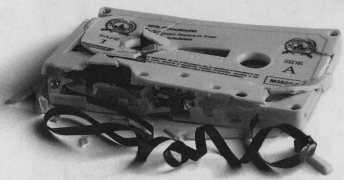

We stand behind our products...
even if someone stands on them!

With the Law School Legends Series you get America's Greatest Law Professors on audio cassette — plus one of the best audio tape guarantees in the business! If you accidentally damage a Law School Legends tape within 5 years from the date of purchase, we'll replace it for free — **no questions asked!**

The Law School Legends Series
America's Greatest Law Professors
on Audio Cassette

Available in Many Popular Titles. All Titles Fully Indexed for Quick Reference.

Administrative Law	Constitutional Law	Family Law	Real Property
Agency & Partnership	Contracts	Federal Courts	Remedies
Antitrust Law	Copyright Law	Federal Income Tax	Sale & Lease of Goods
Bankruptcy	Corporations	First Year Program	Secured Transactions
Civil Procedure	Criminal Law	Future Interests	Securities Regulation
Commercial Paper	Criminal Procedure	Law School Exam Writing	Torts
Conflict of Laws	Evidence	Prof. Responsibility	Wills & Trusts

Call To Order: 1-800-787-8717 or Order On-Line at http://www.gilbertlaw.com

Legalines

Legalines gives you authoritative, detailed briefs of every major case in your casebook. You get a clear explanation of the facts, the issues, the court's holding and reasoning, and any significant concurrences or dissents. Even more importantly, you get an authoritative explanation of the significance of each case, and how it relates to other cases in your casebook. And with Legalines' detailed table of contents and table of cases, you can quickly find any case or concept you're looking for. But your professor expects you to know more than just the cases. That's why Legalines gives you more than just case briefs. You get summaries of the black letter law, as well. That's crucial, because some of the most important information in your casebooks isn't in the cases at all … it's the black letter principles you're expected to glean from those cases. Legalines is the only series that gives you both case briefs and black letter review. With Legalines, you get everything you need to know—whether it's in a case or not!

Administrative Law
Keyed to the Breyer Casebook
ISBN: 0-15-900169-2   176 pages $19.95
Keyed to the Gellhorn Casebook
ISBN: 0-15-900170-6   186 pages $21.95
Keyed to the Schwartz Casebook
ISBN: 0-15-900171-4   145 pages $18.95

Antitrust
Keyed to the Areeda Casebook
ISBN: 0-15-900405-5   165 pages $19.95
Keyed to the Handler Casebook
ISBN: 0-15-900390-3   158 pages $18.95

Civil Procedure
Keyed to the Cound Casebook
ISBN: 0-15-900314-8   241 pages $21.95
Keyed to the Field Casebook
ISBN: 0-15-900415-2   310 pages $23.95
Keyed to the Hazard Casebook
ISBN: 0-15-900324-5   206 pages $21.95
Keyed to the Rosenberg Casebook
ISBN: 0-15-900052-1   284 pages $21.95
Keyed to the Yeazell Casebook
ISBN: 0-15-900241-9   206 pages $20.95

Commercial Law
Keyed to the Farnsworth Casebook
ISBN: 0-15-900176-5   126 pages $18.95

Conflict of Laws
Keyed to the Cramton Casebook
ISBN: 0-15-900331-8   113 pages $16.95
Keyed to the Reese (Rosenberg) Casebook
ISBN: 0-15-900057-2   247 pages $21.95

Constitutional Law
Keyed to the Brest Casebook
ISBN: 0-15-900338-5   172 pages $19.95
Keyed to the Cohen Casebook
ISBN: 0-15-900378-4   301 pages $22.95
Keyed to the Gunther Casebook
ISBN: 0-15-900467-5   367 pages $23.95
Keyed to the Lockhart Casebook
ISBN: 0-15-900242-7   322 pages $22.95

Constitutional Law (cont'd)
Keyed to the Rotunda Casebook
ISBN: 0-15-900363-6   258 pages $21.95
Keyed to the Stone Casebook
ISBN: 0-15-900236-2   281 pages $22.95

Contracts
Keyed to the Calamari Casebook
ISBN: 0-15-900065-3   234 pages $21.95
Keyed to the Dawson Casebook
ISBN: 0-15-900268-0   188 pages $21.95
Keyed to the Farnsworth Casebook
ISBN: 0-15-900332-6   219 pages $19.95
Keyed to the Fuller Casebook
ISBN: 0-15-900237-0   184 pages $19.95
Keyed to the Kessler Casebook
ISBN: 0-15-900070-X   312 pages $22.95
Keyed to the Murphy Casebook
ISBN: 0-15-900387-3   207 pages $21.95

Corporations
Keyed to the Cary Casebook
ISBN: 0-15-900172-2   383 pages $23.95
Keyed to the Choper Casebook
ISBN: 0-15-900173-0   219 pages $21.95
Keyed to the Hamilton Casebook
ISBN: 0-15-900313-X   214 pages $21.95
Keyed to the Vagts Casebook
ISBN: 0-15-900078-5   185 pages $18.95

Criminal Law
Keyed to the Boyce Casebook
ISBN: 0-15-900080-7   290 pages $21.95
Keyed to the Dix Casebook
ISBN: 0-15-900081-5   103 pages $15.95
Keyed to the Johnson Casebook
ISBN: 0-15-900175-7   149 pages $18.95
Keyed to the Kadish Casebook
ISBN: 0-15-900333-4   167 pages $18.95
Keyed to the La Fave Casebook
ISBN: 0-15-900084-X   202 pages $20.95

Criminal Procedure
Keyed to the Kamisar Casebook
ISBN: 0-15-900336-9   256 pages $21.95

Decedents' Estates & Trusts
Keyed to the Ritchie Casebook
ISBN: 0-15-900339-3   204 pages $21.95

Domestic Relations
Keyed to the Clark Casebook
ISBN: 0-15-900168-4   119 pages $16.95
Keyed to the Wadlington Casebook
ISBN: 0-15-900377-6   169 pages $18.95

Estate & Gift Taxation
Keyed to the Surrey Casebook
ISBN: 0-15-900093-9   100 pages $15.95

Evidence
Keyed to the Sutton Casebook
ISBN: 0-15-900096-3   271 pages $19.95
Keyed to the Waltz Casebook
ISBN: 0-15-900334-2   179 pages $19.95
Keyed to the Weinstein Casebook
ISBN: 0-15-900097-1   223 pages $20.95

Family Law
Keyed to the Areen Casebook
ISBN: 0-15-900263-X   262 pages $21.95

Federal Courts
Keyed to the McCormick Casebook
ISBN: 0-15-900101-3   195 pages $18.95

Income Tax
Keyed to the Freeland Casebook
ISBN: 0-15-900361-X   134 pages $18.95
Keyed to the Klein Casebook
ISBN: 0-15-900383-0   150 pages $18.95

Labor Law
Keyed to the Cox Casebook
ISBN: 0-15-900238-9   221 pages $18.95
Keyed to the Merrifield Casebook
ISBN: 0-15-900177-3   195 pages $20.95

Real Property
Keyed to the Browder Casebook
ISBN: 0-15-900110-2   277 pages $21.95
Keyed to the Casner Casebook
ISBN: 0-15-900111-0   261 pages $21.95
Keyed to the Cribbet Casebook
ISBN: 0-15-900239-7   328 pages $22.95
Keyed to the Dukeminier Casebook
ISBN: 0-15-900432-2   168 pages $18.95
Keyed to the Nelson Casebook
ISBN: 0-15-900228-1   288 pages $19.95
Keyed to the Rabin Casebook
ISBN: 0-15-900262-1   180 pages $18.95

Remedies
Keyed to the Re Casebook
ISBN: 0-15-900116-1   245 pages $22.95
Keyed to the York Casebook
ISBN: 0-15-900118-8   265 pages $21.95

Sales & Secured Transactions
Keyed to the Speidel Casebook
ISBN: 0-15-900166-8   202 pages $21.95

Securities Regulation
Keyed to the Jennings Casebook
ISBN: 0-15-900253-2   324 pages $22.95

Torts
Keyed to the Epstein Casebook
ISBN: 0-15-900335-0   193 pages $20.95
Keyed to the Franklin Casebook
ISBN: 0-15-900240-0   146 pages $18.95
Keyed to the Henderson Casebook
ISBN: 0-15-900174-9   162 pages $18.95
Keyed to the Keeton Casebook
ISBN: 0-15-900406-3   252 pages $21.95
Keyed to the Prosser Casebook
ISBN: 0-15-900301-6   334 pages $22.95

Wills, Trusts & Estates
Keyed to the Dukeminier Casebook
ISBN: 0-15-900337-7   145 pages $19.95

Call To Order: 1-800-787-8717 or Order On-Line at http://www.gilbertlaw.com

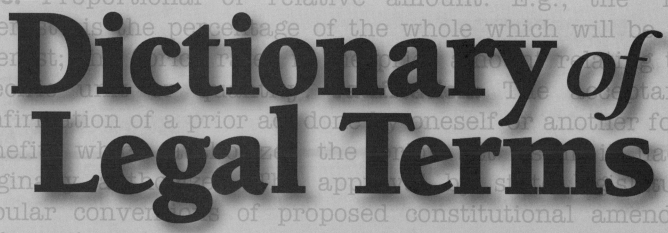

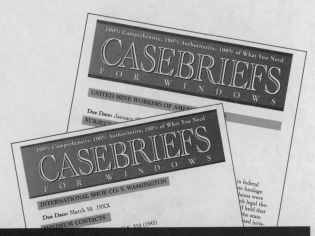

on the Internet!

Employment Guides

A collection of best selling titles that help you identify and reach your career goals.

Guerrilla Tactics for Getting the Legal Job of Your Dreams
Kimm Alayne Walton, J.D.

Whether you're looking for a summer clerkship or your first permanent job after school, this revolutionary book is the key to getting the job of your dreams!

Guerrilla Tactics for Getting the Legal Job of Your Dreams leads you step-by-step through everything you need to do to nail down that perfect job! You'll learn hundreds of simple-to-use strategies that will get you exactly where you want to go. You'll Learn:

- The seven magic opening words in cover letters that ensure you'll get a response.
- The secret to successful interviews every time.
- Killer answers to the toughest interview questions they'll ever ask you.
- Plus Much More!

Guerrilla Tactics features the best strategies from the country's most innovative law school career advisors. The strategies in *Guerrilla Tactics* are so powerful that it even comes with a guarantee: Follow the advice in the book, and within one year of graduation you'll have the job of your dreams … or your money back!

Pick up a copy of *Guerrilla Tactics* today … you'll be on your way to the job of your dreams!

ISBN: 0-15-900317-2 $24.95

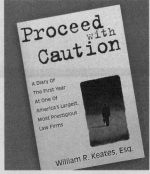

Proceed With Caution: A Diary Of The First Year At One Of America's Largest, Most Prestigious Law Firms
William R. Keates

Prestige. Famous clients. High-profile cases. Not to mention a starting salary approaching six figures.

In *Proceed With Caution*, the author takes you behind the scenes, to show you what it's really like to be a junior associate at a huge law firm. After graduating from an Ivy League law school, he took a job as an associate with one of New York's blue-chip law firms.

He also did something not many people do. He kept a diary, where he spelled out his day-to-day life at the firm in graphic detail.

Proceed With Caution excerpts the diary, from his first day at the firm to the day he quit. From the splashy benefits, to the nitty-gritty on the work junior associates do, to the grind of long and unpredictable hours, to the stress that eventually made him leave the firm — he tells story after story that will make you feel as though you're living the life of a new associate.

Whether you're considering a career with a large firm, or you're just curious about what life at the top firms is all about — *Proceed With Caution* is a must read!

ISBN: 0-15-900181-1 $17.95

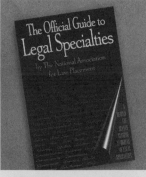

The Official Guide To Legal Specialties
National Association for Law Placement

With *The Official Guide To Legal Specialties* you'll get a behind the scenes glimpse at dozens of legal specialties. Not just lists of what to expect, real life stories from top practitioners in each field. You'll learn exactly what it's like to be in some of America's most desirable professions. You'll get expert advice on what it takes to get a job in each field. How much you'll earn and what the day-to-day life is really like, the challenges you'll face, and the benefits you'll enjoy. With *The Official Guide To Legal Specialties* you'll have a wealth of information at your fingertips!

Includes the following specialties:

Banking	Intellectual Property
Communications	International
Corporate	Labor/Employment
Criminal	Litigation
Entertainment	Public Interest
Environmental	Securities
Government Practice	Sports
Health Care	Tax
Immigration	Trusts & Estates

ISBN: 0-15-900391-1 $19.95

Beyond L.A. Law: Inspiring Stories of People Who've Done Fascinating Things With A Law Degree
National Association for Law Placement

Anyone who watches television knows that being a lawyer means working your way up through a law firm — right?

Wrong!

Beyond L.A. Law gives you a fascinating glimpse into the lives of people who've broken the "lawyer" mold. They come from a variety of backgrounds — some had prior careers, others went straight through college and law school, and yet others have overcome poverty and physical handicaps. They got their degrees from all different kinds of law schools, all over the country. But they have one thing in common: they've all pursued their own, unique vision.

As you read their stories, you'll see how they beat the odds to succeed. You'll learn career tips and strategies that work, from people who've put them to the test. And you'll find fascinating insights that you can apply to your own dream, whether it's a career in law or anything else!

From Representing Baseball In Australia. To International Finance. To Children's Advocacy. To Directing a Nonprofit Organization. To Entrepreneur.

If You Think Getting A Law Degree Means Joining A Traditional Law Firm — Think Again!

ISBN: 0-15-900182-X $17.95

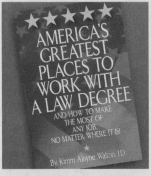

America's Greatest Places To Work With A Law Degree
Kimm Alayne Walton, J.D.

"Where do your happiest graduates work?"

That's the question that author Kimm Alayne Walton asked of law school administrators around the country. Their responses revealed the hundreds of wonderful employers profiled in *America's Greatest Places To Work With A Law Degree.*

In this remarkable book, you'll get to know an incredible variety of great places to work, including:

- Glamorous sports and entertainment employers — the jobs that sound as though they would be great, and they are!
- The 250 best law firms to work for between 20 and 600 attorneys.
- Companies where law school graduates love to work and not just as in-house counsel.
- Wonderful public interest employers – the "white knight" jobs that are so incredibly satisfying.
- Court-related positions, where lawyers entertain fascinating issues, tremendous variety, and an enjoyable lifestyle.
- Outstanding government jobs, at the federal, state, and local level.

Beyond learning about incredible employers, you'll discover:

- The ten traits that define a wonderful place to work … the sometimes surprising qualities that outstanding employers share.
- How to handle law school debt, when your dream job pays less than you think you need to make.
- How to find — and get! — great jobs at firms with fewer than 20 attorneys.

And no matter where you work, you'll learn expert tips for making the most of your job. You'll learn the specific strategies that distinguish people headed for the top … how to position yourself for the most interesting, high-profile work … how to handle difficult personalities … how to negotiate for more money … and what to do now to help you get your next great job!

ISBN: 0-15-900180-3 $24.95

Call To Order: 1-800-787-8717 or Order On-Line at http://www.gilbertlaw.com

Employment Guides

A collection of best selling titles that help you identify and reach your career goals.

National Directory Of Legal Employers
1999-2000 Edition
22,000 GREAT JOB OPENINGS
FOR LAW STUDENTS AND LAW SCHOOL GRADUATES
NALP

The National Directory Of Legal Employers
National Association for Law Placement

The National Directory of Legal Employers brings you a universe of vital information about 1,000 of the nation's top legal employers— *in one convenient volume!*

It includes:

- Over 22,000 job openings.
- The names, addresses and phone numbers of hiring partners.
- Listings of firms by state, size, kind and practice area.
- What starting salaries are for full time, part time, and summer associates, plus a detailed description of firm benefits.
- The number of employees by gender and race, as well as the number of employees with disabilities.
- A detailed narrative of each firm, plus much more!

The National Directory Of Legal Employers has been the best kept secret of top legal career search professionals for over a decade. Now, for the first time, it is available in a format specifically designed for law students and new graduates. *Pick up your copy of the Directory today!*
ISBN: 0-15-900434-9   **$39.95**

SAMPLE PAGE

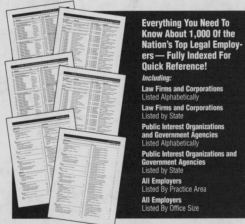

Everything You Need To Know About 1,000 Of the Nation's Top Legal Employers — Fully Indexed For Quick Reference!
Including:
Law Firms and Corporations
Listed Alphabetically
Law Firms and Corporations
Listed by State
Public Interest Organizations and Government Agencies
Listed Alphabetically
Public Interest Organizations and Government Agencies
Listed by State
All Employers
Listed By Practice Area
All Employers
Listed By Office Size

Company Information

1. *Name, Address, and Phone Number Of Hiring Partner*
2. *Demographics*
3. *Primary Practice Areas*
4. *Benefits*
5. *Pro Bono*
6. *Public Interest Fellowships*
7. *Minority Recruitment Efforts*
8. *Non-Discrimination Policy*
9. *Narrative*

Employment Information

10. *Office Size*
11. *Total Firm Size*
12. *Job Opportunities*
13. *Summer Associate Information*
14. *Application Timeline For Summer Associates*
15. *Hiring Criteria For All Job Openings*
16. *Salary Information*
17. *Other Compensation*
18. *Other Data*
19. *Partnership Data*
20. *Other Offices*
21. *Campus Interviews*

THE BEST OF THE JOB GODDESS

The Best Of The Job Goddess
Kimm Alayne Walton, J.D.

In her popular **Dear Job Goddess** column, legal job-search expert Kimm Alayne Walton provides the answers to even the most difficult job search dilemmas facing law students and law school graduates. Relying on career experts from around the country, the Job Goddess provides wise and witty advice for every obstacle that stands between you and your dream job!
ISBN: 0-15-900393-8   **$14.95**

SAMPLE COLUMN

Business Card Resumes: Good Idea, Or Not?

Dear Job Goddess,

One of my friends showed me something called a "business card resume." What he did was to have these business cards printed up, with his name and phone number on one side, and highlights from his resume on the other side. He said a bunch of people are doing this, so that when they meet potential employers they hand over these cards. Should I bother getting some for myself?

Curious in Chicago

Dear Curious,

Sigh. You know, Curious, that the Job Goddess takes a fairly dim view of resumes as a job-finding tool, even in their full-blown bond-papered, engraved 8-1/2x11" incarnation. And here you ask about a business card resume, two steps further down the resume food chain. So, no, you *shouldn't* bother with business card resumes. Here's why.

Think for a moment, Curious, about the kind of circumstance in which you'd be tempted to whip out one of these incredible shrinking resumes. You're at a social gathering. You happen to meet Will Winken, of the law firm Winken, Blinken, and Nod, and it becomes clear fairly quickly that Will is a) friendly, and b) a potential employer. The surest way to turn this chance encounter into a job is to use it as the basis for future contact. As Carolyn Bregman, Career Services Director at Emory Law School, points out, "Follow up with a phone call or note, mentioning something Winken said to you." You can say that you'd like to follow up on whatever it is he said, or that you've since read more about him and found that he's an expert on phlegm reclamation law and how that's a topic that's always fascinated you, and invite him for coffee at his convenience so you can learn more about it. What have you done? *You've taken a social encounter and* turned it into a potential job opportunity. And that makes the Job Goddess very proud.

But what happens if you, instead, whip out your business card resume, and say, "Gee, Mr. Winken, nice meeting you. Here's my business card resume, in case you ever need anybody like me." *Now* what have you done? You have, with one simple gesture, wiped out any excuse to follow up! Instead of having a phone call or a note from you that is personalized to Winken, you've got a piddling little standardized card with your vital statistics on it. Ugh. I know you're much more memorable, Curious, than anything you could possibly fit on the back of a business card.

So there you have it, Curious. Save the money you'll spend on a business card resume, and spend it later, when you have a *real* business card to print, reading, "Curious, Esq. Winken, Blinken, and Nod, Attorneys at Law."

Yours Eternally,

The Job Goddess

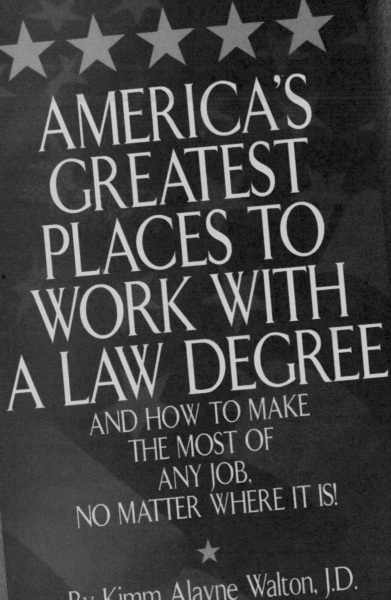